EXPLORATIONS IN SOCIOLOGY

British Sociological Association Conference Volume series

Sami Zubaida (editor)	1	*Race and Racism*
Richard Brown (editor)	2	*Knowledge, Education and Cultural Change*
Paul Rock and Mary McIntosh (editors)	3	*Deviance and Social Control*
Emanuel de Kadt and Gavin Williams (editors)	4	*Sociology and Development*
Frank Parkin (editor)	5	*The Social Analysis of Class Structure*
Diana Leonard Barker and Sheila Allen (editors)	6	*Sexual Divisions and Society: Process and Change*
Diana Leonard Barker and Sheila Allen (editors)	7	*Dependence and Exploitation in Work and Marriage*
Richard Scase (editor)	8	*Industrial Society: Class, Cleavage and Control*
Robert Dingwall, Christian Heath, Margaret Reid and Margaret Stacey (editors)	9	*Health Care and Health Knowledge*
Robert Dingwall, Christian Heath, Margaret Reid and Margaret Stacey (editors)	10	*Health and the Division of Labour*
Gary Littlejohn, Barry Smart, John Wakeford and Nira Yuval-Davis (editors)	11	*Power and the State*
Michèle Barrett, Philip Corrigan, Annette Kuhn and Janet Wolff (editors)	12	*Ideology and Cultural Production*
Bob Fryer, Alan Hunt, Doreen MacBarnet and Bert Moorhouse (editors)	13	*Law, State and Society*
Philip Abrams, Rosemary Deem, Janet Finch and Paul Rock (editors)	14	*Practice and Progress: British Sociology 1950–1980*
Graham Day, Lesley Caldwell, Karen Jones, David Robbins and Hilary Rose (editors)	15	*Diversity and Decomposition in the Labour Market*
David Robins, Lesley Caldwell, Graham Day, Karen Jones and Hilary Rose (editors)	16	*Rethinking Social Inequality*

Eva Gamarnikow, David Morgan, June Purvis and Daphne Taylorson (editors)	17	*The Public and the Private*
Eva Gamarnikow, David Morgan, June Purvis and Daphne Taylorson (editors)	18	*Gender, Class and Work*
*Gareth Rees, Janet Bujra, Paul Littlewood, Howard Newby and Teresa L. Rees (editors)	19	*Political Action and Social Identity: Class, Locality and Ideology*
*Howard Newby, Janet Bujra, Paul Littlewood, Gareth Rees, Teresa L. Rees (editors)	20	*Restructuring Capital: Recession and Reorganization in Industrial Society*
*Sheila Allen, Kate Purcell, Alan Waton and Stephen Wood (editors)	21	*The Experience of Unemployment*
*Kate Purcell, Stephen Wood, Alan Waton and Sheila Allen (editors)	22	*The Changing Experience of Employment: Restructuring and Recession*
*Jalna Hanmer and Mary Maynard (editors)	23	*Women, Violence and Social Control*
*Colin Creighton and Martin Shaw (editors)	24	*The Sociology of War and Peace*
*Alan Bryman, Bill Bytheway, Patricia Allatt and Teresa Keil	25	*Rethinking the Life Cycle*
*Patricia Allatt, Teresa Keil, Alan Bryman and Bill Bytheway	26	*Women and the Life Cycle*
*Ian Varcoe, Maureen McNeil and Steven Yearley (editors)	27	*Deciphering Science and Technology*
*Maureen McNeil, Ian Varcoe and Steven Yearley (editors)	28	*The New Reproductive Technologies*
David McCrone, Stephen Kendrick and Pat Straw (editors)	29	*The Making of Scotland: Nation, Culture and Social Change*
Stephen Kendrick, David McCrone and Pat Straw (editors)	30	*Interpreting the Past: Understanding the Present*
*Helen Corr and Lynn Jamieson	31	*Politics of Everyday Life: Continuity and Change in Work and the Family*
*Lynn Jamieson and Helen Corr	32	*State, Private Life and Political Change*

*Published by Macmillan

Politics of Everyday Life

Continuity and Change in Work and the Family

Edited by

Helen Corr
Research Fellow in Sociology
University of Edinburgh

and

Lynn Jamieson
Lecturer in Sociology
University of Edinburgh

MACMILLAN

First published 1990

Published by
THE MACMILLAN PRESS LTD
Houndmills, Basingstoke, Hampshire RG21 2XS
and London
Companies and representatives
throughout the world

Filmset by Wearside Tradespools
Fulwell, Sunderland

Printed in Hong Kong

British Library Cataloguing in Publication Data
Corr, Helen
Politics of Everyday Life: Continuity and Change in Work and the Family. (Explorations in sociology; 31).
1. Families. Socio-political aspects
I. Title II. Corr, Helen; Jamieson, Lynn III. Series
306.8′5
ISBN 0–333–49365–6
ISBN 0–333–49366–4 pbk

Contents

Acknowledgements

The papers which appear in the revised version were originally presented at the British Sociological Association (BSA) Conference, 'Sociology and History', held at Edinburgh University in March 1988. This is one of four volumes to be produced and it reflects the high quality of the papers and wide-ranging response to the theme. The sister volumes are *State, Private Life and Political Change* (eds) L. Jamieson and H. Corr; *The Making of Scotland: Nation, Culture and Social Change* (eds) D. McCrone, S. Kendrick and P. Straw; *Interpreting the Past: Understanding the Present* (eds) S. Kendrick, P. Straw and D. McCrone. We would like to thank all those who gave papers, the participants, and those who helped with the organisation, all of whom contributed to the success of the conference. We would like to thank the other editors of the conference, Terry Inkster and Lilianne Paterson, for their efficient typing and administrative work in the Sociology Department, and Mike Milotte and Anne Dix of the BSA for their helpful advice.

Acknowledgements

The papers which appear in the revised volume were originally presented at the British Sociological Association (BSA) Conference, 'Sociology and History', held at Edinburgh University in March 1988. This is one of four volumes to be produced and it reflects the high quality of the papers and wide-ranging response to the theme. The sister volumes are: *State, Private Life and Political Change* (eds) L. Jamieson and H. Corr; *The Making of Scotland: Nation, Culture and Social Change* (eds) D. McCrone, S. Kendrick and P. Straw; *Interpreting the Past, Understanding the Present* (eds) S. Kendrick, P. Straw and D. McCrone. We would like to thank all those who gave papers, the participants and those who helped with the organisation, all of whom contributed to the success of the conference. We would like to thank the other organisers of the conference, Terry Tasker and Eleanor Peterson, for their efficient typing and administrative work in the Sociology Department, and Mike Milne and Anne Dix of the BSA for their helpful advice.

Notes on Contributors

Graham Allan has been Lecturer in Sociology at the University of Southampton since 1975. His main teaching and research interests are in informal social relationships and domestic life. His publications include *A Sociology of Friendship and Kinship* (1979), *Family Life* (1985), and *Friendship: A Sociological Perspective*. Together with Graham Crow, he is currently editing a volume entitled *Home and Family* (1989).

Helen Corr is Research Fellow in Sociology at Edinburgh University. She is co-editor with Lynn Jamieson of *State, Private Life and Political Change*. She is currently working on a book on gender, school teachers and education in England and Scotland, 1850–1914.

Graham Crow has been Temporary Lecturer in Sociology and Social Policy at the University of Southampton since 1983. His main publications are in the field of rural sociology, but his teaching and research interests also cover social policy, sociological theory, and the sociology of the family and community. He is currently editing (with Graham Allan) a book on the home, *Home and Family*.

Leonore Davidoff is a Senior Lecturer in Social History in the Department of Sociology, University of Essex. She is co-author (with Catherine Hall) of *Family Fortunes: Men and Women of the English Middle Class 1780–1850* and other books and articles on nineteenth century Britain. She is editor of the journal, *Gender and History*.

Anna Davin is completing a book on girls' childhood in the late-nineteenth-century London working class. She is on the editorial collective of *History Workshop Journal* and is the current organiser of the London History Workshop Seminar. She is a Visiting Lecturer to the State University of New York, Bing Hampton.

Sarah Irwin is a Ph.D. student in the Department of Sociology, Edinburgh University. She has previously held research posts in the Department of Geography, Leeds University, and the Transport Studies Unit, Oxford University.

Lynn Jamieson is a Lecturer in Sociology, Edinburgh University, currently working on childhood (with Dr Toynbee), youth (ESRC 16–19 Initiative) and sexual assault (with Dr Brown, Law, Edinburgh and Ms Burman, Sociology). She is writing a book on Scottish rural childhood with Dr Toynbee and is co-editor of *State, Private Life and Political Change* with Dr Corr.

William Knox is a Lecturer in Economic and Social History, University of St. Andrews; he is author of several articles and books on Scottish Labour History, including a biography of James Maxton, and is currently researching into the development of work and trade unionism in twentieth-century Scotland.

Jane Mark-Lawson is a Senior Research Officer in the Department of Employment: The Training Agency. She has published on women and local politics and industrial restructuring and is co-author of *Localities Class and Gender* (1985).

Kay Sanderson is co-ordinator of the Women's Employment and Enterprise Training Unit in Norwich. She is also a part-time counsellor tutor at the Open University. Her article is based on an unpublished Ph.D. thesis: 'Social Mobility in the Life Cycle of Some Women Clerical Workers' (1988), held at the University of Essex.

Claire Toynbee is a lecturer in Sociology and Social Work, Victoria University of Wellington, New Zealand. Her work includes extensive use of oral histories and genealogies. She is currently writing a book on Scottish rural childhood with Lynn Jamieson.

Sylvia Walby has been a Lecturer in Sociology at the University of Lancaster since 1979 and Director of the Women's Studies Research Centre since 1984. She is the author of *Patriarchy at Work* (1986), editor of *Gender Segregation at Work* (1988), and co-author of *Localities, Class and Gender* (1985) and *Contemporary British Society* (1988).

Anne Witz is Senior Lecturer in Sociology at the City of Birmingham Polytechnic. She has researched and published in the medical division of Labour. Her current research is on Victorian lady doctors in India.

1 Introduction

Helen Corr and Lynn Jamieson

During the past decade in much sociological work there has been a growing sensitivity to the importance of a historical perspective. Both disciplines have shared a growing interest in the social construction and reproduction of gender inequalities in work, politics and the family. Cross-fertilisation between Sociology and History has produced valuable insights into the ways in which the experiences of each sex have been structured. This involves identifying the everyday ways in which gender roles, identities and divisions are shaped in the workplace and the home. Gender relationships are a process of conflict and negotiation, often rife with contradictions. This makes the task of examining the relationship of people to changing social, cultural and political processes a complex one.

A study of the past is crucial to our understanding of the present. However obvious this statement may appear, it holds little or no practical meaning for many young people growing up in contemporary society. A large proportion of school leavers grow up unaware that their field of social relations and work patterns are inherently politically structured and historically gendered. Definitions of what constitutes 'men's work' and 'women's work' are still perceived as unchanging social categories rather than as historical formulations.

One popular misconception is that females are and have always been physically incapable of performing heavy manual labour in the industrial sector of the economy. A prevalent belief is that 'There are certain things that women just can't do and men can't do and it's as simple as that'. (*16–19 ESRC Initiative*, unpublished data). When a female respondent in the East of Scotland was recently asked to support this assertion, she referred to the coalmining industry as always having been barred to women. Yet as Jane Mark-Lawson and Ann Witz point out in this volume, females made up 35 per cent of the coalmining workforce in the East of Scotland during the early Victorian period; but myths die hard. The material significance of the myth is that the search for jobs in the youth labour market is constrained by gender-specific role models. Contemporary attitudes among young people on the subject of feminism also highlight the need for a broader historical and sociological perspective on social movements over time. Within the present generation, there is a tendency to regard sex discrimination as a non-issue, which denotes an air of detachment from the efforts of earlier generations who struggled for the political right to vote and for equality of treatment with men in every area of their lives.

The purpose of the book, therefore, is to view the past and present as an interactive process, and its central focus is on political and social relationships in the overlapping spheres of the home, workplace and family. Gender relationships are historical and fundamental to an understanding of continuities and changes in people's lives across generations. Acquiring a gender identity is part of a political process. The term 'political' is used here in a much wider context than one which is constructed around formal politics such as Government, parties, constitutions, voting patterns and the like. Such an approach adopts a narrow view of politics, and above all, fails to encapsulate the negotiation of power, authority and hierarchy in personal and more general forms of social interaction at an informal level. By placing aspects of everyday lives in a historical context, the articles demonstrate how apparently private matters such as home and family life relate to wider social structures and work processes in the public sphere. The categories of public and private spheres of work and home life were historically formulated in the early nineteenth century (Davidoff and Hall 1987). However, the distinction between public and private lives is elusive in reality – take, for example, the close interplay between the worlds of paid work and household economy.

This theme is poignantly illustrated in a number of articles on patriarchy, employment, home, workplace culture, gender issues and the family. In Part One, all four articles show how the cultural and social meanings attached to the home, childhood, youth and parenting have changed across time. At the same time they recognise that historically the family has displayed continuity in terms of its importance as an economic and social institution. Graham Crow and Graham Allan document how the 'home' has changed since 1945, and how the great diversity of individuals' domestic circumstances and experiences have altered in accordance with gender, age and class differences. The popular theory that implies an evolutionary transition in home life, away from the public domain towards a more private form of domestic relationships, is questioned. Crow and Allan argue instead that past forms of domestic arrangements were never straightforwardly 'public' and that the changes which have taken place are now much more complex than the simple 'public to private' model allows.

Drawing upon a rich historical literature, Anna Davin challenges the notion of childhood, easily assumed to be obvious, but which turns out to be contentious and shifting in Britain during the second half of the nineteenth century. The experience of childhood in the London working class changed dramatically. During the earlier part of the century there were thousands of street children or 'little arabs' who lived by their wits with little or no adult support and were a threat to society. Such children were prepared for adult life since their early experiences equipped them for responsibility and independence. Children could perform the domestic functions of a mother who was ill or had died. However, by the turn of the twentieth century the 'independent' child, though not extinct, was an altogether rarer bird. The chapter focuses on shifts in middle-class and working-class perceptions of childhood in accordance with gender. Davin skilfully shows how the conflict between middle-class ideals and working-class realities of childhood led to increasing state regulation of children's lives.

Sarah Irwin provides a critique of debates on the transitions from youth to adulthood in contemporary Britain. She argues for the construction of a more sophisticated research approach to 'transitions', locating the lifecycle phase, 'youth', in more general understandings of social continuity and change. She breaks down 'youth' into its constituent economic and social relationships. Social and economic demography are used to extend the horizons of existing debates. It is then possible to explore more adequately the implications of the crisis in employment for youth in the 1980s.

The concern of Lynn Jamieson's and Claire Toynbee's article is to identify and explain shifts in the nature of parental authority and control in Western capitalist societies in the twentieth century. It is widely believed that parents in contemporary or industrialised societies are less able or willing to control their children's behaviour than those of previous generations. However, sociological accounts supporting such a belief are few and far between. Drawing on historical research based partly on oral interviews with men and women born before 1912, the authors demonstrate that dramatic changes in familial relationships have taken place since the 1900s. At the turn of the century there was a high degree of parental control over children's time and energy. Jamieson and Toynbee argue that this traditional form of authority has been replaced by a variety of pseudo-democratic styles of family organisation and control.

Part Two further demonstrates interplay between the so-called public and private spheres of work and the family in ideological and practical terms. The chapters by Jane Mark-Lawson and Anne Witz and that by Sylvia Walby assess the relative importance of capitalist and patriarchal relations for an understanding of women's employment. In the first of these chapters, the issue of the theorisation of gender relations within nineteenth-century industrial capitalism is addressed through a historical account of the family division of labour in coal mining. The authors argue that male colliers opposed the exclusion of women from working in mines in districts where the male head of the household operated as a sub-contractor and utilised the family as a unit of labour essentially under his control. For this reason, male hewers did not support attempts, either by individual employers at a local level, or by the state, to remove female labour from the mines. Returning to the evidence of the 1842 commissioners, the authors examine the complex present-day debates surrounding the removal of women from mining under the 1842 Mines (Regulations) Act. This conceptualises the nature of male control over women's labour both within the capitalist labour market and the household as an economic unit.

Sylvia Walby discusses historical changes in gender relations from a sociological perspective, and the concept of patriarchal structures in employment provides her focal point. She pinpoints two main historical models among sociologists: first, that women's employment changes on a cyclical basis consistent with their use as a labour reserve; second, that there is a long-run procession of women into paid employment that depends on the development of capitalism. Both of these approaches, she argues, are empirically and theoretically mistaken. The root of the problem lies in their failure to theorise patriarchal relations and to note the significance of gender struggles around women's employment. She makes a distinction between different forms of patriarchal struggles against women in the workplace, and goes on to trace the significance of these over time.

The next two essays examine the ways in which gender issues spilled over from the workplace into other aspects of nineteenth-century life. William Knox states that since the publication of Braverman's *Labour and Monopoly Capital* (1974) sociologists and social historians have increasingly seen the labour process as central to the problem of class formation and the development of a class ideology. Braverman argues that, in the period 1880–1914, changes in the labour process undermined the skill and the hitherto privileged position of the 'labour aristocracy' which, in turn, radicalised the workers in the direction of independent labour representation and class politics. The previous allegiance by the skilled workers to the liberal/capitalist framework of society collapsed as the balance of power in the workplace underwent a far-reaching restructuring. Knox questions whether changes in the workplace are necessarily harbingers of change in political behaviour, arguing that it is important to see the process of political change as the product of different factors, of which the workplace is only one. (See also Gordon, 1989; Savage, 1989). This chapter draws attention to the role of religious and gender divisions much wider than the workplace in shaping the working class political culture in Scotland.

Through a historical account of sexual politics inside Scottish and English teachers' organisations, Helen Corr's essay demonstrates the dilemmas that women confronted in a male-dominated power structure. Conflict of gender interests is of crucial theoretical importance in understanding workplace and union politics. Gender differences have led to tensions in a range of views on issues such as the struggle for the vote, equal pay, skill, promotions, and professional status in the period between 1870 and 1914, with ideological compromise being more of a feature of women's position in the public sphere. The campaign for equal pay and suffrage raised the difficult ideological question of whether women should place the ideals of their unions first, and their own grievances as a sex second. This essay also refutes the historically received view that women teachers have 'accepted their inferiority with docility' and puts on record their often painful struggle against discrimination.

The issue of women's class position and degree of social mobility is raised in Kay Sanderson's innovative oral-interview study of female civil servants in the inter-war period. John Goldthorpe's extensive study *Social Mobility and Class Structure in Modern Britain* (Oxford: Oxford University Press, 1980), was of male mobility only. The lack of focus on gender was justified on the grounds that women were not easily integrated into traditional studies of social mobility. Sanderson challenges this perspective and argues that women do have a distinctive social position and consequently can be socially mobile. She shows that social position and social mobility can usefully be analysed as components of the biography of the individual: a biography constructed within the socio-economic constraints of a particular historical period. She documents this with the accounts given by female civil servants of their early childhood, education, career, marriage, child rearing and old age.

In Part Three, Leonore Davidoff examines the present relationship of sociology and history, and especially of recent feminist scholarship on the concept of Gender. Here, there is less ready acceptance of received classifications, especially of 'male' and 'female'. She takes a closer look at the historically moulded categories upon which sociological theory was constructed in the nineteenth century: Rationality, Property, The Individual and the Market. Common to these were the notions of independence and dependence as the basis of Victorian manhood and, ultimately, citizenship. At the same time, there was a less widely recognised, albeit important, shift in definitions of sexuality. All of these definitions were implicated in the construction of a private and public sphere and, within the latter, a separation between the economic and the political.

Davidoff follows this in a documented discussion of mid-nineteenth century Britain, the period when sociology was emerging as a discipline. Various masculinities were part of class formation and included new definitions of work and citizenship. By the end of the century, these masculinities had amalgamated with discussions of manhood and war (see also Morgan 1989 and Hearn 1989) and were entered into the definition of the British 'nation'. Her concluding argument maintains that basic sociological categories are premised on and hence limited by certain historically specific notions about gender. Recognising this and giving voice to the 'other' sex should provide concepts elastic enough to embrace the particularities and contradictions which make up the *whole* of social life.

REFERENCES

GORDON E., *Women and Working Class Politics in Scotland, 1900–1914.*

SAVAGE, M., *Urban Politics and the Rise of the Labour Party, 1919–1939.*

MORGAN, D. H. J., *'No more heroes?' Masculinity, Violence and the Civilising Process.*

WEEKS, J., *Sexuality and History Revisited* in Jamieson, L. and Corr, H. (eds), *State, Private Life and Political Change* (Macmillan, 1990).

Part I
Home Matters? The Interplay of Public and Private Worlds

2 Constructing the domestic sphere: The emergence of the modern home in post-war Britain

Graham Crow and Graham Allan

INTRODUCTION

There appears to be widespread agreement that family and home life have been changing, and changing quite dramatically, over the last forty years or so. In essence, what has emerged is a new version of the domestic ideal that encapsulates changed expectations of family relations and housing conditions. As with all such constructions, within this consensus, factual and evaluative statements are run together, combining selective elements of what is with judgements about what ought to be (Davidoff *et al.*, 1976). Thus, the contemporary domestic ideal contains notions about equality and companionship within marriage; it perceives children as being a focal life interest; and it sees the home as a comfortable, relaxed environment in which personally fulfilling family relationships can grow and develop. As sociologists have been at pains to show, domestic life rarely lives up to such aspirations. As well as housing these more desirable features, the home is also the site of conflict and tension, argument and abuse.

This is not to deny that some degree of change along the above lines has been occurring in the domestic sphere. Within sociology the dominant process is frequently represented as one of privatisation. Although taking many different forms and emphasising different elements, the general thrust of these theories is that home life and family relations have become more salient in people's lives; that more personal satisfaction is expected from them than before; and that community, work or other non-domestic fields of activity are less compelling than previously. At their heart is the sense that structural economic and social transformations have cemented relations of interdependence between family members while at the same time increasing their self-sufficiency as a unit.

The aim of this paper is to examine the processes which have been at work in the construction of the contemporary domestic ideal. Its major contention is that the popular theory of the privatisation of the domestic sphere is questionable on several counts. First, it is noted that the idea of privatisation implies an evolutionary transition in home life away from the public domain towards a more private form of domestic relationships. Yet it is difficult to find unambiguous historical evidence to sustain this interpretation. Past forms of domestic arrangements were never straightforwardly 'public', and the changes that have taken place are much more complex than the simple 'public' to 'private' models allow. The second part of the paper examines some of the more important influences that have been at work in shaping the meaning and social significance of the home in people's lives. In doing this, it raises questions about the adequacy of the explanations advanced in a number of models of privatisation. The final section of the paper considers the legitimacy of making generalisations about home-life in the way that privatisation theories tend to, given the great diversity of individuals' housing conditions and domestic arrangements. It argues that there is a good deal of variation in the way people experience the home, depending on their own structural position.

DOMESTIC IDEALS, PAST AND PRESENT

The post-war period is not the first time that a domestic ideal based on the family and on privacy has been present in British society. Davidoff and Hall (1983; 1987) have shown how the period 1780–1850 saw the emergence of new conceptions of the home among the English middle class.

The creation of the middle-class home involved the separation of home and workplace, and the identification of the home as a private place, in which family relationships were to the fore. These family relationships were 'idealized', with 'domestic tranquility' a central part of the emerging domestic ideal, or 'idyll'. Located between the aristocracy and gentry on the one hand and the labouring poor on the other, it was 'the middle ranks who erected the strictest boundaries between private and public space' (Davidoff and Hall, 1987, p. 359). Middle-class houses became places to which access was restricted, and a 'similar desire for privacy-marked property boundaries with gates, drives, hedges and walls around house and garden' (Davidoff and Hall, 1987, p. 361). By the middle of the nineteenth century, then, certain key foundations of the modern domestic ideal had already been laid.

If the idealisation of domestic life came later to the working class than to the middle class, it was not all that much later, speaking in historical terms. Daunton refers to the 'privatization' of Victorian working-class households, whereby 'there was a reorientation of working-class culture from being work-centred to home-centred ... generally, shorter working hours and increased real wages eroded work-centred culture and increased the role of the home as a centre of life' (1983, p. 224). Such developments were, of course, more likely among the artisan and skilled-worker elite of the Victorian working class able to afford them (Marshall *et al.*, 1987; Williams, 1987), but 'aspirations to residential segregation and to house ownership' (Crossick, 1978, p. 149) were not restricted to this group, and over time their ideology and values proceeded to spread further down the class structure. On the basis of what is now extensive evidence relating to the Victorian era, Marshall *et al.* (1987) conclude that privatism (that is, home-centredness and family-centredness) is not a novel feature of contemporary British working-class life, but a long-established one.

Similar arguments have been made concerning later periods also. Thus Thompson has proposed that, being present to a significant degree among the Edwardians, 'the home-centred working-class husband is certainly not a new phenomenon of the more affluent twentieth century' (1977, p. 88). The predominant pattern among the Edwardian working class may still have been for men to withdraw into the public world of 'clubs, friendly societies, trade unions and public houses' (Thompson, 1977, p. 88), but a substantial minority preferred to spend their free time at home. There is some evidence that home-centredness was present among working-class children of this period too (Roberts, 1973), although parent-child relationships still emphasised, in Jamieson's apt phrase, 'the beneficence of the parent, not the marvel of the child' (1987, p. 599).

Coming forward in time, Lewis has written that 'during the inter-war years, evidence suggests that the working-class family became more privatized and more isolated' (1986b, p. 114). Elizabeth Roberts arrives at more or less the same conclusion:

> In the period before 1940, despite the changes in family size and standards of living . . . one is left with a sense of continuity in the lives of working-class women, centred on their homes, families and neighbourhoods. It is difficult to trace in the oral evidence any expansion of their horizons as a result of the lessening of their workload between the wars. Indeed, their sphere probably became *more* domestic; there was less economic need in many families for women to go out to work even part-time, and consequently more opportunity for them to indulge their ambition of staying at home (1984, pp. 202–3, emphasis in original).

There appears in general, then, to be much that is recognisably 'modern' about home life in the worlds of fifty, eighty, or one hundred years ago, or even earlier, leastwise at the level of ideals. However, it is precisely at the level of ideals that some of the most important developments influencing domestic life have taken place.

If it is accepted that 'privatised' lifestyles have been present among both the middle class and the working class (or at least elements of them) for some time, then awkward questions are raised about what precisely is being displaced by privatisation. Perhaps the most common understanding of privatisation is the growth of home-centredness at the expense of work-centredness, but the home/work dichotomy is not the only framework within which privatisation has been conceptualised. Young and Willmott operate with a narrower frame of reference when speaking of the social transitions that have taken place in the changing significance of 'home and street' and in the movement, among working-class men at any rate, 'from bar to home' (1957, pp. 84, 88), while use by other authors of the somewhat broader contrast between 'the home' and 'the community' may be considered to have a more respectable pedigree (Klein, 1965, p. 221).

Whenever any of the above dichotomies is adopted in the analysis of the changes that have taken place regarding the home, it is likely that some serious oversimplification, or even misrepresentation, of the past will be involved. It is difficult to sustain the case that former patterns of people's lives are captured adequately by concepts such as 'work-centredness', 'community-centredness', or 'street-centredness', let alone 'bar-centredness'. Privacy is a central element of the modern domestic ideal, but it was also of vital importance in earlier periods. Even Young and Willmott's old-fashioned Bethnal Greeners, described as 'vigorously at home in the streets' (Willmott and Young, 1960, p. 1), fiercely maintained the privacy of their own homes (Young and Willmott, 1957), and this phenomenon is reported by other writers on the poorer sections of the working class (Hoggart, 1958; Klein, 1965). Klein even goes so far as to suggest that poverty 'may exert pressure to maintain a higher standard of privacy' (1965, p. 252), simultaneously casting doubt on the popularly-held idea that the desire for privacy is positively correlated with affluence.

If the home/community relationship is represented as a dichotomy, it is not at all clear why so much importance should have been attached to the privacy of the home by individuals deeply embedded in local social networks such as those of the 'traditional' working-class community. The answer lies, of course, in the relationship being in reality something other than dichotomous. Thus Hoggart's memories of the inter-war period are of public and private worlds overlapping, and of the need to secure the home's privacy as a defensive measure against that powerful vehicle of neighbourhood criticism, gossip. In a locality where neighbours frequently suffer from over-vivid imaginations, 'the half-length lace curtains keep out most of what little sun there is, but they establish your privacy: the window-ledges and doorsteps scrubbed and yellowed with scouring-stone further establish that you are a "decent" family' (1958, pp. 34–5). Working-class concern with 'respectability' (Gray, 1976) regarding their homes may be compared to middle-class concern with 'gentility' and 'propriety' (Davidoff and Hall, 1987), so long as it is borne in mind that the former was achieved with scarcer resources. In such circumstances, the 'public' face of the home was likely to involve at least a degree of deception, and where a family's public image was maintained this was no mean feat, as Roberts's account of housework indicates:

> The woman's first preoccupation tended to be with outward show – windows shone, framed by immaculate starched white curtains; front doorsteps were unblemished with human footprints ... The interiors gleamed and sparkled in the fire and gas light ... And yet it is very doubtful whether all these houses or their occupants were as clean as they appeared to be. The sanitary inadequacies all militated strongly against the housewives' best efforts, and were of course beyond her powers of remedy (1984, p. 135).

This concern with show, disguising the less-than-ideal conditions of interiors, illustrates the power of the domestic ideal even among those whose material circumstances meant that they could not hope to live up to it in practice. It also illustrates that while outsiders could be debarred from entering the home, a community's standards regarding the organisation of the domestic arena were less easily kept at bay, and exerted a powerful influence on how people conducted their 'private' lives.

It may be observed, then, that the home/community dichotomy is one of dubious utility. Given the close conditions in which they lived, it was simply not open for people in 'traditional' working-class communities to choose between home and community: both were inevitably present in people's lives. As Cronin's discussion of the inter-war period puts it, 'for most working people home and community were not alternative foci, but part of a single world of daily life' (1984, p. 86). Cronin goes on to make the important point that, to the extent that home-centredness had grown at the expense of communal ties and activities, 'it was a slight shift of emphasis rather than any qualitative transformation' (1984, p. 86). Much the same sort of conclusion could be reached for the post-war period, where the growth of home-centredness built on an already well-established foundation, and where the 'loss of community' theme (which was prominent in the literature of the time) overstated the changes taking place. This was so even in such unpromising circumstances as the new suburban housing estates whose populations had had their existing social networks disrupted by the relocation process (Mogey, 1956; Young and Willmott, 1957; Willmott, 1963).

These doubts about models portraying the growth of home-centredness at the expense of community-centredness apply also to the other conceptualisations of privatisation noted above. Whatever area of life that privatisation is said to have displaced, be it community, street, work, pub, or some other place of sociability, it is difficult to find a period in the recent past when home-life has not stood alongside this other focus of people's lives as a central part of their existence. This is particularly true for women, since the other side of the male breadwinner ideology is the full-time housewife, whose place (along with dependent children) is specified as being in the home, but it is true for men, too. Even among 'traditional' working-class men, whose lifestyles have been interpreted as the antithesis of home-centredness, it is still the case that the home looms large in their daily routines. Thus, research conducted in the 1950s found that a coal miner's home

> must provide a sound and comfortable place to eat and sleep for parents and children, a place where they can enjoy privacy if ever they feel the need of it, and, very important, a haven for the tired man when he returns from work; here he expects to find a meal prepared, a room clean and tidy, a seat comfortable and warm, and a wife ready to give him what he wants (Dennis *et al.*, 1969, p. 179).

This instrumental attitude generates a different 'ideal of the home' (Dennis *et al.*, 1969, p. 179) to the modern family-centred one, but it is nevertheless true that the home plays a large part in such men's lives, even if they do not revolve around it as completely as the modern domestic ideal requires.

Thus, proponents of the privatisation hypothesis, by suggesting that life has become more home-centred and family-centred over the post-war period, have tended to exaggerate the scale of this change by understating the extent to which these phenomena were already present in British society by the 1940s, especially among the working class. Very much the same point can be made with regard to another, related, theme of post-war family sociology, the growth of child-centredness; as Pahl has noted, the inter-war years 'comprised a period which emphasized small-scale domesticity centred around young children' (1984, p. 75). While it is undoubtedly the case that growing numbers of people in the post-war era have secured the material resources which allow them to lead more fully 'privatised' lifestyles, this should not distract attention from the fact that this development followed on from a situation in which home-centredness, family-centredness, and child-centredness were already widespread in their occurrence.

When looked at from another angle, however, there is an important sense in which the changes that have taken place have been underplayed, since the meanings of home and family, around which life is supposedly coming to the centre more and more, are not static, but dynamic and variable. This can be seen if the content of the modern domestic ideal is compared with that of earlier periods. Contemporary images of the ideal home are based on the idealisation of a particular family form, and this is not at all the same as the idealised family form which prompted growing home-centredness among the Victorians. Their ideal (in both its middle-class and working-class variants) emphasised the home as an orderly and hierarchical place, a place where women had responsibility for the smooth running of domestic matters, children were expected to be obedient, and men expected to exercise benevolent but firm authority (Davidoff *et al.*, 1976; Davidoff and Hall, 1987; Williams, 1987).

While substantial elements of such ideas survived long into the present century and continue to be reflected in much current practice, it is important to recognise that significant changes have steadily taken place in the way domestic relations are idealised. Thus, for example, much of the religious foundation of the Victorian domestic ideal, so vital to its early development (Hall, 1979; 1982), has been eroded, just as has the material underpinning provided by domestic servants (Taylor, 1979) and their working-class counterparts, 'devoted' daughters (Roberts, 1973). So, while it can be accepted that conceptions of home-life continue to involve men's traditional authority, in recent years the 'good husband' has, as Bell and Newby note, increasingly been 'redefined with greater emphasis placed upon companionship, home-centredness and shared activities' (1976, pp. 160–1). In such a context, conceptions of what constitutes a 'good wife' have also changed from those of the past (Lewis, 1986a), as have (albeit to a lesser extent) conceptions of what constitutes a 'good mother' (Gittins, 1982), with the result that the idea of a woman being the 'angel in the house' (Hall, 1979, p. 15) has become somewhat anachronistic. More generally, the domestic ideal celebrated by the Victorians is now looked back on as one of domestic confinement and drudgery and inequality between the sexes, which post-war changes in domestic technology and the growth of companionate marriage are supposed to have eroded.

Equally, there have been significant shifts in the expectations that people have about their homes. This concerns not just the material standards and amenities of the home but also the cultural conceptions constructed around it. Consider, for example, the changed meaning that 'having a home of one's own' has come to have. Rather than signifying not having to share accommodation with another household, as it did in the quite recent past, with changes in the housing market it is increasingly taken to mean buying one's own home instead of renting it (Wallace, 1987; Holme, 1985b). Thus while recognising the many strands linking present images of home and family life with those held in the past, it is important not to overlook the developing nature of the modern domestic ideal.

INFLUENCES ON THE RISE OF THE MODERN DOMESTIC IDEAL

Thus the development of the modern domestic ideal, in which fulfilling family relationships are enjoyed in the comfort of a private home, has been long and drawn-out, and is still taking place. The processes through which it has emerged have been complex, and frequently contradictory (Davidoff *et al.*, 1976; Gittins, 1982), giving further cause to doubt the simple evolutionism of at least the cruder privatisation models. Privatisation is a diverse phenomenon, with diverse causes, as can be seen from the existence of significant differences in the assumptions and explanations of the accounts of the process of privatisation which are available (Burgoyne and Clark, 1984). Perhaps the most important of these differences relates to the question of choice, the degree to which people's lives are as home-centred, family-centred, and private as they choose them to be. It is not at all uncommon to find writers falling into what Burgoyne has called the 'trap of implying that household structures and domestic lifestyles and strategies are individually and freely chosen' (1987, p. 85). In home life as in other areas of social relationships, choices do exist, but they are restricted by powerful structural constraints.

A good illustration of the presence of structural constraints in the development of contemporary patterns of home-life is provided by the persistence of a distinct working-class variant of the modern domestic ideal despite the growth of affluence. While it can be accepted that the modern domestic ideal is middle-class in origin, the history of its broader adoption is not one of 'diffusion' among the rest of the population (Young and Willmott, 1975), leastwise not when diffusion is understood as operating through the imitation of social superiors as and when material circumstances allow. Of course there were quite direct routes by which the middle-class ideal was transmitted to the working class, not least among them the experience of domestic service, but in general the ideal was not adopted without serious modification. Crossick has noted how Victorian 'labour aristocrats rejected much of middle-class style and values' (1978, p. 129). Moreover those dominant values not rejected 'changed their meaning as they became adapted to the conditions of the artisan world' (Gray, 1974, p. 26). The same phenomenon was noted a century later among affluent workers and their wives, who were more likely to have the 'working-class' normative identification of the 'privatised worker' than the 'middle-class' normative identification of the 'socially-aspiring worker' (Goldthorpe and Lockwood, 1963, p. 150). The achievement by working-class people of levels of income formerly the exclusive province of the middle class does not necessarily bring with it the adoption of middle-class values or ideals.

To the extent that the middle-class domestic ideal was adopted by working-class people, it was not introduced into a vacuum, but into an already existing set of social relationships with its own domestic ideology. There are certain common elements to be found in most ideologies of domesticity, and it is possible to speculate on just how much of the middle-class ideal was already familiar to the working class. To have had any impact at all, the advice and exhortation which 'experts' such as health visitors directed towards working-class women to make their lives more home- and family-centred must have struck a chord in the latter's experience, not least their 'ambivalence towards their wage-earning work' (Roberts, 1984, p. 137). Working-class women were more than simply passive bystanders in the development of the modern domestic ideal, and sometimes gave powerful voice to their distinctive point of view, particularly with regard to housing design (Lewis, 1984). For example, the presence or absence of a parlour in working-class housing became a significant political issue of the inter-war period, and only rarely was the parlour thought by those possessing one to be 'A Living Room too Many' (Mass Observation, 1943, ch. 8), despite often appearing under-utilised from a middle-class perspective. Interestingly in the post-war period Mogey (1956) found that some council-house tenants erected partitions in their L-shaped living room, so as to create a parlour.

This further indicates that particular ideals of the home cannot simply be imposed. Change takes place alongside the persistence of tradition, and researchers have continued to discover distinct middle-class and working-class variants of the domestic ideal. Even among Goldthorpe *et al.*'s affluent workers, who might be thought of as most susceptible to 'diffusion' of middle-class values, the reluctance to entertain non-kin in the home indicates 'the persistence of the long-established working-class belief that the home is a place for kin and for very "particular" friends alone' (1969, p. 92). Such contrasting usage of the home between working-class and middle-class households was reported by other investigators of the time also (Stacey, 1960, p. 114), demonstrating that affluence is not in itself enough to break down the attachment to traditional notions of privacy found among members of the working class. The 'warmest welcome' which Hoggart could remember from his traditional working-class background, '"Mek y'self at 'ome"' (1958, p. 34), was still an invitation extended only sparingly.

The increased affluence characteristic of the first post-war decades was reflected in the improved housing standards of the time, a factor which in turn promoted home-centredness:

> New building and the higher earnings which have made it possible to afford higher rents have given more families a home to themselves. And within the home, whether shared or not, living space is less cramped than it used to be . . . Today's homes are less overcrowded and more comfortable . . . the men stay at home with their wives and children (Young and Willmott, 1957, p. 9).

These changes were assisted by reductions in the length of the working week, and the increasing possession of consumer durables such as televisions also worked to reinforce what Klein labelled the 'home-centred family' (1965, p. 283). Yet while this growth of home-centredness may be associated in some way with rising living standards, it cannot be taken simply as the result of affluence in itself. Aside from anything else, home-centredness did not necessarily need higher levels of income, since, as we have seen, poverty may encourage the desire for privacy and thus foster home-centred activities.

Most importantly, accounts of home-centredness which emphasise affluence are open to the criticism of being male-centred. They usually concentrate on the way in which men have come to spend more time in the home, instead of at work and/or with workmates during leisure-time. Attention needs to be paid alongside this to changes in women's lives, where equally significant developments have taken place, at least at the level of ideology, creating nothing less than a 'new ideal for women' (Wilson, 1980, ch. 2). Part of the background of these changes was Beveridge's concern with housework, and while his contemplation of communal washing, cooking, and childcare was not followed up in the social policy reforms of the post-war years, there was broad agreement in the thinking of the time that improving the lot of housewives was an integral part of post-war social reconstruction, and here Beveridge's idea of marriage as 'partnership' proved more influential.

In the emerging 'new ideal for women', new household technology was held out to offer liberation from the drudgery of housework, allowing women more time and energy to be spent on motherhood and on developing friendship and companionship with their husbands, a previously-neglected side of marriage (Wilson, 1980). Whereas in the past housework had been viewed as burdensome, new technology allowed it to be described in other terms. An authoritative wartime view of 'the kitchen of the future', one planned and fitted out with the latest technology, referred to it as 'The Housewife's Dream' (Denby, 1941, p. 22), building on the immediately pre-war suggestion that 'the Kitchen shows the greatest advance in the modern interior: here the principle of a Laboratory for the preparation of food is tempered by the decorative element which makes it also a Studio for the creation of artistic cookery' (Abercrombie, 1939, p. xvi). This situation was the outcome of 'the application of the principles of domestic science to the planning of kitchens', producing the desired 'mixture of domesticity and efficiency' (Braddell, 1939, pp. 341, 346). In the extreme, this faith in the power of labour-saving devices to transform domestic tasks led to some serious misperceptions, such as Dennis's judgement that with 'improved equipment in the home . . . housework can take on the character of play' (1963, p. 85). When placed against this background, the development of the idea of home as a place where companionate marriage could flourish is more understandable, if no more plausible.

Companionate marriage was itself heralded as one of the main factors drawing men into a more home-centred lifestyle, and sustaining women's home-centredness. However, precisely what companionate marriage entailed was rarely specified. While evidence was readily produced to show that men were more involved in the realm of home and family than their fathers had been (Young and Willmott, 1957; Rapoport and Rapoport, 1971), it was not made clear how far this process would go, except to say that it was always likely to stop some way short of outright equality between spouses (Young and Willmott, 1975), especially where what was being considered was people's behaviour rather than their norms (Edgell, 1980). Klein was right to be cautious in describing closer conjugal relations as a 'touch-and-go transitional phenomenon' (1965, p. 288), with distinct spheres of responsibility between spouses remaining. As Mansfield has said of modern 'companionate' marriages, 'men have entered the kitchen but as visitors rather than co-workers' (quoted in Clark 1987, p. 121). Such limits to sharing in companionate marriage, together with limits to the transformative powers of developments in household technology (Hardyment, 1988), serve to emphasise the 'disjunction between the reality of suburban isolation and idealized images of wives and mothers as creative managers of modern homes' (McDowell, 1983, p. 157). What McDowell (1983, p. 156) terms the 'glorification of domesticity' bears only passing resemblance to the reality of modern home life, even for affluent households. The tensions and contradictions between idealised home-life and less-than-ideal reality set a challenge to the modern domestic ideal founded on the idea of companionate marriage.

Alongside analyses of the growth of home-centredness that focus on affluence and companionate marriage within the household, there are other accounts that set the wider scene by highlighting the role played by the state in the promotion of privatism. There is a long history of state bodies introducing paternalistic reforms, justified in terms of improving living conditions, and an equally long history of regulation with the achievement of social control as its principal objective. In the nineteenth century, undoubted improvements in housing were achieved by a mixture of encouragement, example, and enforcement, used either separately or in combination (Caffyn, 1986). From this perspective, the marked growth of privatism in the later nineteenth century was far more than an indication of a rising standard of living among the population. Daunton has observed how in this period daily life became 'less public and less communal, more private and more introverted. The agencies for change were many. These included imposition from above, out of concern for hygiene and public order' (1983, p. 232).

A similar mixture of concerns can be identified lying behind the state's guidance and regulation of working-class mothers in their performance of domestic and child-rearing duties in the early years of the twentieth century (Lewis, 1984), something which continued into the inter-war period, when state policy in areas such as education and social welfare presumed certain norms to be present in the home-life of its citizens. As Gittens has argued:

> To a great extent, although perhaps inadvertently, the state was actually *defining* what family structure and home life should be; the *size* of council houses, for instance, betrayed what the government felt to [be] the normative, the "right", size of family. The government made it more difficult economically and geographically for married women *not* to have their place in the home (1982, p. 48, emphasis in original).

In such ways, state policies worked to strengthen, if not to bring about, the family form which policy-makers presumed to be ideal.

It is difficult both in theory and in practice to disentangle the twin facets of state action, social improvement and social control, and the two are frequently to be found together, albeit in varying ratios. Lewis has written that, in the inter-war period, 'housing policy generally was formulated more from a fear of unrest by working class men than with the needs of working class women in mind' (1984, p. 29). In this it contrasts considerably with post-war reforms, with all the attention they paid to kitchens and improving the material surroundings of the housewife, and of the working class in general. Post-war reconstruction offered the opportunity to reduce inequalities between classes, particularly in the area of housing, where policy was aimed at avoiding what Bevan called 'a country of East Ends and West Ends' (quoted in Sked and Cook, 1983, p. 51). The other side of this policy has, however, brought with it the prospect of imposed uniformity.

A central feature of post-war reconstruction has been the quite rigid zoning of land for either industrial or residential use. The separation of home and work has been particularly noticeable in the planning of New Towns. Here:

> Neighbourhood units were laid out some distance from the main shopping and recreational facilities in the town centre, with just a few shops within walking distance for daily needs. Men went to the industrial estates, segregated some distance from the main living areas, so that earning and consuming were kept physically separated. There was no expectation that women would want to have employment near to their homes or that opportunities for part-time work might encourage women to combine the care of small children with paid employment (Pahl, 1984, pp. 78–9).

The New Town's achievements in providing people with houses and gardens, the context in which at least some of their planners expected home-centredness could flourish (Aldridge, 1979, p. 10), presumed the desirability of the modern domestic ideal which, in practice, led to women being isolated. The geographical separation of home and work in New Towns and large suburban housing estates also operated to push men into a home-centred existence with few ties to the wider community, as did the fact that such settlements brought together 'a population of strangers' (Lockwood, 1975, p. 22).

The resultant isolation may have been an unintended consequence of state policy, but it nevertheless serves to illustrate the ways in which what Holme has called the 'draw towards the home' (1985b, p. 45) is reinforced by powerful forces imposing privatised lifestyles on households. In the extreme it can be argued that the 'separation of the family from the work place has divorced its activity (and particularly the lifework of the domestic labourer) from the public realm

. . . The home in capitalist societies is architecturally structured to enforce the family's privacy . . . People are literally driven into private' (Seccombe, 1980, pp. 389–90). From this point of view, it is evident that the growth of privatism cannot be understood simply as an exercise of choice; at best, choice is fashioned by structural constraint.

VARIATIONS IN THE EXPERIENCE OF HOME-CENTREDNESS

Despite the romantic appeal of the image of home-life which is associated with the modern domestic ideal, it is clear that people's experiences of home-centredness are not always satisfactory. Moreover the degree of satisfaction achieved by individuals in their home-life is far from being a random occurrence; rather, it is systematically structured around such key sociological variables as gender, age, and class. Women's experiences of home-centredness are different from those of men, and children's are different from those of adults, just as there are differences in home-life between working-class and middle-class households. The modern domestic ideal glosses over these differences, and over the oddity of the idea that a single pattern of domestic organisation might suit the diversity of people's situations, needs, aptitudes, and aspirations. When the full extent of this diversity is borne in mind, it is not surprising to find significant variation in the experiences of home-centredness.

It was suggested earlier that the idea of privatisation offers a male-centred perspective on post-war changes in domestic organisation, since it is among men that the growth of home-centredness has been most marked. Women may experience this trend rather differently, as a growth of constraint rather than one of liberation. For example, the social isolation women so frequently report can be recognised as a prominent, indeed integral, aspect of privatised lifestyles. Thus for women the home can become a place of captivity (Gavron, 1968), of confinement (Hunt, 1980), the setting where they experience 'the isolation that passes for privacy' (Boys *et al.*, 1984, p. 2). In Graham's words, 'home, as the setting in which most caring is carried out, becomes not so much a haven from the rigours of the labour market as a prison' (1983, p. 26). Equally, women's responsibility for the appearance of the home makes it difficult for them to enjoy leisure in the home in the way that men can. As long as the upkeep of the home remains primarily women's responsibility, home-centredness will exercise a constraint on their lives to a far greater degree than it does for men. For example it has been argued that because women are identified with the family, it is harder for them to establish their own, independent identity and corresponding right to individual privacy (Francis, 1984).

Similar points could be made about class differences in how the home is experienced. The modern domestic ideal requires a significant amount of resources, so, as Roberts (1978, p. 83) points out, for working-class women in shared accommodation, it is 'difficult to emulate the ideal wife in the television advertisements when sharing a bathroom, and when the kitchen is a converted landing'. In the context of class inequalities in housing standards, whereby for a good many home-life may be neither private nor peaceful, the idea of the home as 'a private haven from the stresses and strains of the world' can be recognised as a 'bourgeois ideal', beyond the means of those managing tight budgets (Roberts, 1984, p. 196).

In addition to being beyond the poorest members of society, the amount of resources required to achieve the modern domestic ideal is not something static. This is because changes continue to occur in what the home is used for, and here Pahl (1984) suggests that an important dividing line is emerging between those households able to use their dwellings as sites of production and those unable to do so. The existence of domestic production beyond that needed to facilitate consumption has been recognised for some time, but earlier studies tended to play down its significance by giving it the status of a hobby (Willmott and Young, 1960; Willmott, 1963; Zweig, 1961). Pahl offers a somewhat different perspective when he writes that, the 'home as a refuelling and refurbishing base for the urban worker where "he" consumes what "he" has produced elsewhere is becoming less important conceptually and empirically. Rather, dwellings are centres for the production of goods and services supported by a highly productive technology' (1983, p. 377). Such home-based production is possible in most tenure types, but it is given particular encouragement, both material and ideological, by owner-occupation (Pahl and Wallace, 1985), and owner-occupation is, of course, class-related, whether class is understood in conventional terms or in terms of the distinction between 'bourgeoisie', 'middle mass', and 'underclass' (Short, 1982; Pahl, 1984). The existence of important divisions between different groups of owner-occupiers (Forrest and Murie, 1987) does not necessarily contradict this. Divisions between housing groups have persisted at the same time as households have become 'more privatised, inward-looking, home-centred and autonomous' (Pahl, 1984, pp. 319–20).

Clearly there are further dimensions of the diversity of people's lives which raise questions about the ubiquity of the modern domestic ideal. For example Finch's work shows how the privacy of the home can be lost where it is also a workplace. As she argues, where 'work is based in the home, the home is part of the "public" domain, both structurally and experientially, and the notion that there is a clear distinction between the two is called into question' (1983, p. 58). Similarly, in step-families it may be difficult to achieve the degree of privacy and autonomy granted to 'ordinary' families. Burgoyne and Clark, for instance, argue that 'family groups which deviate from the norm of the unbroken nuclear family may experience greater public scrutiny, both formally and informally' (1984, p. 173).

Likewise the domestic ideal does not allow for variation in children's experience. Even if research on the cultural activities of working-class female youth has tended to exaggerate their home-centredness compared to that of male youth (Griffin, 1987), there is nevertheless something to the point. Similar observations could be made about gender differences in the treatment of older children in terms of what contributions to household tasks and what degrees of obedience their parents expect of them (Leonard, 1980). Dependent elderly people also fit only awkwardly into the routines of 'normal' family life (Walker, 1983). In a quite literal sense there is little room for dependent elderly people in the modern domestic ideal, despite their undoubtedly large presence in the reality of their carers' lives (Ungerson, 1987). Like lodgers in the past (Davidoff, 1979; Laslett, 1973), the absence of elderly dependants from the domestic ideal has less to do with their numbers than with their perceived undesirability, not least the threat they pose to domestic privacy.

CONCLUSION

The modern home is then something of a contradictory phenomenon. Aspirations to the modern domestic ideal predominate, despite the diversity of people's situations and evidence of dissatisfaction with certain features of privatised lifestyles, such as social isolation. There is diversity of need in housing, the existence of which those responsible for housing provision have often been slow to acknowledge (Holme, 1985b). The modern domestic ideal and its architectural embodiment, the 'family house', are clearly inappropriate for quite substantial sections of the population, making their persistence a sociological, if not also a social, problem.

People can tolerate or even be satisfied with their current situation and at the same time aspire to a quite different status for the future. Holme's study (1985) reports fairly widespread contentment with their current situation among the young families of her sample, alongside plans to move which were well thought out, and longer-term projects which were highly ambitious. A similar disjunction between short-term goals and long-term ideals was noted by Watson and Austerberry (1986) in their study of homeless women. Consequently housing satisfaction, tied firmly to some standard of what current circumstances allow, may well be achieved without the attainment of a more distant ideal. It is the case, as Rapoport *et al.* note, that 'substandard conditions do not automatically entail misery' (1975, p. 188), although it should be added that, for this to be so, it is generally necessary for the alternatives to be restricted or absent.

Alternatives to the modern domestic ideal do exist, of course, but they are marginalised both ideologically and materially. Conventional housing design and structure reflect assumptions about the nature of family and home life, assumptions which cannot easily be questioned without challenging the whole basis of the modern domestic ideal. Some such questioning is now taking place, not least because of 'the incompatability of single family housing with a more liberalized approach to women's role' (Ungerson and Karn, 1980, p. xiii). Progress towards viable alternative forms of housing and home-life to those of the modern domestic ideal is, however, under current circumstances, likely to be gradual (Watson, 1987). As the history of post-war housing shows, ideas subversive of the modern domestic ideal do not easily take root.

REFERENCES

ABERCROMBIE, P. (1939), 'Introduction' in P. Abercrombie (ed.), *The Book of the Modern House: A Panoramic Survey of Contemporary Design* (London: Hodder & Stoughton).

ALDRIDGE, M. (1979), *The British New Towns: A programme without a policy* (London: Routledge & Kegan Paul).

BELL, C. and NEWBY, H. (1976), 'Husbands and wives: the dynamics of the deferential dialectic', in D. Leonard Barker and S. Allen (eds), *Dependence and Exploitation in Work and Marriage* (London: Longman).

BOYS, J., BRADSHAW, F., DARKE, J., FOO, B., FRANCIS, S., MCFARLANE, B., ROBERTS, M., THORNE, A., and WILKES, S. (1984), 'Introduction', in Matrix Book Group, *Making Space: Women and the Man-Made Environment* (London: Pluto).

BRADDELL, D. (1939), 'The Interior: Kitchens and Bathrooms' in P. Abercrombie (ed.), *The Book of the Modern Home: A Panoramic Survey of Contemporary Design* (London: Hodder & Stoughton).

BURGOYNE, J. (1987), 'Rethinking the Family Life Cycle: Sexual Divisions, Work and Domestic Life in the Post-War Period', in A. Bryman, B. Bytheway, P. Allatt and T. Keil (eds), *Rethinking the Life Cycle* (London and Basingstoke: Macmillan).

BURGOYNE, J. and CLARK, D. (1984), *Making a go of it: A study of stepfamilies in Sheffield* (London: Routledge & Kegan Paul).

CAFFYN, L. (1986), *Workers' Housing in West Yorkshire 1750–1920* (London: H.M.S.O.).

CLARK, D. (1987), 'Changing partners: marriage and divorce across the life course', in G. Cohen (ed.), *Social Change and the Life Course* (London: Tavistock).

CRONIN, J. E. (1984), *Labour and Society in Britain 1918–1979* (London: Batsford).

CROSSICK, G. (1978), *An Artisan Elite in Victorian Society: Kentish London 1840–1880* (London: Croom Helm).

DAUNTON, M. J. (1983), 'Public Place and Private Space: The Victorian City and the Working-Class Household', in D. Fraser and A. Sutcliffe (eds), *The Pursuit of Urban History* (London: Edward Arnold).

DAVIDOFF, L. (1979), 'The Separation of Home and Work? Landladies and Lodgers in Nineteenth- and Twentieth-Century England', in S. Burman (ed.), *Fit Work for Women* (London: Croom Helm).

DAVIDOFF, L., and HALL, C. (1983), 'The Architecture of Public and Private Life: English Middle-Class Society in a Provincial Town 1780–1850', in D. Fraser and A. Sutcliffe (eds), *The Pursuit of Urban History* (London: Edward Arnold).

DAVIDOFF, L., and HALL, C. (1987), *Family Fortunes: Men and women of the English middle class, 1780–1850* (London: Hutchinson).

DAVIDOFF, L., L'ESPERANCE, J., and NEWBY, H. (1976), 'Landscape with Figures: Home and Community in English Society', in J. Mitchell and A. Oakley (eds), *The Rights and Wrongs of Women* (Harmondsworth: Penguin).

DENBY, E. (1941), 'Plan the Home', *Picture Post*, 4 January, pp. 21–3.

DENNIS, N. (1963), 'Secondary Group Relationships and the Pre-eminence of the Family', in J. Mogey (ed.), *Family and Marriage* (Leiden, Netherlands: E. J. Brill).

DENNIS, N., HENRIQUES, F. and SLAUGHTER, C. (1969), *Coal is our Life: An analysis of a Yorkshire mining community* (London: Tavistock).

EDGELL, S. (1980), *Middle-Class Couples: A Study of Segregation Domination and Inequality in Marriage* (London: Allen & Unwin).

FINCH, J. (1983), *Married to the Job: Wives' Incorporation in Men's Work* (London: Allen & Unwin).

FORREST, R. and MURIE, A. (1987), 'The affluent homeowner: labour-market position and the shaping of housing histories', in N. Thrift and P. Williams (eds), *Class and Space: The Making of Urban Society* (London: Routledge & Kegan Paul).

FRANCIS, S. (1984), 'Housing the family', in Matrix Book Group, *Making Space: Women and the Man-Made Environment* (London: Pluto).

GAVRON, H. (1968), *The Captive Wife: Conflicts of Housebound Mothers* (Harmondsworth: Penguin).

GITTINS, D. (1982), *Fair Sex: Family size and structure, 1900–39* (London: Hutchinson).

GOLDTHORPE, J. H., and LOCKWOOD, D. (1963), 'Affluence and the British Class Structure', *Sociological Review* vol. 11, no. 2, pp. 133–63.

GOLDTHORPE, J. H., LOCKWOOD, D., BECHHOFER, F., PLATT, J. (1969). *The Affluent Worker in the Class Structure* (Cambridge University Press).

GRAHAM, H. (1983), 'Caring: a labour of love', in J. Finch and D. Groves (eds), *A Labour of Love: Women, Work and Caring* (London: Routledge & Kegan Paul).

GRAY, R. Q. (1974), 'The Labour Aristocracy in the Victorian Class Structure', in F. Parkin (ed.), *The Social Analysis of Class Structure* (London: Tavistock).

GRAY, R. Q. (1976), *The Labour Aristocracy in Victorian Edinburgh* (Oxford: Clarendon Press).

GRIFFIN, C. (1987), 'Broken Transitions: From School to the Scrap Heap', in P. Allat, T. Keil, A. Bryman, and B. Bytheway (eds), *Women and the Life Cycle: Transitions and Turning-Points* (London and Basingstoke: Macmillan).

HALL, C. (1979), 'The Early Formation of Victorian Domestic Ideology', in S. Burman (ed.), *Fit Work for Women* (London: Croom Helm).

HALL, C. (1982), 'The butcher, the baker, the candlestickmaker: the shop and the family in the Industrial Revolution', in E. Whitelegg, M. Arnot, E. Bartels, V. Beechey, L. Birke, S. Himmelweit, D. Leonard, S. Ruehl and M. A. Speakman (eds), *The Changing Experience of Women* (Oxford: Martin Robertson).

HARDYMENT, C. (1988), *From Mangle to Microwave: The Mechanization of Household Work* (Cambridge: Polity Press).

HOGGART, R. (1958), *The Uses of Literacy: Aspects of working-class life with special reference to publications and entertainments* (Harmondsworth: Penguin).

HOLME, A. (1985b), 'Family and Homes in East London', *New Society* 12 July, pp. 43–6.

HOLME, A. (1985b), 'Family and Homes in East London', *New Society* 12 July, pp. 43–46.

HUNT, P. (1980), *Gender and Class Consciousness* (London and Basingstoke: Macmillan).

JAMIESON, L. (1987), 'Theories of Family Development and the Experience of Being Brought Up', *Sociology*, vol. 21, no. 4, pp. 591–607.

KLEIN, J. (1965), *Samples From English Cultures*, vol. 1 (London: Routledge & Kegan Paul).

LASLETT, B. (1973), 'The Family as a Public and Private Institution: An Historical Perspective', *Journal of Marriage and the Family*, pp. 480–91.

LEONARD, D. (1980), *Sex and Generation: A Study of Courtship and Weddings* (London: Tavistock).

LEWIS, J. (1984), *Women in England 1870–1950: Sexual Divisions and Social Change* (Brighton: Wheatsheaf).

LEWIS, J. (1986a), 'Introduction: Restructuring Women's Experience of Home and Family', in J. Lewis (ed.) *Labour and Love: Women's Experience of Home and Family*, 1850–1940 (Oxford: Basil Blackwell).

LEWIS, J. (1986b), 'The Working-Class Wife and Mother and State Intervention, 1870–1918', in J. Lewis (ed.), *Labour and Love: Women's Experience of Home and Family*, 1850–1940 (Oxford: Basil Blackwell).

LOCKWOOD, D. (1975), 'Sources of variation in working-class images of society', in M. Bulmer (ed.), *Working-Class Images of Society* (London: Routledge & Kegan Paul).

MCDOWELL, L. (1983), 'City and home: urban housing and the sexual division of space', in M. Evans and C. Ungerson (eds), *Sexual Divisions: Patterns and Processes* (London: Tavistock).

MARSHALL, G., VOGLER, C., ROSE, D., and NEWBY, H. (1987), 'Distributional Struggle and Moral Order in a Market Society', *Sociology* vol. 21, no. 1, pp. 55–73.

MASS-OBSERVATION (1943), *An enquiry into People's Homes* (London: John Murray).

MOGEY, J. M. (1956). *Family and Neighbourhood: Two Studies in Oxford* (London: Oxford University Press).

PAHL, R. E. (1983), 'Concepts in Context: Pursuing the Urban of "Urban" Sociology', in D. Fraser and A. Sutcliffe (eds), *The Pursuit of Urban History* (London: Edward Arnold).

PAHL, R. E. (1984), *Divisions of Labour* (Oxford: Basil Blackwell).

PAHL, R. E. and WALLACE, C. D. (1985), 'Forms of work and privatisation on the Isle of Sheppey', in B. Roberts, R. Finnegan, D. Gallie (eds), *New approaches to economic life: Economic restructuring: unemployment and the social division of labour* (Manchester University Press).

RAPOPORT, R. and RAPOPORT, R. N. (1971), *Dual-Career Families* (Harmondsworth: Penguin).

RAPOPORT, R. and RAPOPORT, R. N. with STRELITZ, Z. (1975), *Leisure and the Family Life Cycle* (London: Routledge & Kegan Paul).

ROBERTS, E. (1984), *A Woman's Place: An Oral History of Working-Class Women 1890–1940* (Oxford: Basil Blackwell).

ROBERTS, K. (1978), *The Working Class* (London: Longman).
ROBERTS, R. (1973), *The Classic Slum: Salford Life in the First Quarter of the Century* (Harmondsworth: Penguin).
SECCOMBE, W. (1980), 'The Housewife and Her Labour under Capitalism', in M. Anderson (ed.), *Sociology of the Family: Selected Readings*, second edition (Harmondsworth: Penguin).
SHORT, J. R. (1982), *Housing in Britain: The Post-War Experience* (London: Methuen).
SKED, A. and COOK, C. (1983), *Post-War Britain: A Political History* (Harmondsworth: Penguin).
STACEY, M. (1960), *Tradition and Change: A study of Banbury* (Oxford University Press).
TAYLOR, P. (1979), 'Daughters and mothers – maids and mistresses: domestic service between the wars', in J. Clarke, C. Critcher and R. Johnson (eds), *Working-Class Culture: Studies in history and theory* (London: Hutchinson).
THOMPSON, P. (1977), *The Edwardians: The Remaking of British Society* (London: Granada).
UNGERSON, C. (1987), *Policy is Personal: Sex, gender, and informal care* (London: Tavistock).
UNGERSON, C. and KARN, V. (1980), 'Introduction', in C. Ungerson and V. Karn (eds), *The Consumer Experience of Housing: Cross-National Perspectives* (Farnborough: Gower).
WALKER, A. (1983), 'Care for elderly people: a conflict between women and the state', in J. Finch and D. Groves (eds), *A Labour of Love: Women, Work and Caring* (London: Routledge & Kegan Paul).
WALLACE, C. (1987), *For Richer, For Poorer: Growing up in and out of work* (London: Tavistock).
WATSON, S. (1987), 'Ideas of the family in the development of housing forms', in M. Loney, R. Bocock, J. Clarke, A. Cochrane, P. Graham and M. Wilson (eds), *The State or the Market: Politics and Welfare in Contemporary Britain* (London: Sage).
WATSON, S. with AUSTERBERRY, H. (1986), *Housing and Homelessness: A Feminist Perspective* (London: Routledge & Kegan Paul).
WILLIAMS, P. (1987), 'Constituting class and gender: a social history of the home, 1700–1901', in N. Thrift and P. Williams (eds), *Class and Space: The making of urban society* (London: Routledge & Kegan Paul).
WILLMOTT, P. (1963), *The Evolution of a Community: A Study of Dagenham after Forty Years* (London: Routledge & Kegan Paul).
WILSON, E. (1980), *Only Halfway to Paradise: Women in Postwar Britain: 1945–1968* (London: Tavistock).

WILLMOTT, P. and YOUNG, M. (1960), *Family and Class in a London Suburb* (London: Routledge & Kegan Paul).
YOUNG, M. and WILLMOTT, P. (1957), *Family and Kinship in East London* (London: Routledge & Kegan Paul).
YOUNG, M. and WILLMOTT, P. (1975), *The Symmetrical Family: A Study of Work and Leisure in the London Region* (Harmondsworth: Penguin).
ZWEIG, F. (1961), *The Workeer in an Affluent Society, Family Life and Industry* (London: Heinemann).

3 When is a Child Not a Child?

Anna Davin

By the side of many tall and bouncing young ladies in the establishment, Rebecca Sharp looked like a child. But she had the dismal precocity of poverty. Many a dun had she talked to, and turned away from her father's door; many a tradesman had she wheedled into good humour, and into the granting of one meal more. She sate commonly with her father, who was very proud of her wit, and heard the talk of many of his wild companions – often but ill suited for a girl to hear. But she had never been a girl, she said; she had been a woman since she was eight years old.

(Thackeray, *Vanity Fair*, 1847)

Commonsense tells us that children differ from adults. History tells us that how much they differ, and how, varies with time and place. Childhood, like the family, like marriage, like adolescence or old age, is influenced by cultural and economic context. Its character and ideology cannot be taken for granted. Childhood in Britain in the second half of the nineteenth century is the subject of this paper, and more particularly, how the conflict between middle-class ideals and working-class realities of childhood led to increasing regulation of the conditions of children's lives.

Of the many variables concerning childhood in this period, one stands out: the difference between rich and poor childhoods. Most obviously, the children of the well-to-do were better housed, clothed and fed. But the difference was ideological as well as economic, even if money was needed for creating the childhood they believed in. It was assumed by adults of the middle and upper classes that children were dependent on adults and subservient to them. They did not work; they played and learned. Responsibility for their care and education lay with adults: mother, father, aunt; nursemaid or other servant; governess, tutor, or schoolteacher. They belonged in the home, preferably in separate quarters:

rich houses had day and night nurseries and schoolrooms. Boys were sent to school after about eight, locally at first then sometimes away, and girls too might spend some time in school (Dyhouse, 1981). For both, education was a matter of lessons and books, and of adult teachers – often the mother at first, then paid teachers at home or at school. Whether at home or at school, children were to be segregated from the adult world. They were to accept whatever they were told by adults and ask no questions; girls especially were to know nothing of such adult matters as money or sex, and to be innocent and unworldly. While most boys progressively attained some degree of emancipation from the family in their late teens, through taking a place in other worlds such as college, business or army, their sisters reached adult status through social rites (putting up their hair and coming out; engagement and marriage) which emancipated them from one family only by installing them as dependent in another.

These ideas, though dominant by the mid-nineteenth century, were relatively new. They had developed with the emerging domestic ideology of the expanding middle class (Davidoff and Hall, 1987); the romantic vision of the innocent child (Coveney, 1967) and its sentimentalized Victorian version reinforced them. The precocious responsibility still admired in the early nineteenth century had given way by mid-century to an ideal of childish innocence. Precocity was deplored. It was 'sharpness', and unnatural, even dangerous; it implied corruption. Thus Thackeray's carefully named Becky Sharp was a threat to the innocents of Miss Pinkerton's Academy for Young Ladies. She came from another world, of Bohemian makeshift and disregarded propriety. She was used to adult male company and talk; she knew all about hunger, uncertainty, and debt; she was too 'knowing' for a child. Thackeray drily asked, 'Oh why did Miss Pinkerton let such a dangerous bird into her cage?'; her inappropriate upbringing and knowledge are crucial to her character and so to the plot.

In real life, most children did not live that ideal of the well-to-do. The industrial urban working-class household, like its rural predecessor, was one where children lived huggermugger with adults; segregation was neither possible nor expected. In the 1850s, and often still in the 1900s, it was also an economic unit in which all members but the very youngest played a part, contributing unpaid labour and any earnings. This served economic needs: in London and other large cities much employment was seasonal or irregular, and daily survival was often a struggle. But culturally, too, the expectation was that children learnt to be useful as soon as possible. As young as four they started to help at home with younger siblings and with chores, homework and errands; soon by such help they freed older members to bring in money. They joined in every form of family enterprise: laundry, outwork, wood-chopping, domestic manufacture, shops or market stalls. They earned coppers and food by helping neighbours, or more regular sums working in local shops and on market stalls, or in the workshops where much of London's production still took place. They pursued cheap or free food, queuing for yesterday's bread or for charitable handouts. And they ranged the streets alert for edible or combustible booty.

Such children were clearly not cut off from the adult world. They were prepared for adult life through participation, and their early experiences equipped them for responsibility and independence at an age when their 'betters' were still in the schoolroom. The domestic functions of a mother who was ill or died, or who was sole wage-earner, could be performed by a twelve-year-old; children who lost both parents sometimes managed to hold together as a group; while children who ran away from hunger or from ill-treatment had some chance of getting by on their own.

LITTLE WOMEN: THE CHILD AS ADULT

For those whose children were always children, these real situations were shocking if not alarming. Such reactions crystallised in two contrasting representations of the child-as-adult. The first focused on responsibility for others, and was domestic and female – the 'little woman', or 'little mother'. The second – male, street-based, and emblematic of dangerous independence – was the ragamuffin or 'street arab'.

Charley Neckett, in *Bleak House* (Dickens, 1852–3, ch. 15), illustrates the first figure, the little woman. At thirteen she was 'a very little girl, childish in figure but shrewd and older-looking in the face'; since her mother's death after eighteen-months-old Emma's birth, she had done the 'cleaning and nursing and washing', and looked after Emma and five or six-year-old Tom. Now her father had died and she was in charge. She went out washing and cleaning, with help from neighbours who found her jobs and kept an eye on the little ones (left locked in their attic home); the landlady waived the rent. Dickens exploits the tension between her age and size and her responsibility, while through Jarndyce he reluctantly admires the 'little woman', 'so young and yet with an air of age and steadiness that sat so strangely on the childish figure'. Similar scenes recur not only in Dickens' novels, but in other popular writing of the time. They abound in the Sunday-school-prize waif novels (Bratton, 1981, ch. 4).

The 'little woman' was an emotive figure for middle-class readers. She aroused indignation and pity along with admiration. By taking charge she defended the family, asserting the importance of the close ties between its members and the need for older ones to protect the younger. She was heroic. But her heroism was a sign that things were wrong – it should not be necessary or indeed allowed. She was pathetic, because in that same vision of the family children and females were essentially dependent, not responsible.

Another little woman is recorded from the mid-century, not in fiction but in the work of the journalist and social investigator, Henry Mayhew. His fascinating studies of how poor Londoners lived, based mainly on interviews, started with articles in the *Morning Chronicle* in 1849–50, and continued with his survey, *London Labour and the London Poor*, which appeared in instalments in the early 1850s and in four collected volumes in 1861–2 (Mayhew, 1968; Yeo and Thompson, 1971; Humpherys, 1977). The account of a young watercress seller he met in November 1850 illuminates the gulf between his assumptions about childhood and hers. He opened it with the comment that 'although only eight years of age [she] had entirely lost all childish ways, and was, indeed, in thoughts and manner, a woman.'

> There was something cruelly pathetic in hearing this infant, so young that her features had scarcely formed themselves, talking of the bitterest struggles of life, with the calm earnestness of one who had endured them all. I did not know how to talk with her. At first I treated her as a child, speaking on childish subjects; so that I might, by being familiar with her, remove all shyness, and get her to narrate her life freely. I asked her about her toys and her games with her companions; but the look of amazement that answered me soon put an end to any attempt at fun on my part (Mayhew, 1968, vol. 1, pp. 151–2).

Whether unconsciously or for dramatic effect, he exaggerated her shocking precocity. For despite that 'look of amazement' when he broached 'childish subjects', later in the account she spoke of knowing 'a great many' games, and of playing honeypots and kiss-in-the-ring with the girls in the court sometimes. Play was not so much unknown as hard to fit in. Often she was too tired to play, and her early morning start meant she always went to bed at seven, which no doubt encroached on playing time. She described playthings given her by the Jewish family for whom she was a 'Sabbath goy' (doing necessary tasks which they could not do without breaking the Sabbath). Asked about dolls, she said she'd never had one, and added 'but I misses little sister'. (This suggests she saw dolls mainly in terms of night-time cuddling: till recently the two had shared a bed.) Her 'look of amazement' may well have resulted from surprise at being asked about toys and games by such a person – adult, male, and a gentleman – not from ignorance of play or of fun.

Her account of herself is sturdy and matter-of-fact, and it belies Mayhew's suggestion that she had endured 'the bitterest struggles of life'. She knew cold, hunger, fatigue, and the occasional punishment ('mother . . . don't often beat me; but when she do, she don't play with me'). But she spoke warmly of her mother ('I always give mother my money, she's so very good to me'), and was grateful that she had removed her from school 'because the master whacked me'. She also spoke affectionately of her little sister and of her aunt's baby whom she looked after, and appreciatively of her open-handed Jewish employers. She was proud of what she could do: 'I am a capital hand at bargaining . . . they can't take me in' . . . 'I know the quantities very well'. Her rejection of sweets as childish was an assertion of the will to be strong and responsible, as was her reference to doing housework ('mother don't make me do it, I does it myself'), or her endurance of cold ('I bears the cold – you must'), or her refusal of tears ('No, I never see any children crying – it's no use').

Not surprisingly, Mayhew was dismayed by this child who proudly took on the burden of adult responsibility, insisted that she was not a child, felt no shame about her situation and expected acceptance or even respect rather than pity or alarm. Her strength and self-sufficiency conflicted with his notions of childhood, which were those of his class and time. Indignation at her unchildlike independence perhaps also made it harder for him to see her as part of a domestic unit, with relations of mutual obligation and affection: his emphasis is on the pathetic, unsupported little woman.

CHILDREN AND THE STREET

Mayhew's presentation of the watercress girl was nevertheless more sensitive than the general stereotype of the ragged street child. This was the second figure of the child as adult: antithetical to the little woman, it provoked fear as well as pity – the rough and cunning boy thieves in *Oliver Twist* spring to mind. Again, the stereotype had a basis in reality. Children found many ways to get a living in the street, and were highly visible. They were girls as well as boys, though according to Mayhew (1968, vol. 1, p. 471) boys had a wider range of street opportunities than girls. They emerged from slum courts and rookeries to scratch a living in busy streets and public places – wherever work, charity or pickings might be available. They swept crossings, ran messages, held horses, carried bags, guided strangers, and they turned cartwheels, sang or whistled for coppers. They sold fruit, flowers, cheap toys, and matches or lights for cigars. They picked over market refuse; stared hungrily into food-shops till driven away or bought off with scraps; and watched those who could afford to eat and might throw them a coin or crust. They seized any opportunity to earn money or food, and any chance to help themselves from an unguarded stall, shop, cart or pocket. Some became skilled pickpockets and thieves.

Those who had some form of support had the best chance of survival. To belong to a family, their own or one they lodged with or worked for, made food and shelter fairly sure, even when takings were poor or illness struck. Those who slept rough often had companions. A fictional ragamuffin in the 1860s, newly runaway, was shown the ropes by two other boys, who taught him how to find shelter and how to get a living, and invited him to go partners: 'you works with us, and you grubs with us, and you lodges with us' (Greenwood, 1866, chaps 13–15). For a newcomer such sharing was almost indispensable; for the old hands it was insurance against sickness and bad luck.

According to Lord Shaftesbury, speaking in parliament in 1848, there were some 30,000 'naked, filthy, roaming, lawless and deserted children in and about the metropolis' (Shaftesbury, 1971, p. 228). His estimate certainly included many children with homes, whose relative independence stemmed from their contributory role. The well-to-do seldom distinguished between street children with regular work and those with none, or between those who slept rough, those who paid for a lodging, and those who belonged to households. All were lumped together, condemned by appearance and behaviour alike. They were arabs, urchins, scaramouches, guttersnipes; 'a wild race', 'nomadic', 'a multitude of untutored savages', even (May, 1973, p. 19) 'English Kaffirs' and 'Hottentots'. The labels identified them as heathen and uncivilised, alien to order and progress.

For those who held that children belonged in protecting families, street and home were in total opposition. The street stood for danger and corruption, and no child with a proper home would be freely allowed there. Without a home, or with a deficient one, a child had no sanctuary from the dangers of the street, and no domestic counter to its corrupting influences. So any child who picked up a living in the streets risked moral contamination. With girls the fear, explicit or not, was that they were or would soon be 'on the street', not just in it.

Moreover, such children were not only in danger, they

were themselves dangerous. The thousands who lived by their wits with little or no adult support or control were a threat to society. They eluded (and so challenged) 'natural' adult authority, and indeed even preyed on the adult world, in a hand-to-mouth freemasonry of petty thieving and sleeping rough. Such youngsters swore, smoked, gambled, exchanged coarse repartee, begged, stole – all improper for children. And girls too did these things; the groups sleeping rough were sometimes mixed; and in the worst lodging houses a dozen children might sleep 'squeedged into one bed . . . some at the foot and some at the top – boys and girls all mixed' (Mayhew, 1968, vol. 1, p. 413). Thus 'natural' rules both of age and of gender were breached, and the cry of 'immorality' conveyed the resulting outrage.

DEALING WITH THE 'VAGRANT' CHILD

Attempts to tackle the problem of street children in the middle decades of the century stressed their identity as children, not responsible for their actions. Thus Kay Shuttleworth argued in 1837 that adult paupers might be held responsible for their misfortune (through 'want of industry, skill, frugality or forethought'), but when children were destitute it could not be their fault, since they were by nature dependent. (*Poor Law Commission, 4th Report*, App.B, pp. 145–6; Pinchbeck and Hewitt, 1973, chap. 17). Reformers who campaigned for separate treatment for juvenile offenders took the same line, on humane as well as philosophical grounds, and added that long spells in mixed-aged prisons only corrupted the young and made things worse.

Pragmatic, philosophical and humane justifications were all used by the Bristol reformer, Mary Carpenter, to argue that children and society would be best served by humane methods of prevention and reform. Even if children's behaviour was 'the very reverse of what we should desire to see in childhood', if they were 'independent, self-reliant, advanced in the knowledge of evil', for her they were still 'young beings, susceptible as our own children of privation and suffering' (quoted by Manton, 1976, p. 102). In gaol 'the very repression of all childlike feelings' made the child 'audacious and brazen', so that 'the imposing solemnity of a court [lost] all power to touch him'. Reform instead required kindness and encouragement: children needed to feel loved, and without it they became 'no longer children' (Carpenter, 1851, pp. 300, 74). She deplored the use of 'degrading or revengeful' punishment, and insisted that the important thing was to restore their self-respect by treating them 'with respect, with true Christian politeness': (Carpenter, 1851, pp. 87, 83). Although she spoke from experience, others found it hard to reconcile belief in universal childhood innocence with fears about the dangerous classes. The punitive approach continued influential, though the evangelical Reformatory and Refuge Union (1858) also stressed reform rather than retribution.

The campaign for the child offender to be treated as a child nevertheless had some success. Legislation in 1854 and 1857 empowered courts to send offenders between seven and 16 to reformatory schools. The 'vagrant' child, defined as one under 14 found begging, wandering, without home or visible means of subsistence, or frequenting the company of reputed thieves, could be sent to industrial school; so, after 1866, could those judged 'in need of care and protection' (May, 1973, pp. 26–7; Pinchbeck and Hewitt, 1973, ch. 16). These measures provided an alternative to the imprisonment of children over seven, rather than ending it; and they did not replace punishment by constructive training. But they marked official recognition that children had different needs, and the state an interest in their condition. At the same time they confirmed autonomy as an adult prerogative.

Initiatives around social issues in this period were often voluntary rather than official, and as interest in children grew, so did voluntary work on their behalf. The 'ragged school' movement, with which Carpenter and Shaftesbury were closely identified, put its faith in education. 'Ragged schools' were shoestring classes, often taught by volunteers, set up in city slums to provide basic instruction (in the Bible and in reading, writing and arithmetic) to children excluded from other schools. Later some added industrial training. They offered free shelter and warmth for a few hours, sometimes food and in a few cases dormitories too; and they helped children to repair or replace their ragged clothes

(Carpenter, 1850; Montague, 1904; Manton, 1976, ch. 5). The formation of the Ragged School Union (1844) strengthened the movement, as did the support of Shaftesbury. Ragged schools, he argued in 1848, deserved public subsidy. They reduced the number of predators and so made property safer, rescued children from destitution, taught them habits of decency and order and brought them to a knowledge of salvation. Furthermore, prevention was economically sound – better five pounds a year for a boy at a ragged school, than eleven for him in prison. He also pressed the government to 'transplant' children from the ragged schools to South Australia at the public expense, so as to remove them from vice and temptation and to help resolve colonial labour shortage (Shaftesbury, 1971, pp. 228, 249, 247, 242–3). Government aid was given to a small experimental scheme along these lines in 1849, but not renewed.

Child emigration was not abandoned as a solution, however. Both individuals and organisations were involved, and it had official support and co-operation (Parr, 1980; Wagner, 1982). The 1850 Poor Law Act empowered parish authorities to arrange the emigration of orphans and deserted children under 16. Young offenders from Parkhurst were also sent as emigrants if by good behaviour they earned a provisional pardon. Emigration for child offenders (or potential ones) increased as penal transportation declined.

In spite of ragged schools and emigration, street children were still numerous in the late 1860s, a time of economic crisis. One journalist even claimed improbably that some 100,000 London children were 'destitute of proper guardianship, food, clothing or employment' (Greenwood, 1869, p. 7). When Thomas John Barnardo, a young Irishman planning to be a medical missionary in China, came for training in the East End in 1866, he was shocked by the 'army of outcast boy-life', and stirred up a new wave of public concern. The story was often told of how one freezing cold night he led a party of doubting gentlemen from Lord Shaftesbury's house to search Billingsgate Market for sleeping boys. They found a few under tarpaulins which covered a pile of boxes. Then 'the Good Earl' offered a penny and a free meal to each, and more and more emerged, till the total was 73, aged between 17 and seven (Bready, 1930, pp. 81–6).

(The emphasis on boys was typical, and, like the inclusion of 17-year-olds as children, alerts us to bias in both definition and reporting.) Barnardo's 'philanthropic hunts' continued, and indeed were imitated, as by the Church of England Waifs and Strays Society (Behlmer, 1982, p. 58). His East End Juvenile Mission (1869) was followed by the Stepney 'Home for Lads' (1870), then many more. He also threw himself into temperance campaigns, schooling and rescue work, and sending large groups of children to Canada (Bready, 1930; Parr, 1980).

From the 1870s onwards, vagrant children came under increasing pressure. 'Every year', wrote the sociologist Charles Booth in 1889, street arabs were 'confined within narrowing bounds by the persistent pressure of the School Board and other agencies' (Booth, 1902, vol. 1, pp. 38–9). Police as well as philanthropists cleaned out their lairs. Nine-year-old Arthur Harding had been 'sleeping rough for about three weeks' in 1893 when found by police checking an empty house; and in about 1890, when Charlie Chaplin and his brother were noticed asleep by a watchman's fire at three o'clock in the morning (their stepmother, drunk, had turned them out), police made her take them back, then sent in the NSPCC (Samuel, 1981, p. 62; Chaplin, 1964, p. 39). School attendance officers lay in wait at the usual daytime haunts of children seeking pence, food or fun. Policing at railway stations became more strict, and it was harder to cadge, though carrying luggage from bus or cab to train still paid. Children with no 'proper' homes, were placed under alternative care and discipline in the proliferating orphanages, Homes, industrial schools and reformatories. Rescue stories, exciting or pathetic, but ultimately improving, filled the reports of charitable organisations and the pages of children's Sunday-school-prize books.

PROTECTION OR REGULATION?

With the introduction and enforcement of school attendance, increasingly effective from the late 1870s, any child from five to at least eleven was fair game for the authorities if seen outside the school during school hours. Moreover, since children were not held responsible for their own actions, truancy exposed their parents to sanctions as well. Obviously, parents who let their children 'run wild' were either neglecting or exploiting them, and anyway failing in their parental duty (May, 1973; Behlmer, 1982, ch. 1). Order, hygiene and protection all provided justification for extending official intrusion into the home. From 1880 truancy officers could seek their quarries indoors. Sanitary officers made night raids on low lodging houses to check for overcrowding, and could enter homes where smallpox was suspected; and from 1888 they were allowed to board canal boats and register the age and sex of those who lived on them so as to combat overcrowding and immorality (MacLeod, 1966, p. 111). At the same time the fast growing lobby against cruelty to children extended definitions of cruelty and neglect and argued that ill-treated or neglected children should be removed from their 'unfit' parents. By 1880 official custody might replace parental for three reasons: if parents could not control their children; if they were teaching them to be 'depraved and disorderly'; or if they were in prison. Legislation in 1880 and 1885 allowed children to be sent to Industrial Schools if any part of the house was used 'for immoral purposes'; while the 1889 Prevention of Cruelty to Children Act, the Poor Law Adoption Act (1889), and the Custody of Children Act (1891) added further grounds for removal, mainly based on children's right to 'reasonable' treatment and the parents' duty to provide proper care (Behlmer, 1982, ch. 3).

CHILDISH INNOCENCE AND SOCIAL PURITY

From the 1870s public concern with questions of sexuality began to fuel a campaign around 'social purity'. Practical work took two forms: 'rescue' – finding prostitutes jobs, usually domestic, and tackling their morals; and prevention – supplying economic and social support which would keep vulnerable ('friendless') girls from becoming prostitutes. The Girls' Friendly Society (1874) set up hostels, classes, clubs, and employment registers for working girls. It also asserted that 'virtue is of no class' and emphasised 'personal chastity as the crown of feminine virtue'; and it encouraged middle-class girls in concern for their poorer sisters' virtue and welfare. Similar organisations from the 1870s and 1880s included the Young Women's Christian Association (YWCA) and the Metropolitan Association for Befriending Young Servants (MABYS). Many local clubs and classes sprang up as well.

Ellice Hopkins, a passionate and influential social purity campaigner, argued that preventive and rescue work with women (in which she was very active) must be complemented by a forceful attack on men's unacceptable attitudes and behaviour (Jeffreys, 1985, pp. 9–18). Influenced by her, the Church of England Purity Society (1883), aimed at 'promoting purity amongst men and preventing the degradation of women and children'; while the White Cross Army (also 1883) enrolled men as soldiers for purity (Heasman, 1962, p. 162; Jeffreys, 1985, p. 13). In the evangelical Gospel Purity Association (1884), led by a Salvationist, men's groups pledged themselves to purity while 'Snowdrop Bands' promised to offer no enticement to men (Heasman, 1962, p. 163).

A central demand of social purity campaigners was the raising of the legal age of consent. They argued that this would protect girls by criminalising men who exploited them. (It only applied to girls.) It was raised from 12 to 13 in 1875, then (with more pressure for 'a Bill for the protection of young girls from the evil lusts of wicked men') up to 16 in 1885; but the campaign continued, with 18 or even 21 set by some as the earliest 'age of female responsibility' (Gorham, 1978; Behlmer, 1982, pp. 74–7).

This demand dominated the social purity campaign in 1885, when W. T. Stead, a journalist, caused widespread outrage with an account of sexual exploitation of children and the sale of young virgins (Stead, 1885; Gorham, 1978; Walkowitz, 1982, 1986). The Criminal Law Amendment Act passed that year, in a general onslaught on sexuality, raised the age of consent to 16, introduced sanctions against brothels, and criminalised male homosexual acts (Weeks, 1981; Walkowitz, 1978; Mort, 1987).

The real extent and character of juvenile prostitution is unclear. Stead's 'revelations' focused on young girls tricked, kidnapped or sold into brothels for an upper-class clientele.

But historical evidence on this sector is scant, as such brothel-owners made terms with the police, and their influential clientele could hush up most trouble. According to Walkowitz's authoritative study (1980), arrests for prostitution rarely listed girls under 16; and the inmates of rescue homes and of 'lock' (venereal) hospitals were most commonly 18 or 19. (These sources also show domestic service rather than street selling as the most significant former occupation of prostitutes, which challenges the reformers' notions of 'moral' home and 'corrupting' street.) In prostitutes' own accounts 16 was often the age of sexual initiation, with entry into prostitution a year or two later. Walkowitz even suggests (1980, pp. 17–18) that 'the throngs of child prostitutes' of the 1885 campaign 'must be dismissed as imaginary products of sensational journalism intended to capture the attention of a prurient Victorian public'. Certainly hard evidence is sparse.

Publicity and outrage alike suggest in any case the importance of childish innocence in late-Victorian ideology. The cry 'protection of children', whether from social-purity or anti-cruelty campaigners, mobilised support across the classes. The figure of the pathetic child was already widely familiar, from Dickens and from religious tracts and fiction. Now, with Stead's disclosures and their use in the social purity campaign, it was taken a stage further, to become the helpless (female) child victim of adult (male) lust.

The campaign of the mid-1880s drew support from the respectable working class as well as the middle class. In both, humanitarian indignation was probably compounded by the need to believe that homes were havens and families loving, and that adult men protected women and children. Stead's use of 'one of the most popular themes of nineteenth-century melodrama, street literature and women's penny magazines' – 'the seduction and exploitation of the daughters of the people by vicious aristocrats' – also spoke to both middle and working classes (Walkowitz, 1982, p. 83; 1986, p. 42). Conversely, accusations of cruelty and debauchery among the poor were easily believed both by those for whom the lower classes were outside cultured society, scarcely human and highly sexual (see Davidoff, 1979), and by members of the respectable working class hostile to the 'rough' who gave their class a bad name.

RHETORIC AND REALITY

Of course protection of children was desirable, from sexual exploitation as from cruelty and neglect. But its application inevitably drew on middle-class views concerning childhood and family. Not only a 13-year-old girl, but even an 18-year-old, came well within the middle-class definition of childhood; and those who wanted 21 to be the age of consent presumably saw childishness as lasting still longer.

Most working-class girls were wage-earners at 14 or earlier. They were well on the way to adult responsibility and awareness, and often to adult freedoms, though respectable parents expected to maintain considerable control, and might even try to prolong their dependence. Freedom (like responsibility) came earliest amongst the very poor and in rough culture, where peers had more influence than parents. Observers noted the 'young woman of the East End [who] may be 16 or even 14'; the 'factory girls with big hats and frizzled fringes, romping with their youthful lovers'; the 'horseplay between lads and lasses in the streets [which] leads one to suppose that there must be a good deal of loose living among them'; or the couples who 'had to get married' (Bewicke, 1879, p. 395; Compton, Earl, 'The Homes of the People', *New Review* 1, June 1883; Booth mss B292, p. 97; Besant, 1903, p. 60). Coster couples still often set up in their mid-teens. But as Harding recalled the rough East End girls of the 1890s, 'they wasn't easy prey for anyone' (Samuel, 1981, p. 52). Such girls knew how to look after themselves, even in the dangerous streets of Stead's scenario. Those who turned to prostitution were less probably drugged or trapped into it by wicked men than making a choice: they couldn't make ends meet; they knew other girls made money that way and decided to try it; or their 'chap' or landlady or friend urged them to it. Nor was it a life sentence: marriage and other employment remained possible (Walkowitz and Walkowitz, 1973; Walkowitz, 1977; Finnegan, 1979).

The campaign for revising the age of consent blurred the boundaries of childhood, prolonging it to 18 or even 21. It also blurred differences between common-law marriage, promiscuity and prostitution. Adolescent girls and young women were claimed as children, weak and defenceless, unfit to look after themselves or make responsible decisions, incapable of sexual choice. The campaign and the ensuing legislation reinforced the image of children as helpless, and prolonged the duration of childhood for girls. This meant an extension of social regulation, of childhood on the one hand, and of sexual behaviour on the other, though veiled by ideals of the innocent child, of marriage and of the family. As 'family' and 'home' became more rigidly defined and more prescriptive, outrage at 'child' victims or 'little adults', and concern about early and 'irresponsible' marriage among the unrespectable poor (or, still worse, neglect of it) validated further official intrusion into home and private life. Domestic 'sanctity' could be breached when prescribed standards were not met. Even the shocking stories of brutality and neglect publicised from 1884 on by the expanding Societies for the Prevention of Cruelty to Children must be placed in this context, though of course without condoning the behaviour which they described.

The coercive aspects of the protection of children placed the poor and unrespectable at a disadvantage. (Similarly, class and cultural difference compounded by racism led more recently to official abduction of aboriginal children in Australia, and of gypsy children in Switzerland.) Charges of neglect, which rather than assault was overwhelmingly the issue in NSPCC cases by the 1900s (Behlmer, 1982, p. 181), were especially liable to class bias. Many commonplaces of poverty (drink, fights, 'disreputable' means of support, unmarried parents, spells in prison, letting children find street work or 'run wild') were used to label parents as unfit, especially if they had no one from church or chapel to speak for them. And protection was about punishing parents, as well as rescuing children. When children 'in need of care and protection' were sent to Industrial Schools, the parents were required to contribute to their maintenance, being thus simultaneously deprived of parental rights and forced to fulfil parental duties. A proposal to punish mothers with prison if their daughters 'fell' below the age of 16 was supported by the Reformatory and Refuge Union in the 1900s, but rejected by civil servants who thought it 'absurd to make a mother criminally responsible for the seduction of her daughter', impossible 'to turn a careless or stupid mother into a clever and careful one by Act of Parilament', and undesirable to make her a criminal (Public Record Office files HO45 10285 107840/1–2).

Advocates of 'child-saving' and rescue work in this period deployed both the threatening figure of the street arab and the pathetic figure of the waif. Yet many children admitted into Homes were not rescued waifs or arabs but casualties of domestic emergency, brought in by parents or other relatives, who expected to retrieve them once the crisis was weathered. More than half of Barnardo's young emigrants between 1882 and 1908 were admitted to the Homes on purely economic grounds, and 'moral' grounds alone accounted for only 11 per cent (Parr, 1980, ch. 4, esp. pp. 62–4). But accusations of parental immorality and improvidence abounded, and were invoked to justify restriction of contact between children and their families, 'philanthropic abduction' of children to the colonies without their parents' consent, and suppression of letters (Parr, 1980, ch. 4; Wagner, 1982, ch. 8). Even when contact was maintained, and before emigration, retrieval was hard. Barnardo 'fought over 80 attempts by parents to reclaim their children through the courts' (Wagner, 1982, p. 147).

So the rhetoric of rescue hid 'a tension between the families' descriptions of their own needs and the child-savers' accounts of the children's needs' (Parr, 1980, p. 63). It proclaimed the righteousness of middle-class ideology, and the duty to intervene in working-class life. It asserted the sanctity and safety of the (conforming) home, and the dangers of the street. And, at the same time, it confirmed the passive, dependent role of children, whether victims or rescued.

CHILDREN AND RESCUE

Street children themselves sometimes defended their independence. Even ragged schools provoked resistance at times, though as children were not compelled to attend, discipline could not be too severe. Street children were 'not accustomed to ordinary rules; they [had] never been subjected to domestic discipline, and they [had] no notion of being forced'

(Shaftesbury, 1971, p. 238). The child-savers believed that such children had to be disciplined for their own good. Not surprisingly, children who had learnt to survive, and who had known authority as harsh and restrictive, were wary of rescue. A cabbie recalled a night hunt with Barnardo when they found two nine-year-olds sleeping rough: 'We got 'em in the cab, but they licked us; as soon as we opened the door they shot out like two eels' (Clapham, 1938, pp. 51–3). Inmates of the Homes who found the discipline and routine hard to accept were labelled 'unruly', 'audacious' and 'insubordinate', and attempts to subdue them were never abandoned. Some, too, 'could not bear to be closed in'. But those who ran away were often picked up again, and returned runaways were heavily punished.

Homes suited some, however, even if autobiography never provides as glowing a picture as fiction and journalism. They offered support for those whom disease, accident or inheritance had handicapped (Heasman, 1962, chaps 11, 12). The adaptable enjoyed the regular food and relative comfort, and avoided trouble. Harding, three years in Barnardo's Leopold House, was 'only a penny tram ride from home' and he was allowed back every Saturday, probably because his mother cunningly passed as decent however poor (Samuel, 1981, p. 62). In smaller Homes children could meet with kindness and understanding. In large ones, authority was impersonal, and strict discipline, loneliness, and even bullying were likely. But even there 'the carefully instilled conviction that they would enjoy life in Canada' might console when institutional life bore hard (Parr, 1980, p. 71).

Although in the outside world employment was considered inappropriate for children and strengthened the case for their 'rescue', rescued children supplied much of the daily domestic labour in Homes. This was seen as good training and discipline, and kept costs down. There was probably also an element of punishment, or at least, as with 'rescued' prostitutes, a notion of purification through work, especially washing. Children swept and scrubbed, carried water and coal, chopped firewood, helped in the kitchen, 'learnt' laundry work or cobbling, sewed clothes and household linen for the establishment and sometimes for sale, and kept clothes and other articles in repair. Darning stockings was one of the heaviest chores. In the Orphan Working School on Haverstock Hill, for instance, during one year (1878), the 243 senior girls mended 16,554 pairs of stockings and 35,480 'other articles' for the 277 senior boys and the 93 boys and 57 girls of the junior school. Making kept them busy, too: they made dresses, pinafores, skirts, shirts, stockings, aprons, sheets, pillowcases, towels, handkerchiefs and so on: 3,487 items in all. As for schooling, the children all did basic subjects; and in addition boys were offered Acoustics, Light and Heat, Botany, Euclid and Algebra, but girls only Domestic Economy – the theory to match their practice. Older girls in such institutions were sometimes made half-timers to cope with the work. The same pattern prevailed in the workhouse schools of the early twentieth century. At nine, Ada Bennett was one of the girls 'sent to help feed and change the babies'; and on Wednesday afternoons, instead of school, she went back to the dormitory to 'sew buttons on or to mend and darn socks' (Peckham People's History, 1983, p. 86). Since girls' future was to be domestic, such work counted as training.

Emigrants apart, the girls taken into Homes and other institutions were usually kept until 15 or 16 (both for their protection and for their labour), though boys might leave at 14. Then they were placed in employment, preferably residential, and for girls almost always domestic service. Those brought up in institutions often found it hard to adjust to the unfamiliar routines and relative independence of everyday life outside. Many Homes kept in touch for a while, and encouraged their girls to join organisations like the Girls' Friendly Society, MABYS and the YWCA (see above), which would provide suitable company and support in the longer term.

Protective philanthropy also extended to the young outside institutions. For young people from working-class homes, boys especially, there was a surge of provision from the 1880s. The Boys' Brigade and the cadet movement (both mid-1880s) shared militaristic methods and reforming ends (Springhall, 1986, pp. 151–2). Clubs, too, proliferated, run by missions and settlements (often those linked to public schools), churches, chapels, and individuals. Their leaders were influenced both by the concerns of the social purity movement, and by growing anxiety about the prospects and activities of working-class boys and young men, or adolescents, as they were coming to be known (Gillis, 1974 and 1975; Musgrove, 1964; Springhall, 1986). Although they varied in style and content, their common aim was to promote temperance, purity and other moral and behavioural conventions, and to keep young people off the street and out of the penny gaff or the music hall by providing alternative activities and interests after the day's work. Refining effects on rough girls were claimed from 'even only few months intercourse with ladies'. Clubs forbade swearing and encouraged temperance; and one settlement head claimed that club members were marrying at 25 or 26 instead of 18 or 19.

CONCLUSION

Rescue and protection, then, apparently uncontentious and wholly admirable aspects of nineteenth-century philanthropy and social progress, seem more complex on closer examination. Their well-meaning protagonists inevitably held to the beliefs and practices of middle-class ideology. Where working-class practice was different, they saw it as their duty to intervene, directly or indirectly. Whether working with the inmates of Homes, or with children and young people who lived in their own homes, they taught the values and conventions of their class, adapted to suit servants. Industry, punctuality, a neat appearance and knowing your place – in age, gender and class terms – were encouraged; challenging authority and convention were deplored. Their ideas about childhood and the family had profound effects for the poor and powerless. Laws requiring children to be sent to school, laws enforcing parental responsibility or permitting children's removal, laws against cruelty to children and children's employment – all affected the daily lives of the poor. At the same time charitable help discriminated between the 'deserving' and the feckless, and rewarded conformity to convention.

The notion of childhood itself, again easily assumed to be obvious, turns out to be contentious and shifting. By the end of the nineteenth century the wholly or even partly independent child, though not altogether extinct, was an altogether rarer bird. Reasons for this include a substantial rise in living standards (Hobsbawm, 1968); the impact of compulsory school and of protective measures, both legislative and voluntary; and the erosion of 'rough' working-class culture by the lapping waves of respectability. By the turn of the century the dominant view (in the respectable working class as well as above it) of children who fended much for themselves was that they were neglected and pathetic. The transition had been made from street arab to waif.

This did not mean that a homogeneous, cross-class practice of childhood had emerged (Davin, 1987). True, most urban working-class children in the early twentieth century attended school for six to eight years and grew up in households whose main wage-earners were adult: often the father alone or with teenagers, though mothers' earnings were also sometimes needed. But working-class children did still have responsibilities and did still work. Girls and sometimes boys were the mother's auxiliaries in domestic labour, especially for child care, chores and shopping. Before school, after it, in the dinner hour, and on Saturdays, many boys and girls earned money, and they could seldom keep all they earned. Institutional children were expected to work as well, especially girls, even though the importance of sheltering children from work and responsibility dominated both the rhetoric of rescue and the critique of the working-class family.

If the need for children's earnings had diminished in some households, the need for their domestic labour had not. Improved circumstances meant more to do and perhaps higher standards. The family that was no longer crammed into one room had more space, more windows, more furniture and more ornaments, which meant more scrubbing, dusting, sweeping and polishing; it probably had curtains to be washed, bed linen to be changed; more clothes to be kept clean and neat, a copper and probably a front doorstep to be kept white. Food prepared in a proper kitchen, on a stove blackleaded every day, was eaten more formally at set meals. Children had to be scrubbed and tidy for school and Sunday school at least.

This was all the task – and pride – of the housewife (Ross, 1985). But the custom of children contributing to the household economy and learning through work allowed her to delegate to them. At the same time, the association of domestic work with the sphere of women, reinforced now by the domestic emphasis in girls' education and the greater importance given to the attendance of boys, meant that more help was expected from girls. And the increased policing of the streets and the restrictions (especially after the 1908 Children's Act) on children's street employment limited outside earning but not unpaid domestic work. Respectability, too, kept girls close to home but let boys roam.

Children of the labouring poor in the 1900s, then, were largely dependent (though girls especially gave work) until at 14 they escaped school and most of the restrictions on their employment. Even then, family expectations usually kept them contributing money and labour to the family economy; family rules held them in check socially and still more sexually; and clubs and youth organisations tried to contain them in the no man's land of adolescence. They still bore much more responsibility than their middle-class coevals, however; they had more experience of work, money and other 'adult' preserves; they knew they would soon be able to support themselves; and they could not be manipulated through expectations of inheritance or corralled into 'suitable' marriages. At the same time, the conventions of gender difference skewed the development of new childhood patterns. The street arab and the waif were no more; and children spent more time in school and home (or Home). But if boys could not be boys, girls were often still little women.

REFERENCES

BEHLMER, G. K. (1982), *Child Abuse and Moral Reform in England, 1870–1908* (California: Stanford University Press).

BESANT, W. (1903), *As We Are and As We May Be* (London).

BEWICKE, A. (1879), 'Recreation for Girls', *Social Notes* 3.

BOOTH, C. (1902), *Life and Labour of the People in London* (London: Macmillan).

BRATTON, J. S. (1981), *The Impact of Victorian Children's Fiction* (London: Croom Helm).
BREADY, J. W. (1930), *Doctor Barnardo, Physician, Pioneer, Prophet: Child Life Yesterday and Today* (London).
CARPENTER, M. (1850), *Ragged Schools: their Principles and Modes of Operation, by a Worker*.
CARPENTER, M. (1851), *Reformatory Schools for the Children of the Perishing and Dangerous Classes*.
CHAPLIN, C. (1964), *My Autobiography* (London: Bodley Head).
CLAPHAM, W. E. (1938), *The Good Fight at Bow* (London: Hodder & Stoughton).
COVENEY, P. (1967). *The Image of Childhood* (Harmondsworth: Allen Lane).
DAVIDOFF, L. (1979), 'Class and Gender in Victorian England: the Diaries of Arthur J. Munby and Hannah Cullwick', *Feminist Studies* 5.
DAVIDOFF, L., and HALL, C. (1987), *Family Fortunes: Men and Women of the English Middle Class, 1780–1850* (London: Hutchinson).
DAVIN, A. (1987), 'Edwardian Childhoods: Childhood and Children, Image and Diversity', in J. Beckett and D. Cherry (eds), *The Edwardian Era* (London: Phaidon).
DICKENS, C. (1852–3), *Bleak House* (London).
DYHOUSE, C. (1981), *Girls Growing Up in Late Victorian and Edwardian England* (London: Routledge & Kegan Paul).
FINNEGAN, F. (1979), *Poverty and Prostitution: a study of Victorian Prostitutes in York* (Cambridge University Press).
GILLIS, J. (1974, revised 1981), *Youth and History* (New York: Academic Press).
GILLIS, J. (1975), 'The Evolution of Juvenile Delinquency in England, 1890–1914', *Past and Present* 67.
GORHAM, D. (1978), '"The Maiden Tribute of Modern Babylon" re-examined: Child Prostitution and the Idea of Childhood in late-Victorian England', *Victorian Studies* 21.
GREENWOOD, J. (1866), *The True History of a Little Ragamuffin* (London).
GREENWOOD, J. (1869), *The Seven Curses of London* (London).
HEASMAN, K. (1962), *Evangelicals in Action: An Appraisal of their Social Work*.
HUMPHERYS, A. (1977), *Travels into the Poor Man's Country: the Work of Henry Mayhew* (University of Georgia Press).
JEFFREYS, S. (1985), *The Spinster and her Enemies* (London: Pandora).
MACLEOD, R. M. (1966), 'Social Policy and the Floating Popula-

tion: the Administration of the Canal Boats Acts, 1877–1899', *Past and Present* 35.

MANTON, J. (1976), *Mary Carpenter and the Children of the Streets* (London: Heinemann).

MAY, M. (1973), 'Innocence and Experience: the Evolution of the Concept of Juvenile Delinquency in the mid-19th century', *Victorian Studies* 17.

MAYHEW, H. (1968). *London Labour and the London Poor*, [1861–2] (New York: Dover).

MONTAGUE, C. J. (1904), *Sixty Years in Waifdom, or the Ragged School Movement in English History.*

MORT, F. (1987), *Dangerous Sexualities: Medico-Moral Politics in England since 1830* (London: Routledge & Kegan Paul).

MUSGROVE, F. (1964), *Youth and the Social Order* (London: Routledge & Kegan Paul).

PARR, J. (1980), *Labouring Children: British Immigrant Apprentices to Canada, 1869–1924* (London: Croom Helm).

PECKHAM PEOPLE'S HISTORY (1983), *The Times of Our Lives: Growing up in the Southwark area, 1900–1945* (London: Peckham Publishing Project).

PINCHBECK, I. and HEWITT, M. (1973), *Children in English Society*, vol. 2 (London: Routledge & Kegan Paul). *Poor Law Commission, Fourth Report*, PP 1838 xxviii.

ROSS, E. (1985), 'Not the Sort that would Sit on the Doorstep: Respectability in Pre-World War I Neighborhoods', *International Labor and Working-Class History* 27.

SAMUEL, R. (1981), *East End Underworld: Chapters in the Life of Arthur Harding* (London: Routledge & Kegan Paul).

SHAFTESBURY, Lord (Anthony Ashley Cooper) (1868, reprinted 1971), *Speeches of the Earl of Shaftesbury upon Subjects Having relation chiefly to the Claims and Interests of the Labouring Class* (Shannon: Irish University Press).

SPRINGHALL, J. (1986), *Coming of Age: Adolescence in Britain, 1860–1960* (Dublin: Gill & Macmillan).

STEAD, W. T. (1885), *The Maiden Tribute of Modern Babylon (Report of the Pall Mall Gazette's Secret Commission)* (London).

THACKERAY, W. M. (1847–8), *Vanity Fair* (London).

VALLÈ, J. S. (1884), *La Rue à Londres* (Paris).

WAGNER, G. (1982), *Children of the Empire* (London: Weidenfeld & Nicholson).

WALKOWITZ, J. (1978), 'The Making of an Outcast Group: Prostitutes and Working Women in Plymouth and Southampton', in M. Vicinus (ed.), *A Widening Sphere: the Changing Roles of Victorian Women* (Bloomington: Indiana University Press).

WALKOWITZ, J. (1980), *Prostitution and Victorian Society: Women, Class and the State* (Cambridge University Press).

WALKOWITZ, J. (1982), 'Male Vice and Feminist Virtue: Feminism and the Politics of Prostitution in nineteenth-century Britain', *History Workshop Journal* 13.

WALKOWITZ, J. (1986), 'Science, Feminism and Romance: the Men's and Women's Club, 1885–89', *History Workshop Journal* 21.

WALKOWITZ, D. and WALKOWITZ J. (1973), '"We are not Beasts of the Field": Prostitution and the Poor in Portsmouth and Southampton under the Contagious Diseases Act', *Feminist Studies* 1.

WEEKS, J. (1981), *Sex, Politics and Society: the Regulation of Sexuality since 1800* (London: Longman).

YEO, E. and THOMPSON E. P. (1971), *The Unknown Mayhew* (London: Merlin).

4 Transitions in the Youth Debate: A Critique

Sarah Irwin

INTRODUCTION

This paper presents a discussion of rites of passage from youth to adulthood in contemporary Britain. It is guided by an interest in youth as a historically variable social category as well as a life-cycle stage. A review of the debate on the transition from youth to adulthood is presented. The terms of the debate have developed in a way which encourages more explicit interest in locating youth as a life-cycle stage with historically contingent meaning. Literature in social and economic demography is drawn on in arguing that the terms of the debate need to be spread still more widely in order to address the methodological challenges presented by the study of life cycle and structure.

The main issues are as follows:

(1) The youth debate has centred on employment circumstance and continued a tradition of concern with the school-to-work transition. The focus has been on youth as a life-cycle stage. Youth non-employment has been interpreted as undermining the achievement of adult status, that is, the period of youth has undergone structural change. However, the equation of adulthood with a secure wage (or motherhood) has limited the scope for historical comparison, and the focus on the life-course of contemporary cohorts has constrained the development of understandings of structural change in the period of youth.

(2) Employment circumstance is of central importance, but it needs to be understood in terms of its relationships with other variables indicative of the attainment of adult independence and responsibilities. Early life-course events include leaving school, entering the labour force, leaving the parental home, establishing an independent household, mar-

riage and family formation. These events label change in household and family circumstance. A definition of youth in terms of sets of events as they occur in relation to economic circumstance would allow for the development of broader historical bases for comparison. This would enable an exploration of economic processes in structuring patterns of progression from youth to adulthood. Only by an analysis of process is it possible to consider the extent to which structural change holds differential meaning across socio-economic groups.

(3) Economic circumstance is important to the timing of events, but the form of the relationship remains unclear. Demographic evidence shows interesting patterns of change in the timing of early life course events. It is important to incorporate into the analysis of youth a more critical understanding of these patterns and of the literature which attempts their explanation. This should improve understandings of the economic and social relationships and of change in the experience of youth and early adulthood.

YOUTH AND EARLY ADULTHOOD IN REVIEW

This section presents a discussion of the youth transition debate from the 1960s to the mid-1980s. Important developments and continuities in the youth debate are outlined. A serious problem for the debate has been the form of its definition of youth as a life-cycle stage. While arguments around structural change in the position of youth have recently been advanced, the associated research frameworks have constrained the development of understandings of change.

In the 1960s and 1970s, years of relatively full employment, research was developed in terms of the perceived discontinuity between separate institutions. Analysis was of processes that would explain apparently 'smooth' transitions from school to work. Social-psychological models were predominant here, and continuities between school and work were explained in terms of family, school and work socialisation (see Roberts, 1968; Ashton and Field, 1976). The literature presented the period of youth in terms of the perceived psychological problems of the transition to adulthood. The youth and employment issue was set up in terms of entry into working life.

Roberts, for example, in the late 1960s, wrote a critique of earlier psychological models and stressed the importance of social environment in structuring young people's conceptions of their interests and capabilities. Earlier writers had interpreted careers as being a working out of young people's ambitions. Education and home circumstances influenced occupational allocation through their effect on vocational aspirations. Roberts criticised the ideology of free occupational choice implied in these models, arguing that ambitions were to be explained by social location rather than conversely. He posited an alternative model whereby school leavers' careers derived from the employment opportunity structure, with youth placed with differing degrees of access to different types of employment. 'Social proximity' to types of employment, malleable orientations to occupational roles and socialisation explained the smoothness of entry into work (Roberts, 1968).

Ashton and Field, in the mid-1970s, similarly argued the existence of a general fit between school and work in terms of orientations and socialisation. They distinguished groups in terms of temporal orientations, wherein different social-economic classes hold different perspectives, from a focus on the immediate present through to long-term planning. Socialised orientations to work are confirmed on entry into different 'career' routes. Work and career structures, then, confirm orientations acquired at home and school (Ashton and Field, 1976).

The work of these authors emphasised the significance of employment opportunities in structuring apparent choices, and was important in laying to rest models of unconstrained choice. However, by focusing on the period of transition to work, point of entry into the labour force was emphasised at the expense of a more general theoretical understanding of youth.

More recent work has been increasingly concerned with youth unemployment, and attention has been directed to structural change. The theoretical emphasis on point of entry into the labour force has continued. This presents difficulties for arguments of structural change, an important theme in contemporary literature. While life-cycle change ('transition from youth to adulthood') is part of structural change, the latter cannot be accessed by the focus on a single cohort. Cross-sectional analysis cannot specify the mechanisms whereby structural change is possible, since it ignores the dynamic implied in arguments of change. While the bulk of youth research published through the 1980s has been concerned with structural change in the circumstance of youth, the narrow conceptualisation of youth has inhibited arguments of change.

Before I discuss this literature, I shall briefly describe the circumstance which it was addressing. The literature developed in response to the huge increase in youth unemployment, and in response to government policy on youth training, employment and youth wages. The number of school-leavers entering the labour force without the guarantee of a secure wage was a cause of increasing political and social concern. The percentage of 16–18-year-olds in Britain who were unemployed or on training schemes grew from 10.1 in 1979 to 27.0 in 1984 (DES figures, quoted in Raffe, 1985, who provides a discussion of trends and changes in unemployment estimates). Aggregate earnings statistics are also indicative of interesting changes in the economic relationships of youth and early adulthood. Mean earnings for young age groups have been increasing over the years, albeit at a slower rate than among older age groups. There has been a significant reduction in the earnings of young men, relative to full adult wages between 1979 and 1986. Median and quartile measures provide a slightly more detailed picture, and show a drop in real earnings for some (age defined) groups between the mid 1970s and the mid 1980s (from New Earnings Survey data). Earnings data then, as well as the extent of non-employment among young people, are suggestive of potential problems for some groups in securing the resources that underwrite the acquisition of adult responsibilities and independence. With new youth-training and social security arrangements the Government is reducing state commitment to providing resources that underwrite paths to independence. (See Harris, 1988 for a review of change in social security arrangements.)

The research focus in the early 1980s, then, was concerned with the nature of changes in the position of youth. If earlier work was conceived in terms of the perceived psychological problems of the transition to adulthood, this more recent literature was set up in relation to the perceived structural problems of making the transition to adulthood. Roberts, writing in the 1980s, argued that through the 1950s and 1960s there was sufficient consistency between school leavers' ambitions and the occupational structure for the majority to make 'smooth transitions'. He suggested that the main problems surrounding work were never to do with the nature of transition, but rather rooted in the quality of available jobs. He noted the importance of opportunity structures as determinants of school-leaver trajectories, and argued that, with mass unemployment, a collapse in these structures has occurred (Roberts, 1984).

Two main branches of the literature published earlier this decade are discussed below. The first presented a critique of the New Right and its appropriation of the political agenda for youth. The second branch was concerned with the nature of change in employment processes and its consequences for youth, that is, studies directed towards analysis of change in labour demand. While these aspects of the youth debate remained quite distinct, they hold parallels in their conceptualisations of youth. In both, youth is defined in terms of labour force circumstance, and this is the only axis used in arguments of structural change.

The critique, by a number of authors, of the Youth Training Scheme (YTS) as social control again focuses attention on point of entry into the labour force: a critical moment in the reproduction of labour power and one which has been appropriated by the New Right. The literature charted the growth of the Manpower Services Commission (MSC) through the early 1980s, and examined the ideological underpinnings and resonances of its policy.

Benn and Fairley, for example, argued that the New Training philosophy was being used to break working-class young people into accepting a lifetime of low wages and long periods of poor employment. The implementation of the Conservatives' political philosophy 'has meant progressively – and largely secretly – planning to close down work for everybody under eighteen' (Benn and Fairley, 1986, p. 3).

The subordination of the needs of young people to the needs of industry was also a theme of Finn. He argued that mass youth unemployment had brought about a need to intervene to ensure a disciplined, productive and malleable labour force (Finn, 1982; 1987). Finn saw a dramatic problem being posed for the state by potential political and social unrest, and he constructed the issue of training as a kind of mind management. State training policy was conceptualised as an attempt to ingrain the work ethic deeply enough for youth to survive long periods of unemployment. The work by Walsgrove, where unemployed youth are argued to fantasise about a normal employed lifestyle, provides an interesting contrast. (See Walsgrove, 1987.) Similarly, Markall and Gregory argued that the MSC had amplified the myth that unemployment was a result of the mismatch between young people's abilities and those required by employers. YTS was training young people into a mute acceptance of the work ethic (Markall and Gregory, 1982).

The critique of the deficit model implied in YTS was a theme which connected the writings of several authors. The politically motivated assault on the transition into the workforce was criticised also in discussions of social and life skills: a cultural deficit model which guided the content of training (see the collections of papers in Bates *et al.*, 1984; and Rees and Atkinson, 1982).

The arguments, then, were set up in terms of the perceived discrepancies between labour demand and supply, and of the ideological gelling of the two. These were evidenced in a deficit model of youth implicit in YTS, which served to hide the inadequacy of a training policy where the real problem resided in the lack of jobs. Government policy was argued to reify the popular myth that the fault lay with young people and not in the economic structure. The critiques led to very generalised policy recommendations, from arguing for a participatory debate on the kind of work society needed (Benn and Fairley, 1986), to teaching 'subversive skills' (Atkinson *et al.*, 1982).

The explanatory models were often explicitly conspiratorialist. While they focused attention on the period of youth and argued that it had changed its meanings, the frameworks were established in terms of unemployment, youth training and the ideology of the New Right. They did not consider the definition of youth outside these terms, which inhibited the possibility of broader, analytical explanations of change.

The other main branch of youth research in the early 1980s was a debate over the nature of unemployment. Arguments hinged on the issue of whether youth unemployment is a structural or cyclical phenomenon. The literature was important for its emphasis on YTS as an integral part of the labour market: a better understanding of employment processes was needed in order to understand the operation of YTS as it fitted into these processes. This provided a difference in emphasis to that outlined above, where YTS was seen as an ideological intervention and considered within these terms of reference.

Ashton and Maguire examined the changing structure of job opportunities and YTS was considered within that context (Ashton and Maguire, 1986). They argued that, in the organisations surveyed by them, the implementation of YTS had made no major changes either in the number of young people recruited, or in their access to different types of jobs. The authors conducted an interview survey of 18–24-year-olds in four towns in England chosen for their differing employment structures. They examined the job movement of young adults and the connection between early work experience and entry into the adult labour market. Their arguments were based on a conceptualisation of the youth labour market as being distinct from that of adults, and differing in its entry patterns and in the selection criteria used by employers. This conceptualisation was central to their argument that the youth labour market was undergoing specific forms of structural change, an argument heavily contested by Raffe (Raffe, 1986).

Ashton and Maguire argued that changes in the industrial structure were having a differential impact across market segments. The shift in importance from the manufacturing to service industries had increased the number of openings in higher occupational segments and decreased the number in manual segments, where effects were intensified by economic recession. There were hints at a growing gap in opportunities for young people, exemplified by the lack of training opportunities for those aged 18 or more and without training. Those who had not already been absorbed into the labour market at 16 or 17 were destined for jobs without age barriers, jobs that tended to be in less-skilled occupations. Further, technologically advanced industries were argued to be closing their internal labour markets to school leavers. New technologies, then, were argued to signal a permanent contraction in employment opportunities for young people (Ashton and Maguire, 1986. Also, see Roberts, 1986).

The arguments of the importance of structural change presented by Ashton and his colleagues, and a number of other authors (see Finn) were criticised by Raffe, who supported his argument with evidence from the Scottish school-leavers surveys. His contention was that youth unemployment was caused almost wholly by recession. Only if expanding industries employed smaller proportions of school-leavers than contracting industries could young people be affected by structural change. On the basis of his own statistical evidence, Raffe argued that this had not happened to any significant extent. He criticised arguments of structural change for their internal contradictions, and the lack of supporting empirical evidence. Youth unemployment, he argued, could for the most part be explained by recession (Raffe, 1986).

In its concern with work trajectories, this debate, then, had a somewhat different focus from the earlier research discussed. Arguments of structural change suggested an increasing polarisation in the resources and employment opportunities available to young people. Raffe argued that the case for structural change had not been proven in the terms which its proponents had set up. It is an argument of this paper that it was the terms which presented the difficulties, and that the interest in structural change *is* important.

GENDER DIVISIONS IN THE TRANSITION TO ADULTHOOD

This section presents a discussion of conceptualisations of the transition from youth to adulthood as it varies among young men and women. There is a general recognition that adulthood is a variable concept, holding differing meanings across sex and class. Male and female adulthood, then, have been considered as holding very different sets of meanings. This argument, however, seems to have become a basis for seeing discrete paths to separate locations, rather than seeing structural relationships between the two.

There have been frequent references to male adulthood being defined by work, and female adulthood being defined by motherhood (Bazalgette, 1978; West and Newton, 1983; Busfield, 1987; Dunnell, 1979). Surveys which asked young people about their expectations of the future found 'gender typical' expectations. These were argued to '... reflect a prevailing view in society ... that adulthood for the male is generally marked by his entry into the world of work, whereas adulthood for the female appears to be contingent upon her marriage' (West and Newton, 1983, p. 162). These sorts of arguments were made, without discussion of the inter-relationships between male and female rites of passage to adulthood. This is a serious problem once male and female routes to adulthood are seen to be structured in relation to each other.

There has been some debate over the relationship between work and motherhood for young women. For example, Burgogne emphasised the differences between women who obtain a professional qualification, or who follow occupational careers, and those for whom motherhood confirms the wisdom of choosing motherhood as their main career (Burgogne, 1987). Also, the relationship between work and home lives has been argued to be one of conflict for many women, where there is a clash in household and work responsibilities (see Kiernan and Diamond, 1983).

Cockburn provided a recent statement of gender inequality among youth, and the progression, via YTS, to adult sexual inequality (Cockburn, 1987). This was based on her survey of YTS training providers and of young people on YTS in London, between 1984–86. She argued that it was the political and economic context of YTS which made it a machine for mass producing sex inequalities. She addressed the problems involved in setting up gender inequality, and particularly sex segregation, in terms of 'choices' made at 16, and she argued that the relations of training and work feed back to young women, and act as a deterrent to making gender-contrary choices.

The point that inequalities in YTS are an integral part of inequalities in employment is an important one and deserves emphasis. In Cockburn's analysis, gender segregation, while it was not always a result of overt discrimination by employers, or of gender policing by young people themselves, was still explained at the level of ideas. There is a tension here in her argument that ideas have changed. She argues that there is a structural underpinning to gender conformity – that the context of high unemployment would involve particular risks in daring to be non-conformist. Many of her interviewees were quite liberal in terms of who could do what types of work, but this 'openness at the level of ideas coexists with an actual behaviour that is almost always conformist' (Cockburn, 1987, p. 198). In what sense can ideas be separate from, indeed contradict, social and economic structure? This question is an important one, and is returned to later in a discussion on methodology.

In the literature on youth there has been a tendency to emphasise the distinctness of male and female paths to adulthood; to set up the general impression that youth somehow crystallises the divergence of the paths that young men and women will follow. It is argued here that there are important interdependencies between male and female routes to adulthood, and that these need to be explored further than has been the case.

A SUMMARY OF ANALYTICAL PROBLEMS RAISED BY THE LITERATURE

The debate on youth and the transition to adulthood raises questions over the adequacy of conceptualisations of life cycle and social structure and the relationship between them. It is argued that models of transition have not succeeded in locating youth as a historically specific social category. The focus on youth as a period of transition, and the tendency to define youth and adulthood in terms of labour force circumstance placed limits to the arguments of structural change which have been made in the literature.

Claims have been made that there is a prolonging of the period of youth and there is an implied deferment of adulthood. There has been an alleged collapse in the paths along which some young people negotiate adult life styles. Where there is an inability to achieve a secure income there is a corresponding disruption in rites of passage to adulthood. Young adults are then said to experience 'frozen transitions' (Willis, 1985).

The idea of young adults being 'trapped as teenagers' holds substantive issues for research. It implies that, as a consequence of problems related to employment, the ability to leave home, get married, start a family and so on is no longer financially underwritten. However, these relationships have been largely assumed. The relationships between work and other transition variables were not explored systematically. To say that some young adults experienced frozen transitions remained a euphemism for their problematic employment status. Further, there is an implication that change has occurred, that to be young now holds a historically specific meaning. Such arguments, cast solely in terms of labour force circumstance, provided limited scope for comparing the experience of youth in the 1980s to that of earlier periods.

In order to consider structural change it is important to find a means of exploring change in the construction of youth and early adulthood as a life-cycle stage. It will therefore be useful to define the relationships of youth and early adulthood in terms that are broader than those presented in the earlier literature. In order to explore structural change in the period of youth and early adulthood it will be useful to develop understandings of the relationship between labour force circumstance and household circumstance. Changes in the latter may be accessed through indices that define rites of passage to adulthood more broadly. Leaving school, entering the labour force, leaving the parental home, setting up an independent household, marriage and birth of first child all pinpoint important changes in social and economic relationships.

The events and changes in circumstance that have been suggested as appropriate indices for the attainment of adult status are clearly not universally experienced, and do not provide a rigid definition of adulthood. Exceptions to the pattern should not be considered deviant within such a model. Their experience is expected to be structured in relation to societal norms. Frameworks that include indices of social and economic relationships provide a more adequate conceptualisation of the progression from youth as dependency to forms of adult independence and responsibilities.

Understandings of the relationship between change in labour force circumstance and change in household and family circumstance lead to a broader definition of youth and early adulthood as a life-cycle stage. Historical comparison, established in the same terms, would enable an exploration of structural change in the period of youth and early adulthood. These become unshackled from the static equation of work and motherhood with male and female adulthood respectively.

The next section summarises some demographic trends to show variations in event timing, indicative of change in the relationships of youth and early adulthood. Explanations of trends have been the subject of macro-level social-democraphic analyses. Issues stemming from such analyses as they are pertinent to the study of youth are discussed. The final section returns to more recent sociological studies of youth in transition that take on board patterns of event timing. It is argued that the explanation of structural change in rites of passage from youth to adulthood would be aided by resolving the contradictions between different levels of analysis.

RESTRUCTURING RITES OF PASSAGE: DEMOGRAPHIC CHANGE

An understanding of youth and of rites of passage to adulthood necessitates an explanation of patterns of event timing. A consideration of demographic processes, which show changes in the patterning of event timing, is therefore of fundamental importance to the analysis of youth.

On patterns of leaving home and establishing an independent household there is limited evidence, but see Kiernan, 1984; Wallace, 1987a; 1987b; Jones, 1987b and Murphy and Sullivan, 1986. For a discussion on state 'privatisation' of youth dependency see Harris, 1988.

On changing patterns in ages at marriage and birth of first child, the last two decades have seen a reversal of the long-term trend this century to lower ages at family formation, a trend which was quite marked in the 1950s and 1960s. The 1970s witnessed a change which has continued and become more pronounced through the 1980s (OPCS data). Since the early 1970s there has been a significant decline in marriage rates, most dramatic among younger age groups. Birth rates have also declined. The number of births per thousand women aged under 20 fell by 40 per cent between 1971 and 1986, and by 39 per cent for those aged 20–24 (Social Trends, 1988, figures for England and Wales). The 1970s also saw an increasing interval between marriage and the first birth to married couples, with a median interval of 20 months in 1970s, 31 months in 1978 and 28 months in 1981 (Kiernan, 1983).

Data provided by Thompson shows that the generation born in 1955 shows a significant change in the timing of first births. While up to the age of 18 its rate of fertility was higher than that of earlier generations, it shows a pattern of delayed starts in childbearing, reaching its peak for mid-20-year-olds, that is two to four years older than among earlier generations. Women of this generation who had not had a child by the age of 18, in 1973, then significantly delayed having children (see Thompson, 1980). Other evidence indicates delays in family formation across all social groups, but it is more pronounced among social classes 1 and 2 (Joshi, 1985).

The figures presented by Joshi suggest a fairly neat relationship between husband's social class and the age of mother at first birth; the less skilled the occupation the lower the age at childbirth. However, results from an analysis of data collected in the Medical Research Council's Survey of Health and Development, where occupational groupings are based on last full-time job held at the age of 26 for both men and women, suggest the strong likelihood of skilled male workers having a child at an earlier age than their unskilled counterparts (Kiernan and Diamond, 1983). These authors argued the inadequacy of the usual dichotomy between manual and non-manual workers. While women who were classified as unskilled in their own right have the highest rate of early childbirth, the probability that men in skilled manual occupations would be fathers at the age of 22 was 80 per cent greater than for those in non-manual occupations, but also 30 per cent greater than for those in semi-skilled and unskilled occupations; that is, there is no straightforward correlation between socio-economic groups and age at childbirth. An important research question is the extent to which this patterning is underlain by economic resources.

There have been various attempts at explaining the relationship between economy and demographic change; and at explaining patterns of marriage and fertility as they are related to the economy, the state of the housing market, and the pattern of women's attachment to, and rewards from work, relative to men. Models presented in such analyses tend to be based on large data sets, and draw on economic theory in explaining patterns of event timing and demographic change. Macro-level explanations that rest on theories of micro-level behaviour have been made, but are not informed by empirical analysis at a micro level. This is the case in the explanations provided by Oppenheimer, 1982; Hogan, 1981 and Ermisch, 1983. For example Ermisch models marriage and childbirth patterns on the basis of household utility maximisation decisions, which may fit as a broad model (Ermish, 1983), but as an explanation of individual decision-making this is problematic. If people do not behave in the manner specified in the models then the patterning of their behaviour needs to be considered anew.

Work at both levels of analysis has addressed event timing as it varies across class. Marriage and family formation would seem to be patterned over lifetime earnings profiles (see Oppenheimer, 1982; Wallace, 1987). Broadly it appears that event timing may display a logical pattern in terms of lifetime resources. Steep profiles, where there is a significant rise in earnings at least until the middle years, mean benefits through the postponement of family formation. Relatively flat lifetime earnings profiles exclude such benefits of deferment. Generational continuities within these patterns have led a number of authors to draw on cultural explanations.

Kiernan and Diamond presented explanations of the timing of childbirth in these terms. As well as concluding the importance of qualifications, occupational class and so on in predicting the age at first birth, they argued the importance of family of origin in explaining the age at which men and women became parents. Those whose parents married and had children early were themselves more likely to become parents at an early age. The relationship held after controlling for educational and occupational experience. Therefore, the authors argue, there is some transmission of norms between generations in reproductive behaviour (Kiernan and Diamond, 1983). Dunnell presented figures on age at marriage that show differences in family-formation patterns persist between women in similar jobs (before marriage) in different socio-economic groups. She also looked at the relationship of expectations and resources to family-building patterns. Educational differences could not completely account for differences between socio-economic classes. She argued that there were additional powerful cultural and attitudinal factors leading women in manual classes to marry early (Dunnell, 1979).

This intergenerational transmission of norms has itself been the subject of analysis in some research (see Mott *et al.*, 1982 and Shaw and Statham, 1982). In the first of these the authors examined the effect of mothers' working on their daughters' work behaviour, and found a relationship which operated in the opposite direction to that hypothesised. The certainty of some relationship in the terms set up led the authors to look at mothers' attitudes to work, which they found to be a better predictor of daughters' labour force participation.

Continuities of event timing between generations, then, have been explained in the literature by various quantifiable factors. These leave an unexplained residual variation in empirical evidence which has been accounted for in terms of a 'transmission of norms'. Normative causes then come to be distinguished from structural causes in the explanatory models presented.

It is argued here that the social structure a person matures in is more important to event timing than the social structure his/her parents grew up in. Patterns of intergenerational continuities in event timing may have more to do with being born into a particular set of circumstances with respect to the social economic structure, than with a transmission of norms. A more critical understanding of the location of groups with respect to the social-economic structure should help develop understandings of the residual variation that has been explained in the literature by normative factors. It would also allow for specification of socialised norms as they are rooted in structural circumstance.

Earlier it was emphasised that an understanding of change in the circumstance of contemporary youth necessitates appropriate historical bases for comparison. The next section returns to recent sociological contributions to the youth debate. The research of Wallace (1987) and Jones (1987a, 1987b) has made advances in broadening definitions of youth and early adulthood which should help historical comparison. Some problems raised by their work are drawn together with issues stemming from the literature on generational continuity and change.

RECENT DEVELOPMENTS IN EXTENDING DEFINITIONS OF YOUTH AND EARLY ADULTHOOD

Some recent work has been significant in addressing the relationships between labour force circumstance and other 'transition variables'. Two examples are discussed, but see also Hutson and Jenkins, 1987; Murphy and Sullivan, 1986.

Wallace, in her work on the Isle of Sheppey, interviewed a cohort of 16-year-olds in 1979, which she followed up one year later, and again in 1984 (Wallace, 1987). Her work was set up partly as a critique of earlier studies that focused on the articulation of the education system and the economy and examined the reproduction of labour in this context. She criticised the notion of transition as a smooth process and argued that, in a context of high youth unemployment, there are fractures in the reproduction of work roles. By taking a longitudinal format she was able to look at change in individuals' life courses, and was able to examine the relationships between labour force circumstance and change in household circumstance. She raised some interesting points which are highlighted below.

Wallace argued that there is not a straightforward reproduction of labour, and that it is through other pressures that people come to accept the discipline of labour. She argued that acquiring a family is more effective in these terms than Government training schemes could be. In exploring the relationships between employment circumstance and family formation, Wallace made an important point concerning event timing: that it is better to conceptualise domestic careers as determined by, rather than determining, economic circumstances. This argument is emphasised since, as Wallace maintains, it is desirable to avoid an essentially deficit model, where working-class transitions are seen to pull young people into a vortex of disadvantage. Wallace argued that what constitutes 'planning', and what is premature in terms of event timing, varies across social groups and can be related to economic and social circumstances.

Wallace's 'new model of social and cultural reproduction' was partly set up as a critique of studies that presented the transition from school to work as if these were two institutions with a clean break between them. She argued that a longer time sweep is necessary for understanding transition, and the process is not a smooth but a ragged one. The model posits 'layers of reproduction' with the movement from school into the labour force running in parallel with the movement from family of origin to family of destination. The model does not theorise how the 'layers' interact. Wallace argued that work trajectories were important to domestic trajectories. So, for example, she examined attitudes and actions with respect to starting a family. The majority of her sample held attitudes against the idea of getting married and having children while unemployed. She argued that 'unemployment would appear to inhibit "normal" family transitions in principle' (Wallace, 1987, p. 167). She presented data showing that for those who had had children, eight out of 13 had a long-term unemployed background. She suggested that this confirmed the idea that the unemployed 'drift' into parenthood. Two points will be made on this. Firstly, Wallace presented data for those who had already had children by the age of 21, and set this against the attitudes of the sample as a whole. This does not support the argument of a contradiction between stated attitudes and action. Secondly, her table shows that of those with children by the age of 21, only four were male, and of these two were regularly employed. No male who had never worked had a child at the age of 21.

A significant problem for Wallace's argument is that although she attempted to relate work circumstance to family formation, her cohort data stopped at the age of 21; that is, the data fell short of the terms in which the argument was set up, yet this was not addressed as a methodological problem. The broader definition of youth is a significant advance, but it needs to be carried further by developing analyses of 'equivalent' events across a broad social spectrum necessitating a wide age bracket.

Jones, in her work on the General Household Survey (GHS) and the National Child Development Survey (NCDS), also addressed some of the problems identified in earlier analyses of youth (Jones, 1987). She noted the lack of success in integrating ideas about youth as a period of transition and the positioning of youth and young adults in a social structure. She pointed to the lack of models of stratification which might be appropriate for examining youth, a period characterised in her argument by high levels of occupational mobility. Importantly, she addressed problems which stem from any cross sectional analysis of youth. Current socio-economic position is an inadequate indicator of future class location as defined by occupational career trajectories. She developed a typology of 'youth classes' that defined youth by its occupational position relative to fathers' occupational position (as the most stable indicator of class background). She argued that this would provide a framework for analysing inequality and class differences in the move to independent housing, family formation and in labour market behaviour during the transition to adulthood (Jones, 1987a).

In her analysis of GHS and NCDS data she examined inter-generational stability and continuity in the class structure. She identified changes in early careers, and the tendency for increasing similarity with fathers' occupational class as sons and daughters age. She argued that while intergenerational class stability is more immediate for the working class, it tends to occur through a process of downward, then counter-mobility for the middle class.

Jones' emphasis on youth and early adulthood being defined over a longitudinal period is particularly important, as is her definition of adult status as being gained through marriage and family formation (Jones, 1987b). Further, her 'youth classes' have, by definition, an intergenerational foundation. This is important for enabling analyses of structural continuity and change. The 'youth classes' are explicitly rooted in a manner which allows an empirical investigation of intergenerational, a form of structural, continuities. She argued that for the middle classes intergenerational stability is achieved through a process of downward, then counter-mobility. This mobility is, however, relative to a single occupational position, that of fathers' occupations when children left school. If fathers were mobile in their careers then it is possible that downward and counter-mobility is in fact a historically removed *replication*, where patterns of life-cycle change are repeated.

The work of Wallace and Jones has been argued to provide a break with some limitations of the earlier literature on transitions. Their work has broadened definitions of youth and early adulthood, and emphasised the importance of exploring the relationships between changes in labour force and household circumstances. It has located youth as a life-course stage in terms of its constitutive relationships, and it has begun to outline frameworks for an empirical investigation of structural change.

This literature, then, presents the argument that, in considering the processes underlying change, it is important to examine intergenerational as well as intra-generational relationships. The structuring of differences between groups can only be accessed through a historical understanding. An argument of polarisation, or any kind of change cannot be sustained through cross-sectional analysis. It is only by comparing the experience of different cohorts and generations that it is possible to analyse structural change. It is argued that in Jones' study it would have been useful to have a record of fathers' and mothers' occupational careers. Work and household trajectories of contemporary youth could then be explored in relation to parents' work and household trajectories. An intergenerational comparison could be made across the relationships by which youth and early adulthood have been defined.

As suggested previously, there is not a straightforward correlation between socio-economic groups and event timing. The form that the patterning takes has not been clearly defined, and nor have the processes by which macro-level patterns must involve, simultaneously, micro-level understandings. Aggregate changes indicate processes and the task becomes one of explaining how these are operating at an individual level, and in turn, how such understandings can inform interpretations of aggregate level changes.

Addressing these problems of explanation needs to be an integral part of any explanation of change in patterns of progression from youth to adulthood. Explanations of change at an aggregate level maintain the importance of economic structures in helping to explain event timing. Research on youth conducted at a micro-level has faced difficulties in demonstrating a patterning between event timing and economic resources, and in demonstrating hypothesised inter-relationships between change in labour force circumstances and household circumstances. A valuable direction for youth research to follow is in designing means to connecting disparate macro- and micro-level explanations.

Continuity between generations must be seen in relation to changes in standards of living. Change between generations may be examined at an aggregate level, but would be of particular interest if it were disaggregated in order to examine differentials within a population. To impose categories of homogeneity from outwith available data may be limiting and ultimately misleading. Cross-sectional indices, say of occupational position, are not definitive predicators of future circumstance. Disaggregating a contemporary cohort along different dimensions and comparing the chronology of their event timing with that of their parents, might show differential patterns of change across social classes. (It is, of course, important to be aware that cohort comparisons abandon any certainty that like is being compared with like; and intergenerational comparisons abandon any steady historical time control.) In disaggregating data on a contemporary cohort it would be possible to define homogeneous groups with respect to event timing, to resources, and to attitudes, and to explore co-variations between them. Intergenerational comparisons of event timing could then be made. Processes underlying variation in the experience of youth and early adulthood could then be accessed and explanations of structural change advanced.

A methodology based on these ideas should help in an account of dynamics. It would bridge generations but also allow for historical change in ideas about acceptable living standards. It would allow for intergenerational continuity, or reproduction of relative position in the social structure, and for change, or restructuring, of the whole.

SUMMARY

The youth debate in Britain has centred on youth as a specific life-cycle stage, currently undergoing crisis. The collapse of work, and of expectations of a secure wage for many, have undermined the resource base through which young people achieve adult life styles. In earlier literature, the implied change in the experience of youth was difficult to access because youth itself was established as a fixed concept. It was fixed as a life-cycle stage, with suggestions that it may be lengthening, but with little research on the relationship between labour force circumstance and other elements that are constitutive of adult status. It was limited as a historical explanation because the only basis for comparison with other generations or cohorts was set up in terms of work.

More recent work has broadened the definition of youth and early adulthood and freed it from a static equation with labour force circumstance. While the latter is still of central interest, this is in terms of its relationship with other elements of adulthood, in particular with household and family circumstance. Employment circumstance is expected to be significant to patterns of leaving home, household formation, marriage and childbirth. By examining the interactions it is possible to conceive more broadly of youth as a life-cycle stage and to locate youth as a historically specific category.

'Youth' as a social category, then, has been defined in more recent literature in terms of its broader constituent economic and social relationships. These have been summarised by indices of employment and household/family circumstance, or demographic events. It has been argued in this paper that changes in event timing are indicative of changes in the relationships and experience of youth and early adulthood.

Recent sociological literature, however, has not attempted a critical understanding of macro patterns of change in event timing, nor addressed the explanatory problems faced by the social-demographic literature in accounting for these changes. Discrepancies between macro- and micro-level explanations of event timing need resolving. This is central to the task of understanding patterns of event timing and thereby understanding the economic and social relations and experience of youth.

REFERENCES

ASHTON, D. N. and FIELD, D. (1976), *Young workers: the transition from school to work* (Sussex: Wheatsheaf).

ASHTON, D. N. and MAGUIRE, M. J. (1986), *Young adults in the labour market*, Department of Employment RP no. 55.

ATKINSON, P. *et al.* (1982), 'Social and life skills: the latest case of contemporary education', in T. L. Rees and P. Atkinson (eds), *op. cit.*

BATES, I. *et al.* (1984), *Schooling for the dole? The new vocationalism* (Basingstoke/London: Macmillan).

BAZALGETTE, J. (1978), *School and work life. A study of transition in the inner city* (London: Hutchinson).

BENN, C. and FAIRLEY, J. (eds) (1986), *Challenging the MSC on jobs, training and education* (London: Pluto).

BURGOGNE, J. (1987), 'Change, gender and the life course' in G. Cohen (ed.) *Social Change and the life course* (London: Tavistock).

BUSFIELD, J. (1987), 'Parenting and parenthood' in G. Cohen (ed.) *op. cit.*

COCKBURN, C. (1987), *Two track training. Sex inequalities and the YTS* (London: Macmillan).

DUNNELL, K. (1979), *Family formation 1976* (London: OPCS, HMSO).

ERMISCH, J. (1983), *The political economy of demographic change* (London: Heinemann).

ELDER, G. H. (1974), *Children of the Great Depression* (University of Chicago Press).

FINN, D. (1987), *Training without jobs: new deals and broken promises* (Basingstoke: Macmillan).

FINN, D. (1982), 'Whose needs? Schooling and the "needs" of industry', in T. L. Rees and P. Atkinson (eds), *op. cit.*

HARRIS, N. (1988), 'Social security and the transition to adulthood', *Journal of Social Policy* 17 (4) pp. 501–23.

HOGAN, D. (1981), *Transitions and social change. The early lives of American men* (New York: Academic Press).

HUTSON, S. and JENKINS, R. (1987), 'Family Relationships and the Unemployment of Young People in South Wales', in White, M. (ed.), 'The Social World of the Young Unemployed', Discussion paper no. 19.

JONES, G. (1987a), 'Young workers in the class structure', *Work, Employment and Society* 1 (4), pp. 487–508.

JONES, G. (1987b), 'Leaving the parental home: an analysis of early housing careers', *Journal of Social Policy* 16 (1), pp. 49–74.

JOSHI, H. (1985), *Motherhood and employment: change and continuity in post-war Britain* (London: OPCS Occasional Paper 34).

KIERNAN, K. (1984), *The departure of children: the timing of leaving home in the life cycles of parents and children* (Centre for Population Studies Research, paper 84–3).

KIERNAN, K. (1983), 'The structure of families today: continuity or change?' in *The Family* (British Society for Population Studies, OPCS Sept 1983).

KIERNAN, K. and DIAMOND, I. (1983), 'The age at which childbearing starts – a longitudinal study', *Population Studies* 37, pp. 363–80.

MARKALL, G. and GREGORY, D. (1982), 'Who cares? The MSG interventions: full of Easter promise', in T. L. Rees and P. Atkinson (eds), *op. cit.*

MODELL, J., *et al.* (1976), 'Social change and transitions to adulthood in historical perspective', *Journal of Family History* 1 (1), pp. 7–33.

MOTT, F. L., STATHAM, A. and MAXWELL, N. L. (1982), 'From mother to daughter: the transmission of work behaviour patterns across generations', in F. L. Mott (ed.), *The employment revolution: young American women in the 1970s* (Cambridge, Mass/ London: MIT Press).

MURPHY, M. and SULLIVAN, D. (1986), 'Unemployment, housing and household structure among young adults', *Journal of Social Policy* 15 (2), pp. 205–22.

OPPENHEIMER, V. K. (1982), *Work and the family: a study in social demography* (New York: Academic Press).

RAFFE, D. (1986), 'Change and continuity in the youth labour market: a critical review of structural explanations of youth unemployment, in S. Allen *et al.* (eds), *The Experience of Unemployment* (Basingstoke: Macmillan).

RAFFE, D. (1985), *Youth unemployment in the UK 1979–1984*, Centre for Educational Sociology Working Paper 8513 (CES: University of Edinburgh).

REES and ATKINSON (eds) (1982), *Youth unemployment and state intervention* (London: Routledge & Kegan Paul).

ROBERTS, K. (1968), 'The entry into employment: an approach towards a general theory', *The Sociological Review* 16 (1), pp. 165–84.

ROBERTS, K. (1984), *School leavers and their prospects. Youth and the labour market in the 1980s* (Milton Keynes: OUP).

ROBERTS, K., DENCH, S. and RICHARDSON, D. (1986), 'Youth labour markets in the 1980s', *Employment Gazette*, July.

SHAW, L. B. and STATHAM, A. (1982), 'Fertility expectations and the changing roles of women', in F. L. Mott (ed.), *op. cit.*

THOMPSON, J. (1980), 'The age at which childbearing starts – a longitudinal study', *Population Trends* 21, pp. 10–13.

WALLACE, C. (1987a), *For richer, for poorer. Growing up in and out of work* (London: Tavistock).

WALLACE, C. (1987b), 'Between the family and the state: young people in transition', in M. White (ed.), *op. cit.*

WALSGROVE, D. (1987), 'Policing yourself: social closure and the internalisation of stigma', in G. Lee and R. Loveridge (eds), *The manufacture of disadvantage* (Milton Keynes: OUP).

WEST, M. and NEWTON, P. (1983), *The transition from school to work*, (London: Croom Helm).

WILLIS, P. (1985), *The social condition of young people in Wolverhampton 1984* (Wolverhampton Borough Council).

5 Shifting Patterns of Parental Authority, 1900–1980

Lynn Jamieson and Claire Toynbee

INTRODUCTION

It is widely believed that parents in contemporary Western industrialised societies are less able or willing to control their children's behaviour than those of previous generations. This is evidenced in the blaming of parents for a variety of social ills – a recurring refrain among Conservative politicians and newspaper columnists. Some go so far as to suggest that parental authority has collapsed (except, implicitly, in their sort of families: usually middle class, white, privately educated). We challenge this view through a discussion of the changing economic, social and political contexts of parenting. This paper identifies changes in the nature of parental authority and control in Western capitalist industrial societies within the twentieth century, using primary source data from New Zealand and Scotland[1] and secondary material from other English speaking countries.

The community studies we draw on generally agree that parents typically no longer inhabit social worlds that unequivocally support 'traditional' parental authority. Seeley summarises the position well:

> the parents, who are still held legally responsible for the rearing of the children, are, at the same time shorn of the moral sanction they once had for the exercise of absolute power over the subordinate children, an authority then thought to follow 'naturally' from age and the dominant economic position of the parents (particularly the father) and further buttressed supernaturally by traditional religious norms (Seeley *et al.*, 1956, p. 167; a view reiterated more recently by Harris, 1983).

At any one time, a variety of styles of parenting can be found; for example, a range in the prescriptions and prohibitions parents impose on their children. Throughout the century children might occasionally have observed that others were allowed to do what they were not or that other children were provided with what they were denied. This was true for the first decades, not just recent years (Jamieson, 1984; Toynbee, 1986). In the first decades of this century, middle-class British parents were far from being a homogeneous group in terms of their proscriptions for children's behaviour (Jamieson, 1983). It is only when the parental right to lay down the law is less taken for granted that variation can be experienced as a question mark over parental judgement. Variation in the past was not such a potential challenge.

Using our own work and drawing on a variety of authors, we can include the following in the list of hypothesised factors prompting shifts in parental authority this century: changes in family size, domestic technology and conditions of employment resulting in parents having more time and money for 'spoiling' their children; changes in patterns of consumption and the development of children and youth as markets, increasing parents' opportunities for indulging children on the one hand, and for 'youth' to express tastes in contradiction to those of their parents on the other; industrial restructuring and/or increased geographic and social mobility resulting in the break-up of homogeneous communities and placing parents in positions of uncertainty and contradiction concerning 'the rules' of good parenting. With similar effect, affluence and the Welfare State have made a support network of kin and neighbours redundant; likewise secularisation and the subsequent loss of religious back-up to parental authority; more awareness on the part of children and parents of the possibility of leading lives differently, due to the development of mass media; hegemony of experts on childrearing (psychologists, educationalists, paediatricians and the like) through mass media and state intervention, further weakening parental autonomy and confidence; shifts in dominant ideas concerning children's needs, good mothering, good fathering and the appropriate divisions of labour between mother and father, parents and the state (the ideological outcome of multifaceted demonstration and proselytising by 'the experts' and less powerful unofficial bodies such as the Women's Movement).

This does not add up to a theory of social change but indicates key analytical levels: that of material circumstances, the 'economic context' of mother/child and father/child relationships; the articulation between family household and 'community' – the ways mothers, fathers, sons and daughters, are tied into wider social networks; and what has sometimes been called the politics of parenthood – the process by which particular views concerning children and parents become pervasive and become the dominant ideologies concerning childhood and parenting. We are unable to go beyond this to offer a more integrated theoretical account. Much space is necessarily devoted to the task of summarising and clarifying the changes that have taken place. We conclude that while it is undoubtedly the case that there have been dramatic changes in parent-child relationships during the twentieth century, these do not amount to a collapse in parental authority, but rather the substitution of more pseudo-democratic forms of control for 'traditional authority'.

Parents' power and the concept of traditional authority

The fundamental basis for parental power lies in their control of resources. Parents have access to a wealth of material resources not directly available to the child. At the outset parents have vastly superior strength which makes physical coercion possible. In addition they have the intellectual ability to outwit their children and they may also draw on emotional sanctions. Their power is not total, however, since children may also trade on their parents' vulnerabilities.

Socio-historical contexts generate socially acceptable standards for both parents and children. These are set down formally in law and religion and informally in sets of more or less clearly defined everyday norms which set limits on the behaviour of both parents and children. Nevertheless, within such contexts parents have the *potential* to use their power, legitimated or otherwise.

We use the term 'traditional authority' in association with

parent-child relationships in the first decades of this century because of the general absence of challenges to legitimacy – it was taken for granted that children did as they were told and parents 'knew best'. Traditional authority appears natural, immutable, since it is legitimised by 'the sanctity of the order and the attendant powers of control as they have been handed down from the past' (Weber as quoted in Bell and Newby, 1978).

Bell and Newby (1978) have conceptualised contemporary husband/wife relationships in terms of 'traditional authority'. They refer to the dialectic existing between the opposing concepts of differentiation and identification which characterise all relationships involving the use of traditional authority: the 'deferential dialectic'. By differentiation, Bell and Newby mean the sub-superordinate relationships based on both gender and generation within the family. Identification refers to positive affect, the common bond of love (1978).

By extrapolation, contemporary parents seeking to exercise 'traditional authority' must steer a steady course between differentiation and identification in order to maintain a stable relationship. If they are too hard on their children, there is a danger that the children will perceive an injustice and withdraw their love and trust. On the other hand, overindulgence on the part of the parent may create a situation in which the children seek to upstage the parent. In appropriate socio-historical contexts indulgent parents may choose to 'swing the norms', allowing the children to have their way, at the same time seeking to retain a lesser measure of power, sacrificing differentiation to their desire for love. It is only in a weak sense, where parents need to work hard to maintain the fiction of a 'natural' or 'god-given authority', that we would expect to find instances of 'traditional authority' in the present.

PARENT-CHILD RELATIONSHIPS IN THE EARLY TWENTIETH CENTURY

In this section we will use our own data for early twentieth century Scotland and New Zealand to show how parent-child relationships in many families were constrained by the need for children's labour to help maintain themselves and others. It is important to note, however, that the use of traditional authority and a distinct social distance between parents and children was not confined to those requiring children's services for survival.

Child contributions to the household economy

By the early twentieth century only a very small minority of households in Western 'industrialised' societies generated their livelihood in association with kin. Our interviews show that farming and crofting families were often largely self-sufficient, supplementing the produce of their land and labour with fishing, hunting and gathering activities. In these cases children were readily absorbed into the family work-force. The majority of the working-class families were still close to subsistence, and here too all members of households, except very young children, were expected to contribute labour through a range of money-making or money-saving activities. Most girls, especially older daughters, were heavily involved in housework and/or cared for younger siblings.[2]

Depending on circumstances, children usually started making some contribution when they were very young, This gradually increased as they grew into young adulthood, when it was common for virtually all their earnings to be paid into the household purse. Parents often needed their children to help them maintain an acceptable standard of living, while young adults helped provide for ageing parents or their younger siblings in large families. This is in marked contrast to the level of contemporary parental demands on children in which instrumental responsibilities lie overwhelmingly on parents.

Children at the service of adults

The essentially adult-centredness of virtually all families was obvious in parental demands for socially appropriate behaviour (as defined by the parents and in terms of their interests) in the home generally, at meals, and for compulsory attendance at Church/Sunday School, as well as in children's respectful and deferential demeanour to their elders ('children should be seen and not heard'). To a varying extent, parents also controlled the comings and goings of children, their playmates and the way they spent their time when not in school. In the case of working-class parents and small farmers, such control was generally restricted to enforcing a bedtime and the priority of housework, errands and homework over play.

There was variation within families in that individual children felt the weight of parental authority to a greater or lesser degree. Eldest children, especially daughters, might have been marked by their mothers to take over some of their chores, continuing to shoulder their heavy responsibilities while younger children were 'let off' relatively lightly. In many urban homes, especially working-class ones with large numbers of children, girls tended to be heavily involved in domestic labour while some boys got off 'scot-free'. Even when children could see that they were being treated more harshly than siblings, fatalistic resignation was the most common, although not the only response.

It appears that the rights of parents to children's services was so universally accepted, that our most compliant respondents reacted with some puzzlement when we asked questions about how their parents got them to carry out their chores. Some people said that they had no other expectations. Other children in their neighbourhood were similarly involved and had the same standards of behaviour expected of them by their parents: 'We were all doing the same thing'.

Social distance between parents and children

There was a marked degree of social distance between most parents and their children. This was expressed in a variety of ways. Emotional coolness on the part of many parents made it difficult or impossible for children to approach them with problems (McCrindle and Rowbotham, 1979; Vigne 1975; Thompson 1975). Strong emotional ties did not necessarily dissolve social distance, however. Working-class respondents who, throughout childhood, were painfully aware of their mother's struggle to provide a decent living on their behalf, typically expressed their devotion through silent admiration and redoubled efforts at contributing to the household.

Dialogue between parents and children was often minimal. During the interviews, a whole range of questions about politics, religion, sex and other matters, elicited the kind of answers which made it quite clear that these matters were often never discussed in front of children, regardless of class. In general, fathers were perceived by children of both sexes to be much more remote than mothers, physically, in the sense that they worked long hours, and socially, because they did not expect to have their leisure life interrupted by children.

In upper-middle-class families, the physical separation of parents and children was quite common (Thompson, 1977; Vigne, 1981). A few of our respondents were largely cared for by nursemaids and educated by governesses, eating separately in the nursery and seeing their parents only for short times each day. Lower down the social scale, cramped living conditions made any form of privacy or physical separation impossible, but here too it was clear that most parents constrained their children's ability to communicate freely either with themselves or with siblings, through demands for silence and 'good' behaviour.

Social distance, hierarchy and demands for deference at home were matched or, for some children, exceeded in the school. Although at any one time there was a range of practice, teachers generally adopted what would now be regarded as authoritarian styles, making liberal use of corporal punishment. This was not simply a matter of lack of resources (although teachers in many working-class schools did have to cope with very large classes and few materials), but also of a pedagogical focus on disciplining the will of the child despite the long history of more liberal views of education.

In general, our data show a high degree of differentiation between parents and children, tight control over children's behaviour, requirements for obedience and the absence of forms of behaviour which challenged parental legitimacy. Differentiation was maintained in a myriad of ways which emphasised the fact that children were not on a par with their elders in general, and parents in particular. This differentiation did not threaten the stability of the parent-child relationship, rather it was a taken for granted aspect of their mutually defining positions. Love between parents and children was also an inexpressible fact of life, typically more akin to the love between the gods and lesser mortals than that of friendship between equals.

Parents and Teenagers

The general statements above largely apply to teenagers as well as young children. Although earning from the age of 14, working-class young people were not generally in command of their earnings until their late teens or early twenties. Mothers continued to demand housework from daughters, whether they were earners or not. Curfews were in operation for both sons and daughters, although more strictly observed for daughters. Working-class young people had their own worlds of dance-halls and gathering places which provided the equivalent escape to the world of street play for children. But, as yet, there were few elaborate props associated with working-class youth. Middle-class young people remained in education longer and outside school they were more integrated into a class-specific world of adult supervised sociability.

PARENT-CHILD RELATIONSHIPS SINCE 1950

We have chosen to contrast the early 1900s with the period since 1950 because the changes to which we refer are most clearly established after World War II.

Parents at the service of children?

On the whole, parents now make far fewer demands for service or financial assistance from their school-aged children. Indeed, many service their children rather than sharing chores with them or being serviced by them. In the words of Michael Anderson 'children have almost totally ceased to be part of an interdependent resource-generating system' (1980). Goodnow's studies of children's work in Australia (1986, 1987) suggest that parents' demands are restricted to individual 'cleaning up your own mess' sort of tasks, motivated by a desire to teach respect for themselves and others. Her studies recall the possible motives of some of our middle-class children's mothers who required both boys and girls to make their own beds and other light tasks, that is, individual rather than social reproduction.

Affluence and the disappearance of children's work

Throughout the century, employment opportunities for children have diminished as a result of mechanisation, bureaucratisation and legislation. In addition statutory requirements for schooling have lengthened.

Significant shifts have occurred not only in the sphere of employment and income distribution but also in the nature and distribution of goods for consumption. For example, due to changes in domestic technology, retailing and patterns of consumption, most of the unpaid jobs that formed the bulk of working-class children's work in the early decades of the century have now disappeared, for example, daily shopping (in the case of urban children, shopping included special trips for such items as broken biscuits, yesterday's bread, chipped eggs), collecting fuel and cutting wood for open fires, cleaning cutlery, polishing brasses and black leading ranges.

The disappearance of children's jobs does not necessarily mean there is literally nothing for children to do in the present. Although fewer households are struggling to subsist, time spent in housework has not radically diminished with modern conveniences and smaller families (Cowan, 1983; Bitman, 1988). Since the 1950s, it has become increasingly common for married women to return to the labour force, and at younger ages, with the result that increasingly larger proportions of family households enjoy two incomes. Indeed, two incomes may be required for the family to be able to achieve an acceptable living standard.

Employed mothers often suffer from work overload as they carry the 'double burden', while the burgeoning of 'do-it-yourself' means that work around the home is a main 'leisure time' activity for a significant minority of men and women. The greatly reduced participation of children in the unpaid work of the household is a result of changes in the ideas as well as material conditions; parental attitudes no longer pervasively and unequivocally support the notion that children should 'do their bit'.

Changing demands for children's services

Different contexts result in parents having different economic interests in their children, with implications for parent/child relationships. It has generally been assumed that traditional authority is most thoroughly underwritten when parents hold key resources, such as land or capital, which will be passed from parents to children (Goode, 1970; Anderson, 1980). Throughout this century, the overwhelming majority of parents were not in this position. They were and are urban-based proletarians with no ownership or control of means of generating income other than their own labour power. It could be argued that even into the first decades of this century working-class parents still had an economic interest in controlling their children. Many households needed the contribution of their children to the household economy in order to maintain a decent standard of living, or, in some cases, bare subsistence.

It is tempting to explain the demise of traditional authority in terms of reduced material motives for keeping a firm control of children's behaviour, with increased affluence and the eradication of opportunities for paid work on the part of children being the structural factors leading to this change of heart. This is too simplistic. When it is believed that children *should* be at the service of adults, then parents need not be so specifically motivated by the need for help. Our upper-class children were not exempted from the traditional style of authority, despite children's position of total economic dependence (Jamieson, 1987). The absence of an economic motive need not necessarily result in the exclusion of children from providing services to their parents, nor is that exclusion necessarily linked to the demise of traditional authority.

The position of teenagers

This picture of children being served by parents is less clear for young people over sixteen. Leonard's 1960s study of young adults from a variety of class backgrounds suggests that neither young male nor female adults living at home prior to their impending marriage are expected to contribute much to their parents' household in either money or domestic work (see Barker, 1972; Leonard, 1980). They are equally and unselfconsciously 'spoiled'. However, the overwhelming majority of British young people who continue to live 'at home' are expected to (and do) pay towards their keep, once in receipt of an independent income (Cusack and Roll, 1985, '16–19 Initiative', unpublished data). But this does not amount to the same sort of parent/child relationship expressed in the contribution made by young earners earlier in the century. There is no intermediate phase of complete adult management of their wage as there was then.

There is some reason for further qualifying Leonard's picture of youth as a period relatively free from parental demands for service, at least in areas of economic depression during the 1980s. Some more recent work (Hutson and Jenkins, 1987; Wallace, 1988; Corr and Jamieson, 1988) does suggest that a minority of girls continue to make a substantial contribution to the household economy in domestic labour, and that some young people also make a substantial contribution in income, with parents in some cases demanding several times the going rate for 'digs money'. It may be that in some households which are seriously under-resourced parents are attempting a more absolute control of their children's labour power and earnings. In contrast to the early 1900s, however, resentment and discontent is an inevitable outcome. At the same time the state is weakening the ability of many young people to contribute to the household, through measures reducing their independent income (Harris, 1988). The balance parents and their children had negotiated between the 'freedoms of youth' and 'paying your way' is inevitably disrupted.

Closeness between parents and children

According to community studies conducted in the 1950s, many parents of the time felt that the emotional and social distance between them and their children was markedly less than between their parents and themselves. British parents of the 1950s were often very conscious of the contrast between themselves and their own parents: Mrs Glass of London's working-class Bethnal Green community said, 'We're different with our boy: we make more of a mate of him' (Young and Wilmott, 1957). The same is expressed quite clearly by a number of the Newsons' respondents; for instance, the 'driver's wife', who remarked that 'they can talk to me a lot easier than I ever could with my mother – even though she was a real good mother, I mean she was a wonderful person really, but you just couldn't get through to them in those days, I don't think, same as mine do to me' (1974). There are fewer studies of middle-class parents in the 1950s, but one change is clearly documented: the virtual disappearance of the domestic servant. Studies of middle-class mothers in the 1960s could not paint a sharper contrast with the beginning of the century, when many did the more skilled housework leaving the 'rough work' and much of the childcare to the servant.

The extent to which parents have moved away from 'traditional authority' is exemplified by changed attitudes to 'cheek'. Depending on the particular family, the child may feel free to object to what he or she considers unreasonable parental requests or to make judgements on the behaviour or opinions of parents without inviting their wrath, or causing parental loss of face. Whereas any kind of 'talking back' or questioning of parental authority was considered a heinous crime in former times, parents nowadays appear to invite 'discussion', viewing the talking-over of any problems as part of caring and sharing in family life.

Wanting to be a pal to the children means wanting to spend more time with them. This can have unanticipated penalties, as Seeley *et al.* slightly gloatingly observe in the North American context. It is difficult for parents to reconcile their closeness with their children when they, as teenagers, abandon family company for the peer group (1956). Barker's middle-aged parents anticipated the 'empty nest', and schemed to keep their adult children 'close' by spoiling them, deliberately creating reciprocities through which they expected to bind their children to them throughout life (Barker, 1972).

We can afford to spoil them

Some research of the 1950s and 1960s allowed working-class parents to speak for themselves of the significance of changes in the standard of living. Reflecting on both the severity of their own parents and their own relative 'softness', many said they wished to spare their children from the hardships of their own childhood: 'I try to give these what I didn't have' (postman's wife, Newson and Newson, 1963). They themselves linked their greater affluence with their less disciplinarian treatment of their children, acknowledging that they could afford to give their children leeway in such matters as faddiness with food, buying them clothes, toys and taking them on holidays. Not only were these parents deeply appreciative of the changing conditions that made it possible to indulge their children, some also acknowledged the grind and worries of poverty which had made their own parents irritable and severe in their dealings with children (Klein, 1965; Zweig, 1961).

In summary, it is clear that parents now are less concerned to maintain hierarchical distance, and are much more concerned with 'having a good relationship' with their children than were the parents of our elderly respondents. The tension between differentiation and identification is largely resolved by giving priority to the latter, but may bring in its wake new problems.

Variations and inconsistencies in styles of parenting

There is sufficient evidence of variation in the somewhat scattered sociological literature on parent-child relationships to ring a cautionary bell about identifying any single dominant pattern of parental control of young children or teenagers. Firstly, the work of parenting is gendered – 'mothering' is not the same as fathering. Those studies which have focused on both mothers and fathers, demonstrate how inappropriate it is to be talking about 'parents' as if they acted as one person. In the study undertaken by the Ritchies in the 1960s, for example, fathers tended to be rather shadowy figures, whose identification with their young children was expressed in occasional displays of horseplay and gift-giving. Their 1970s study reveals a substantial change. Fathers were much more likely to be involved in bathing their children, reading them stories and so on, demonstrating a significant move towards child-centredness on their part. Although these observations are echoed in work in Britain and North America, how much *real* change has taken place in the role of fathers remains controversial (McKee and O'Brien, 1982). Up to the present, more young people feel able to confide in their mothers than their fathers (unpublished data '16–19 Initiative').

In the second place, a number of studies identify class as an important variable in predicting parental attitudes and behaviour towards children (Lynd and Lynd, 1929; Newsons, 1968, 1976; Ritchie and Ritchie, 1970, 1978). There are some indications that wanting to spend more time with and enjoy the children might not have had the same meaning in all households.

In general, working-class parents have been shown to be stricter, more concerned about noise and mess, and more punitive than middle-class ones. On the other hand middle-class mothers may feel more burdened by their children. Bott's 'well educated' mother who quipped 'You must excuse me if I sound half-witted. I've been talking to the children all day' (1957) obviously found spending time with the children harder work than is suggested by the working-class response of 'we make more of a mate of him'. It is unclear from existing studies whether persistent class differences are due to fundamental differences in attitude or to the presence or absence of resources that alter the priorities of parenting.

Thirdly, the contemporary scene is complicated by findings indicating that many parents are not entirely consistent in their handling of their children. For instance, the Ritchies conclude their investigation of child-rearing in New Zealand in the early 1960s (1970) by remarking that, although in general the mothers could be described as relaxed and easygoing in their relationships with their children, other factors intervened. In particular, they mention the prevalence of house-pride among these mothers. Conflict occurs when children create their normal chaos in their mothers' well ordered workplaces. Prevailing norms prescribe a perfectly-kept home as well as encouraging permissive child-rearing methods (see also Oakley 1974). The Ritchies imply that this conflict has diminished for mothers in their 1970s study (1978); mothers had shifted their interests more decisively from home to children, from house-pride to a more permissive, encouraging approach to children and a greater degree of warmth in everyday interaction.

Understanding the child: the antithesis of traditional authority?

Perhaps the parenting style farthest removed from the taken-for-granted adult-centred approach of our elderly subjects' parents, come from studies involving middle-class parents. Seeley *et al.* rather disapprovingly describe the absence of differentiation between parents and children in their Canadian families of the 1950s: 'These children are not led to believe there are certain adult privileges which children cannot share' (1956).

The most detailed recent sociological study of contemporary parents' attitudes to their children is offered by Backett (1982). Her highly educated middle-class British parents are clearly child-centred. For them, understanding the child is the main task of parenting. Both parents see children as having special child-specific needs and both respond (in different, and gender-related ways) to an overwhelming sense of responsibility for fulfilling these needs. The parents expect to have, and they promote, emotionally intense relationships with their children, while at the same time worrying about smothering them and impairing their individualism.

Although sometimes consulting 'experts', the mothers in Backett's study were confident that they were *the* experts with respect to their own children. Evidence that some parents were becoming much less confident in the roles comes from the Newsons, interviewing in Nottingham in the 1960s. They quote at some length an exceptionally child-centred parent, 'Mrs West', the 'thirty-eight year old mother of three children and wife of a craftsman setting up his own business', perhaps anticipating that her concerns were to become more pervasive.

> People nowadays think more about what's good for the children, from the children's point of view . . . Nowadays, if they don't turn out right you wonder where *you've* gone wrong, don't you? It used to be, they made you do this and do that, and you did it, and if things went wrong it was the child's fault, not the parents', they could never be wrong. I think we're not so happy about *ourselves* these days, we blame ourselves, not the child (Newson and Newson, 1963, p. 258).

This quotation is particularly interesting in that it implies a radical departure from traditional authority. Parents who blame themselves, or are blamed by others, for the way their children turn out, cannot believe that they have God-given or 'natural', immutable rights as parents. It does not mean that they have no control, rather that they have to work harder to resolve the tension in family relationships between differentiation and identification. By accepting responsibility and seeking closer ties with their children, they become vulnerable to children's demands and more open in seeking new ways of coping.

DISCUSSION

The Economic Context

A particular set of material and economic circumstances, shared by a number of industrialised nations, set the conditions permitting increased dependence of school-aged children on parents, the near independence of older teenagers and the 'spoiling' of both by parents. Changes in the relationship between the household and the economy occurred at a number of levels. It is an oversimplification to observe simply that more mothers and fathers have time and money to spend on children. But shifts in this direction have been important and are in themselves the result of a number of factors: improved conditions of employment giving full-time earners more time, money and good humour to spend (which many then spent at home); smaller family size among all classes; and improved domestic technology. All reduce the burden of housework (still carried by women) necessary for the most basic level of comfort. The increase in the labour-force participation of mothers since the 1960s does not necessarily contradict these factors – many chose hours of paid work that minimised their unavailability to their children and simultaneously reduced the time they spent on housework.

Post-war periods of boom were associated not only with increasing wages and full employment, but also an exponential growth in the range of goods available for mass consumption, many of them for the embellishment of the home or for enjoyment at home. 'Youth' and children, became (gendered) specific markets. Parents had the option of providing children with props of childhood that they had never had. But if parents sought gratitude for this they could find themselves wrong-footed; their children necessarily lacked their sense of the past and took a higher standard of material provision for granted. The development of 'youth' as a market also introduced a potential new arena of conflict between parents and their children. Since at least a portion of 'youth' were independent wage earners; 'youth products' could more readily develop in directions offensive to parental tastes.

The shift to the 'affluent consumer society' has been associated not only with the multiplication of goods provided for children by parents, but also a reduction in the contributions made by children and young people to their family household. This is in spite of the fact that many parents, particularly mothers, suffer from work-overload. Young people do make some material contribution, however. Those receiving an independent income generally pay a fixed sum of money to the household in exchange for the domestic services they receive. And some parents, perhaps particularly in those households that are seriously under-resourced, continue to demand much more.

The social context – the loss of close-knit community?

Many authors have suggested that the social context of parenting has shifted in ways that mean parents no longer receive support for laying down the law to their children. There is no mutually supporting chorus of proscriptions and prescriptions from Church, kin, grandparents or neighbours to 'honour thy father and thy mother'. Rather, parents and children are presented with a variety of models originating from various sources in the social environment. This may take the form of directly or indirectly supported State intervention that seeks to impose middle-class models based on current versions of what the 'experts' consider desirable. Models may also be suggested by the example of others in the mother's, father's, or child's social network.

Accounts of social change often refer to the break-up of homogeneous 'communities' and the break-down of the social support networks they contained. Studies that have contributed to the 'loss of community' thesis (Bulmer, 1986) focus on social settings where the respondents are geographically and often also socially mobile, for example, the boom town, the new town, the new housing estate. These are settings in which people are to an extent cut off from their families of origin and their old contacts. Bott (1956, p. 81) notes that 'change in the climate of opinion makes parents less certain about the proper way to treat their children. The strain is most severe on those who are not surrounded by others of their own tradition'. A potent source of parental vulnerability in this context are the children themselves, whose own social networks provide knowledge of alternative, more liberal parenting styles and examples of extravagant generosity with which to torment their own parents. Clearly, the extent of the parental vulnerability will vary with the degree to which parents fear to lose their children's love in the face of invidious comparisons with others. Harris (1983) suggests that the extent of this vulnerability is related to alternative sources of identity for parents – their place in wider social networks, their relationship to employment, for example. Mothers are often more vulnerable than fathers.

One response to the higher wages, better standards of housing and potentially new reference groups of the 1950s and 1960s is the unfolding of desires for further material improvements, and an openness to different lifestyles. Following Mogey (1956), Klein talked of an increase in the acquisitive aspiring sector of the working class. They are portrayed as particularly susceptible to the messages of the mass media, with its offerings concerning the ideal home and family. Here 'social norms have to be created because the old ones are no longer congenial' (Klein, 1965).

The chapter by Crow and Allan notes that the contrasts between 'traditional' and 'new' working-class 'communities' have been overdrawn. In both, the privacy of the home is protected and residents suffer from the insecurities of 'keeping up with the neighbours'. For instance, in 1956, Dennis *et al.* suggested that for mothers in Ashton, buying new clothes for their children at Christmas and Whitsun was important for their public profile and self-esteem. Dennis *et al.* condemn these miners' wives for spending 'as much as possible on clothes and toys for the children, often uneconomically'. Here, the authors reveal their own biases and priorities in the area of child-rearing, based on middle-class ideologies of psychologically oriented child-centredness. However, from the point of view of the mothers in question, to be seen as a 'good' parent, the yardstick was not psychological development of the child, but what Dennis *et al.* call 'the outward signs – new clothes, new toys, well-fed children', exactly those things which they and their neighbours might well have particularly valued as a result of their own materially deprived childhoods (Dennis 1956; see also Harris, 1983).

The effect, then, of 'break-up' of 'community' should not be overstated. Changing material conditions had an impact even in the 'traditional working-class community'. Nevertheless, rehousing and residential mobility did mean that many young mothers would no longer be in close touch with their own mothers. Their social networks, consisting of neighbours and friends in the same position as themselves, would provide greater heterogeneity in ideas and practices. More formally, they would be likely to have at least minimal contact with health professionals espousing current theories and practices. This was occurring at the time when the mass media were increasingly reaching into every home. We would also expect considerable unevenness by class and region in acceptance of new practices (Busfield, 1974).

The political context – competing ideas of good parenting

Powerful collectivities have a vested interest in defining 'good' parenting. Since the nineteenth century, governments have become increasingly engaged in population management – the reproduction of a number and 'quality' of citizens appropriate to the interests of the state. The twentieth century has witnessed the blossoming of state-sanctioned professions claiming appropriate knowledge and practice in the management of children: educational professionals (teachers and their academic teachers); health and welfare professionals (doctors, paediatricians, health visitors, child-psychologists and psychiatrists, social workers). Much of 'expert' writing and talking about child development, psychology, health, education and training has been directed to mothers as the primary carers of chidren and therefore those best placed to influence their development. The dominant messages to mothers (there have always been a range of messages at any one time, sometimes contradicting one other) have changed over the century. McDonald (1978) talks of a shift after World War II, from seeing children predominantly as a social capital in which the state invests, to an emphasis on fulfilling the psychological and emotional needs of children. Ostensibly many professionals have been striving for a more 'child-centred' approach, although the needs of children are defined by the experts, not the chidren themselves. More recently there is a concern with the rights of children (McDonald, 1978). Changes in parenting to more child-centred styles are therefore in line with shifts in the dominant orthodoxy of 'experts', although we remain unclear about precisely how much causal weight to give this.

Certainly the views of experts have not simply resulted in writing and talking, they have also been translated into practical interventions. However, the history of any particular intervention – for example, the establishing of 'schools for mothers' – involves more than the will of 'experts', but also the co-operation of less official bodies representing more 'grass roots' views. Mothers themselves always have an interest in defining what is necessary for 'good' parenting and have formed their own organisations to express their views – from women's guilds to the women's movement.

The history of particular forms of 'expert' intervention is well documented, most notably the advice and practical management of child physical and psychological health (Ehrenreich and English, 1979; Hardyment, 1983; Lewis, 1980; Reiger, 1985). There are histories of child-rearing manuals and of how state-sanctioned medical personnel have increasingly managed and supervised birth and early infant care and feeding. The influence of Sir Truby King in New Zealand, Australia and Britain is perhaps the best example in respect of infant care designed to safeguard state investment in social capital while retaining the traditional authority of parents. His highly regimented and 'scientific' schedule was one in which mothers had what one might regard as delegated responsibility from the experts for controlling their own babies' feeding times and letting the babies know at an early stage who was boss.

In keeping with new principles of infant and child care informed by psychological theories, and widely adopted since the early 1960s, babies are much more likely to be fed on demand, and to be eased into potty training when it suits them, rather than according to an 'expert' schedule. Mothers are now encouraged to put 'baby's sense of timing' before their own. Infants are now regarded as psychological beings, whose every need must be met if they are to fulfil their potential.

Just as 'expert' views on infant feeding and potty training have changed, so notions of good teaching method have been modified considerably over the century, although vestiges of 'the old style' remain in practice. Many teachers (like parents) have sought some reduction in the distance between themselves and the children they teach, for pedagogical reasons modifying their view of what constitutes 'cheek' from a child, and encouraging more discussion with pupils. The use of physical punishment has been increasingly abandoned, official sanction for corporal punishment having been withdrawn in many countries. Maintaining discipline remains a daily concern of the teaching profession, however, and moral entrepreneurs refer to exceptional discipline problems as proving the need for more disciplinaire styles of teaching and/or parenting. Generally, teachers still receive parental back-up for punishments inflicted on children in school, although this is now often sought more formally (requiring parents to sign punishment exercises for example).

The history of attempts to influence standards of domesticity and motherhood through the school is also well documented (Corr, 1983; David, 1980; Lewis, 1980; Reiger, 1985). From early this century until quite recently, most girls have been required to learn cooking and sewing at school as part of the regular curriculum. State intervention into domestic standards has taken the form of school attendance inspection, dental care, medical inspections (for clean neck and nails, lice, impetigo and other evidence of unhealthy living), free milk (often clandestinely disposed of!), and the imposition of uniforms or other standards of dress (for example, polished shoes).

While there is plenty of evidence of the proliferation of activities of professionals of many kinds involved in directing or influencing parental activity, there is little research documenting their impact on ordinary parents, either in the earlier decades of this century or in more recent times. Indeed, attempts at assessing the impact of professional 'experts' on child-rearing must necessarily suffer the same methodological problem as an investigation of the effects of the mass media which often carry their messages. It is extremely difficult to disengage the particular effects of something so pervasive and diverse in content. It can only be assumed that such a barrage of messages must have some effect.

CONCLUSIONS

It is probably true to say that many contemporary parents are closer to their children and treat them in a less authoritarian way than their own parents did. Indeed, there is a good deal of evidence supporting the claim that parents have become far more child-centred. It appears that many of today's parents have given up being distant and dignified, voluntarily relinquishing the trappings of traditional authority, which has become increasingly difficult to sustain.

In the past, traditional authority did not need to be authoritarian in the sense now defined by psychologists: punitive, restrictive, and parent-centred. 'Authoritarian' makes no sense as an insult when child labour was generally needed to maintain a decent standard of living for the household. In the past, the successful exercise of parental authority, benevolently practised, exempted many children from physical punishment.[3] Contemporary parents trying to maintain traditional authority in the present are much more likely to find negotiation cannot always be resolved in their favour. They then have to resort to the ultimate back-ups of their authority – the power of the hand and the purse. Indeed, parents striving for more democratic styles have not abandoned imposing their will when all else fails. In this sense their democratic styles remain pseudo-democratic. Some parents wish to minimise or remove the distance that being an authority implies. What they seek is mutual respect and admiration, accepting that they learn from their children as well as teach them. A relationship of equality is elusive, however, as the material basis of parents' power typically remains into the young adult life of the child. Parents, therefore, are constantly tempted to pull power when the going gets rough.

We have suggested that the changes in family relationships are the combined effect of a variety of factors that have influenced the process of negotiation between parents and children. We have discussed these factors under the heading of the economic, social, and political context. In reality they are not separable. It is not possible, for example, to understand an individual's response to the vagaries of economic context without an appreciation of the social relationships in which he or she is embedded, both within and outside the household. Similarly, the effect and often the occasion of exposure to different ideas is mediated by relationships. Moreover individuals do not simply live in the present. Current orientations are a product of past experience and contain a sense of future. It is particularly important to remember this with respect to parents and children. Parents commonly use their children in an attempt to rework their own past, while young people often struggle to 'modernise' their parents.

NOTES

We would like to thank the following people for helpful comments on an earlier draft: Michael Anderson, Colin Bell, Helen Corr, Chris Harris, David Pearson. This paper draws on material from the 16–19 Initiative funded by the ESRC.

1. Our own material was drawn from the oral histories gathered by both authors for their independent research in Scotland and New Zealand respectively (Jamieson, 1983; Toynbee, 1986), with the addition of a sample of rural Scottish informants gathered after the Ph.D. research was completed. Both writers were originally inspired by the work of Paul Thompson (1977) whose interview schedule and methods formed a common basis for their Ph.D. work. Respondents were chosen in such a way as to provide enough cases from rural and urban locations, and from a range of class situations. Usable interview material from 210 men and women born before about 1912 was achieved, 85 from New Zealand and the remainder from Scotland.
2. The work of children has been well documented in working-class autobiographies and in the steady stream of oral histories published in recent years (see for instance Thompson, 1975, 1977; Vigne, 1975, 1981; Roberts, 1984; Burnett, 1982; McCalman, 1984; Facey, 1981).
3. A notable characteristic of the early twentieth century families was the general absence of physical punishment on a day-to-day basis. To be sure, some children had the misfortune to have (usually one) punitive and/or sadistic parent. Status anxiety (the top of the working class and lower middle class) was quite commonly associated with slapping by mothers. Many had either experienced a beating themselves

or remember such an incident in their own family without having been beaten personally. In such cases the offence was usually a serious one involving brushes with the law or school authorities or danger to life or property. These generally applying characteristics of our sample families in respect of obedience, compliance with heavy parental demands and the relatively low incidence of frequent punishment, are powerful indicators of the general belief of the times in the right of parents to control their children's lives (McDonald, 1978).

REFERENCES

ANDERSON, M. (1971), *Family Structure in Nineteenth Century Lancashire* (Cambridge University Press).

ANDERSON, M. (1980), *Approaches to the Study of the Western Family 1500–1914* (London: Macmillan).

BACKETT, K. (1982), *Mothers and Fathers: A Study of the Development and Negotiation of Parental Behaviour* (London: Macmillan; Edinburgh Studies in Sociology).

BARKER, D. (1972), 'Young People and their homes: spoiling and "keeping close" in a South Wales Town', *Sociology Review* 20 (4), pp. 569–90.

BARKER, D. L. and ALLAN, S. (eds), *Dependence and Exploitation in Work and Marriage* (London: Allen & Unwin, 1976).

BELL, C. and NEWBY, H. (1976), 'Husbands and wives: the dynamics of the deferential dialectic', in D. L. Barker and S. Allen (eds), pp. 152–68.

BOTT, E. (1957), *Family and Social Network* (London: Tavistock, 1964 edn).

BULMER, M. (1987), *The Social Basis of Community Care* (London: Allen & Unwin).

BURNETT, J. (1982), *Destiny Obscure: Autobiographies of Childhood, Education and the Family from 1820s to 1920s* (London: Allen Lane).

BUSFIELD, J. (1974), 'Ideologies and reproduction' in Martin Richards, (ed.), pp. 11–36.

CARTER, I. (1979), *Farmlife in Northeast Scotland, 1840–1914: The Poor Man's Country* (Edinburgh: John Donald).

COHEN, P. and MURDOCH, G. (eds) (forthcoming), *The Making of the Youth Question 1880–1914* (London: Macmillan).

CORR, H. (1983) 'The schoolgirl's curriculum and the ideology of the home, 1870–1914' in Glasgow Women's Studies, *Uncharted Lives* (Glasgow: Pressgang).

CORR, H. and JAMIESON, L. (1988), 'Earning your keep: the

politics of dependence', Working Paper presented at 16–19 Initiative Workshop, Harrogate.

COWAN, R. S. (1983), *More Work for Mother: The Ironies of Household Technology from the Open Hearth to the Microwave* (New York: Basic Books).

CROW, G. and ALLAN, G. (1988), 'Constructing the domestic sphere: the emergence of the modern home in post-war Britain, (Paper presented at the British Sociological Association Annual Conference, Edinburgh; revised version this volume).

CUSACK, R. and ROLL, J. (1985), *Families Rent Apart*, Poverty Pamphlet no. 65 (London: Child Poverty Action Group).

DAVID, M. (1980), *The State, the Family and Education* (London: Routledge & Kegan Paul).

DAVIN, A. (1982), 'Child labour, the working-class family and domestic ideology in 19th century Britain', *Development and Change*, 13 (4).

DENNIS, N., HENRIQUES, C. and SLAUGHTER, C. (1956), *Coal is Our Life* (London: Eyre & Spottiswoode).

EDGAR, D. and OCHILTREE, G. (1983), *The Changing Face of Childhood* (Melbourne: Institute of Family Studies).

EHRENREICH, B. and ENGLISH, D. (1979), *For Her Own Good: 150 Years of the Expert's Advice to Women* (New York: Anchor Press).

ELIAS, N. and SCOTSON, J. L. (1965), *The Established and the Outsiders* (London: Frank Cass).

FACEY, A. B. (1981), *A Fortunate Life* (Melbourne: Penguin).

GOODE, W. (1970), *World revolution and family patterns* (New York: Collier Macmillan).

GOODNOW, J. J. (in press) 'Children's housework: its nature and function', *Psychology Bulletin*.

GOODNOW, J. J. (1986), 'Children's household work: differentiating tasks and styles of assignment' (Paper presented at the meeting of the Society for Research in Child Development, Baltimore, Maryland, under the title 'The distributive justice of work: children's household tasks').

HARDYMENT, C. (1983), *Dream Babies: Child Care from Locke to Spock* (London: Jonathan Cape).

HARRIS, C. C. (1983), *The Family and Industrial Society* (London: Allen & Unwin).

HARRIS, N. (1988), 'Social security and the transition to adulthood' *Journal of Social Policy* vol. 17, no. 4.

HUTSON, S. and JENKINS, R. (1987), 'Family relationships and the unemployment of young people in Swansea', in M. White (ed.), *The Social World of the Young Unemployed* (London: Policy Studies Institute).

JAMIESON, L. (1983), 'A Case Study in the Development of the Modern Family: Urban Scotland in the Early Twentieth Century', Unpublished Ph.D. Thesis in Sociology, University of Edinburgh.

JAMIESON, L. (1984), 'Growing up in Scotland: Class and Gender', in Glasgow Women's Studies Group, *Uncharted Lives* (Glasgow: Press Gang).

JAMIESON, L. (1986), 'Limited resources and limiting conventions: working-class mothers and daughters in urban Scotland 1890–1920', in J. Lewis (ed.) (London: Blackwell, 1986) pp. 49–69.

JAMIESON, L. (1987), 'Theories of family development and the experience of being brought up', *Sociology*, vol. 21, no. 4.

JAMIESON, L. (1989), 'State norms, parental authority and adolescent sexuality in Edwardian society' in P. Cohen and G. Murdoch (eds), *The Making of the Youth Question 1880–1914* (London: Macmillan, forthcoming).

KLEIN, J. (1965), *Samples From English Culture*, vol. 1 (London: Routledge & Kegan Paul).

KOOPMAN-BOYDEN, P. G. (1978), *Families in New Zealand Society* (Wellington: Methuen).

LEONARD, D. (1980), *Sex and Generation: A Study of Courtship and Weddings* (London: Tavistock); see also Barker.

LEWIS, J. (1980), *The Politics of Motherhood* (London: Croom Helm).

LEWIS, J. (ed.) (1986), *Labour and Love* (London: Blackwell).

LYND, R. and LYND, H. (1929), *Middletown* (New York: Harcourt, Brace & World).

McCALMAN, J. (1984), *Struggletown: Public and Private Life in Richmond, 1900–1965* (Melbourne University Press).

McCRINDLE, J. and ROWBOTHAM, S. (eds) (1979), *Dutiful Daughters: Women Talk about Their Lives* (Harmondsworth: Penguin).

McDONALD, D. J. (1978), 'Children and young persons in New Zealand society', in Koopman-Boyden, pp. 44–56.

McKEE, L. and O'BRIEN, M. (eds) (1982), *The Father Figure* (London: Tavistock).

MOGEY, J. M. (1956), *Family and Neighbourhood: Two Studies in Oxford* (Oxford University Press).

NEWSON, J. and NEWSON, E. (1963), *Patterns of Infant Care in an Urban Community* (London: Allen & Unwin).

NEWSON, J. and NEWSON, E. (1968), *Four Years Old in an Urban Community* (Harmondsworth: Penguin).

NEWSON, J. and NEWSON, E. (1974), 'Cultural aspects of chidrearing in the English-speaking world', in Richards (ed.) (1974), pp. 53–83.

NEWSON, J. and NEWSON E. (1976), *Seven Years Old in the Home Environment* (London: Allen & Unwin).

OAKLEY, A. (1974), *The Sociology of Housework* (London: Martin Robertson).

REIGER, K. M. (1985), *The Disenchantment of the Home: Modernizing the Australian Family 1880–1940* (Melbourne: Oxford University Press).

RICHARDS, M. P. M. (ed.) (1974) *The Integration of a Child into a Social World* (Cambridge University Press).

RITCHIE, J. and RITCHIE, J. (1970), *Child Rearing Patterns in New Zealand* (Wellington: A. H. & A. W. Reed).

RITCHIE, J. (1979), *Child Rearing Patterns: Further Studies* (Hamilton, N.Z.: University of Waikato, Psychological Research Series No. 11).

ROBERTS, E. (1984), *A Woman's Place: An Oral History of Working-Class Women* (Oxford: Basil Blackwell).

ROSENBERG, C. E. (ed.) (1975), *The Family in History* (University of Pennsylvania Press).

SEABROOK, J. (1982), *Working-Class Childhood* (London: Victor Gollancz).

SEELEY, J. R., SIM, R. A. and LOOSLEY, E. W. (1956), *Crestwood Heights: A Study of the Culture of Suburban Life* (New York: John Wiley & Sons).

THOMPSON, P. (1977), *The Edwardians: The Remaking of British Society* (London: Paladin).

THOMPSON, P. (1975), 'The war with adults', *Oral History*, 3, 2, 29–38.

TOYNBEE, C. (1986), 'Her Work, His Work and Theirs: the Household Economy and the Family in New Zealand, 1900–1925' (Unpublished Ph.D. Thesis in Sociology, Victoria University of Wellington).

VIGNE, T. (1975), 'Parents and children 1890–1980: distance and dependence', *Oral History*, vol. 3, no. 2, 6–13.

VIGNE, T. (1981), *Edwardian Childhoods* (London: Routledge & Kegan Paul).

WALLACE, C. (1988), *For Richer for Poorer: Growing Up In and Out of Work* (London: Tavistock).

WEARING, B. (1984), *The Ideology of Motherhood: a Study of Sydney Suburban Mothers* (Sydney: Allen & Unwin).

YOUNG, M. and WILMOTT, P. (1957), *Family and Kinship in East London* (Harmondsworth: Penguin).

ZUCKERMAN, M. (1975), 'Dr. Spock: The Confidence Man', in Rosenberg (ed.) (1975), pp. 179–207.

ZWEIG, S. (1961), *Worker in an Affluent Society* (London: Heineman).

Part II
Politics at Work: The So-called Public Sphere

6 Familial Control or Patriarchal Domination? The Case of the Family System of Labour in 19th Century Coal Mining

Jane Mark-Lawson and Anne Witz

INTRODUCTION

There is considerable debate and disagreement about the concept of patriarchy, both over the precise referent of the concept and whether or not it has any utility in explanations of women's position in modern capitalism. Some participants in the debate exhibit extreme caution regarding the use of the term 'patriarchy' and, at most, are prepared to admit only a historically specific, *generational* use of the term to refer to the power of the father over women and younger men (see Barrett, 1980). The stance of extreme caution may be broadly associated with the Marxist-feminist current (Barrett, 1980; Rowbotham, 1981; Vogel, 1983). Barrett (1980) argues that although categories of Marxism cannot allow an exhaustive account of women's oppression under capitalism, at the same time the concept of patriarchy cannot replace those categories. For Barrett, patriarchy remains a trans-historical and solely descriptive term when it refers to all expressions of male domination within a society. The concept of patriarchy to which Barrett takes exception is that in current usage among feminist social historians and sociologists; broadly a *gender*-based concept of the domination of women by men. Rowbotham (1981) is similarly troubled by the use of the term 'patriarchy' to distinguish women's subordination, as a sex, from class oppression, objecting to its use on the grounds of its alleged universalism and biologism. Curiously, though, Rowbotham (1981) takes the referent of the term 'patriarchy', to which she objects, to be the 'power of the father', and yet this is precisely what Barrett (1980) takes to be an acceptable, restricted use of the term. Generally, though, what we may broadly define as the Marxist-feminist current insist upon the adequacy of Marxism to the task of analysing women's oppression in capitalist society, while acknowledging the family as a site of male power inadequately treated within Marxist theory (see Vogel, 1983). When the concept of patriarchy is introduced into Marxist feminist analyses, then its use is (largely) derived from a Lacanian psychoanalytic problematic and patriarchy is treated as a relatively autonomous structure of psychic relations responsible for the production of sexed subjects (see Kuhn and Wolpe, 1978). But, as a structure relatively autonomous of the capitalist mode of production, patriarchy is limited in its effectivity to the family as the site for the production of sexed subjects.

On the other hand there are those feminist social historians and sociologists who, albeit in a variety of ways, have sought to salvage the term 'patriarchy' from theoretical neglect and recast it in such a fashion as to further our understanding of the ubiquity of male dominance and the complexity of gender relations and inequality in the family, the labour market and the state. Patriarchy is seen as an all pervasive system of male dominance, not restricted to the family, but pervading other sites of social relations. Walby (1986) defines patriarchy as a system composed of inter-related structures of social relations in the domestic division of labour, paid work, the state, male violence and sexuality. In their defence of patriarchy, Alexander and Taylor (1981) argue, in our view correctly, that sexual divisions and antagonisms need to be analysed with concepts for that forged purpose.

Accordingly, the gender-based concept of patriarchy currently in vogue describes the power relations between men and women, in which men are dominant and women are subordinate, that is, it speaks of a societal-wide *system* of male dominance. Inevitably, there are divergent formulations of the lynch-pin or basis of such a system and a variety of material bases of patriarchy have been identified. Firestone (1970) specifies reproduction, Delphy (1984) husbands' control over their wives' labour within the marriage relation, Rich (1980) compulsory heterosexuality, and Hartmann (1979) men's control over women's labour, both inside and outside the household, as the material underpinnings of patriarchy. When it comes to considering the inter-relations between patriarchy and capitalism, Eisenstein (1979, 1981) employs a notion of one system of capitalist-patriarchy, whilst Hartmann (1979, 1980) works with a dual-systems model of separate sets of capitalist and patriarchal relations that inter-relate to form a 'partnership' of patriarchal-capitalism.

Here we argue the case for the explanatory relevance of the gender concept of patriarchy, and adopt a dual systems framework associated with Hartmann (1979). Hartmann defines patriarchy as:

> A set of social relations which has a material base and in which there are hierarchical relations between men and solidarity among them which enable them in turn to dominate women. The material base of patriarchy is men's control over women's labour power. Their control is maintained by denying women access to necessary economically productive resources and by restricting women's sexuality . . . the material base of patriarchy, then, does not rest solely on childbearing in the family, but on all the social structures that enable men to control women's labour (Hartmann, 1980, pp. 14, 12).

The main strength of Hartmann's analysis lies in her theorisation of patriarchal relations as systemic relations. Employing a notion of patriarchal capitalism, she demonstrates how patriarchal relations persist within capitalism both within the capitalist labour market and within the family. Women's oppression in these two spheres is seen as dynamically inter-related and reinforcing. Hartmann's thesis pivots around an analysis of the exclusionary strategies of organised male workers, which, together with the demand for a family wage for men, and the development of the notion of the male 'breadwinner', were the major means whereby working-class men simultaneously restricted the role of women in paid employment and secured their unpaid services within the home.

Hartmann's thesis is not without its problems. For one thing, the rate of male trade unionism in the nineteenth century was so low that if the maintenance of patriarchal relations pivoted around the organised pursuit of exclusionary strategies, then 'patriarchal-capitalism' could hardly be said to exist prior to 1900 (Brenner and Ramas, 1984; Sen, 1980). And the family wage should not be treated as an actuality but as an imperfectly realised demand on the part of organised male workers (Barrett and McIntosh, 1980). In a recent article Seccombe has called for greater historical appreciation of the generation of the norm of the male breadwinner (Seccombe, 1986). In this paper we question the centrality accorded to the supposed support of male workers for protective legislation which, in the course of the nineteenth century, increasingly restricted the range of occupations open to women.

Humphries (1981) is generally sceptical of the patriarchal-capitalism thesis (and generally unwilling to countenance that the concept of patriarchy has any weight in explaining women's position in capitalist society). Using evidence from the 1842 Report of the Commissioners on the Employment of Children (Mines) (the report which preceded the 1842 Mines Regulation Act), Humphries tests several of the main points of Hartmann's argument. This was, after all, a piece of protective legislation which brought about the direct exclusion of women from one occupation, providing an apparently incontrovertibly patriarchal instance of male workers' successful exclusion of women from underground mining. But was it? Humphries (1981) finds it paradoxical that coal-mining men should have supported state intervention to remove female and child labour from underground mining when, as she shows, coal-mining men benefited from the system of family labour that existed in coal mining prior to the 1842 Act.

Under this system the male collier was able to maximise family income by sub-contracting work among family members rather than non-family members and, because the coal-mining workforce was divided into 'non competeing groups distinguished by age and sex', women's labour underground did not pose any threat to men. Neither does Humphries find any evidence that the male collier saw his wife's underground labour as in any way threatening his patriarchal privileges in the domestic sphere. There were no material grounds, argues Humphries, for male hewers to become embroiled in the pursuit of exclusionary practices either as a result of competitive threats to their jobs and wages levels, or to their familial authority. Humphries is then left with a paradox:

> What is remarkable, under these circumstances, is that male colliers almost universally wanted state intervention to regulate the labour of women and children, and the overwhelming majority of hewers believed that women should be prohibited from working below ground. This is true even of those husbands, fathers and brothers whose economic interests were directly served by their wives, children and sisters working (Humphries, 1981, pp. 15–16).

In our view, Humphries' evidence does raise doubts about the adequacy of the concept of patriarchy, as it has been commonly used, to look at the case of the 1842 Mines Regulation Act. But unlike Humphries, who insists upon the adequacy of Marxist categories of analysis to the task of analysing women's position in modern capitalism, we shall argue that it is impossible to analyse the constellation of interests which came into play around the 1842 Mines Act, without recourse to a theory of patriarchal as well as capitalist interests. Nonetheless, Humphries' careful analysis of the 1842 Mines Regulation Act in order to test several points of Hartmann's broad-ranging thesis does raise, in our minds, the question of whether there is more space for a fruitful interchange between the macro-structural focus of patriarchy theory (as demonstrated by Walby's chapter in this collection), which addresses the neglected question of a societal-wide system of male dominance, and the micro-historical viewpoint.

In the remainder of this chapter we examine the system of family labour in nineteenth-century coal mining and its demise due to the passing of the 1842 Mines (Regulation) Act. We argue that the system of family labour was an internal contract, whereby the exploitation and management of labour was delegated to the male hewer by coal owners and managers. The case study of early nineteenth-century coal mining provides an example of how the family functioned as a unit of labour within the mining labour process, and this adds an interesting new twist to Medick's (1976) thesis of the proto-industrial family. The burden of our argument is that the system of family labour within nineteenth century coal mining provides a case of the constitution of patriarchal control relations within the capitalist labour process. Using a concept of patriarchy our analysis of the family system of labour cuts through the ongoing debate concerning the relative importance of capitalist or patriarchal relations for the theorisation of gender relations in nineteenth-century, and indeed contemporary, industrial capitalism. This debate is mainly represented here through the writings of Hartmann (1979, 1980) and Humphries (1977, 1981), although other writers have addressed the major points of contention in this debate, which centres on whether the structural determinants of women's oppression are patriarchal, capitalist or both (see Eisenstein, 1979, 1981, 1984; Alexander and Taylor, 1981; Rowbotham, 1981; Cockburn, 1983; Barrett and McIntosh, 1980; Barrett, 1980; Beechey, 1979; Walby, 1986).

By looking again at the family system of labour in nineteenth-century coal mining and at the reasons for its demise, we resolve Humphries' *paradox* of why coal-mining men should have supported moves to abolish a system of family labour from which they benefited, and refine Hartmann's thesis of patriarchal capitalism. Although we use categories of analysis derived from a theory of patriarchy we also recognise the continuing need to *refine* the concept of patriarchy and with this aim in mind we are taking up the gauntlet of those critics of the concept who insist that more historically specific studies are needed (see Beechey, 1979; Seccombe, 1986).

THE FAMILY SYSTEM OF LABOUR IN COAL MINING

The use of family labour, which was very extensive in the seventeenth and eighteenth centuries, survived as a historically specific mode of patriarchal control over women's labour in pockets of nineteenth-century capitalism. We will show that, under such a system, men were able to oversee the labour of women and children, as well as exercise control over the distribution of material benefits and the allocation of work tasks. The family labour system described here is one in which the capitalist employed only the principal worker (the hewer in the case of coal mining) whose task it was to recruit, train and pay his assistants. It may be seen as a form of internal contract (see Hobsbawm, 1964; Littler, 1982). The hewer was paid piece rates for his work and in turn was responsible for the remuneration of those who worked under him and, as Humphries (1981) shows, he almost always preferred to employ family members. In areas like Ayrshire and Lanarkshire, where women's employment in mining was fairly common, the hewer generally employed two female bearers and might share a third 'fremit' (non relative) with another hewer (John, 1984, p. 22).

We should be clear at the outset as to why the hewer preferred to work with his family, a point not really discussed by Humphries. There were two main reasons for this. Firstly, his already given position of authority in the household mutually reinforced his position of authority in the work place. As one witness to the 1842 Commissioners Report explained:

> 'I think the reason why girls are employed is because the colliers like to have the children more under their command and bring their own girls in preference to employing other people's boys' (P.P. 1842, vol. XVI, p. 237, quoted in Humphries, 1981, p. 13)

The control exercised by hewers is evident in the interviews with witnesses in the 1842 Report. Numbers of children spoke of their dislike for the work when they first started it and how their fathers 'made them like it'. Ann Harris, a fifteen-year-old hurrier in the east of Scotland, started mining partly because she '. . . could get no other profitable work' and partly because she was '. . . obliged to do the work, as father houks (hews) below' (P.P. 1842, vol. XV, p. 29). A 37-year-old Bolton woman said:

> 'My feller (husband) has beaten me many a time for not being ready. I were not used to it at first and he had little patience. I have known many a man beat his drawer.' (P.P. 1842, vol. XV, p. 27)

The man who used family members to work under him could expect both loyalty and a range of services beyond those available to the normal sub-contractor or employer. In Yorkshire the hurriers were '. . . hired and paid by the colliers whose servants they are (and they) must do whatever work is set them by these men' (P.P. 1842, vol. XV, p. 72).

The second reason why the male hewer preferred to use the labour of household members was because the wages he paid to his assistants then went directly into his own household, a factor which suggests he would have had to pay more to buy in assistants from outside. Indeed, this may explain the discrepancy between the wages that employers claimed hurriers earned (the amount they included in the hewer's wage for that purpose) and the amount that the hewers said they actually got. As an underlooker in the Lancashire and Cheshire district explained:

> 'One reason why women are used so frequently as drawers in the coal pits is that a girl of 20 will work for 2s. a day or less, and a man of that age would want 3s. 6d.: it makes little difference to the coal master, he pays the same whoever does the work . . . the only difference is that the collier can spend 1s. to 1s. 6d. more at the ale house, and very often the woman helps him spend it.' (P.P. vol. XV, 1842, pp. 26–7)

Under these circumstances it is clear that the hewer would benefit from the use of his wife and daughter to provide subsidiary labour, and that the family as a whole would also benefit, since no part of the hewer's wage was going into another household. But in many cases where women and girls were working for husbands and parents they received no separate wage. One girl in the east of Scotland explained how she 'began working at ten years of age; father took sister and I down; he gets our wages' (P.P. vol. XV, 1842, p. 29). Even where a daughter worked for other men in the pit, her father might collect her wage. A 17-year-old girl at Barnsley said: 'I am not paid wages myself; the man who employs me pays my father; but I don't know how much it is.' (Quoted in Pinchbeck, 1981, p. 258.)

If the position of the male hewer in the family labour system gave him a good deal of control over family members, both in the household and in the workplace, it also seems to have allowed him a good deal of control and autonomy over the work process itself: control not only in terms of his own craft skill, but also in terms of the labour of his 'team'. The male hewer allocated work tasks to those who worked for him, and so determined both the sexual division of labour in the coal mining process and the amount and speed of his output. Work discipline, in the sense in which E. P. Thompson (1974) described it, was almost entirely absent in those coal fields where the family system of labour prevailed. Normally, the hewer went to work several hours before his hurriers or drawers, giving him time to cut the coal before they started to move it. But these areas saw 'St. Monday' and sometimes 'St. Tuesday' as a regular occurrence. The hewer who took time off at one end of the reckoning (usually a fortnight in the east of Scotland) could expect those who worked under him to make superhuman efforts later on to make up output.

> 'The Monday after the pay is always a holiday . . . and I am informed by the proprietors that many of them will not settle to work before the middle of the week following the pay. In this manner the drawers are kept employed for two or three days at the beginning of the reckoning and towards the end of it they are worked past their strength to make up for the lost time.' (P.P. 1842, vol. XV, p. 124)

Although it differed depending on the individual hewer, this system could mean that every so often hurriers had to work right through the night. Elizabeth Dickenson, who worked in Scotland with two brothers and two sisters, worked 24 hours once every two weeks. The male hewer, then, could unilaterally and arbitrarily allocate work tasks and intensify the effort-reward bargain struck between him and his team of family workers.

We are suggesting that the family system of labour created

a workforce organised on the basis of patriarchal control and that it endowed the principal male worker with certain benefits. It gave him the status of an independent sub-contractor, and it allowed men *direct* control over women and children's labour within the labour process, as well as control over the distributive and allocative processes of the household. Humphries, on the other hand, sees the family system of labour as primarily a means of monitoring and supervising the workforce, an element of capitalist control of the work process. The existence of this system also challenges Hartmann's view that patriarchal control is dependent on the *exclusion* of women from the workforce. The system of family labour, in which the male sub-contractor mediated between capital and the woman worker, represented an *alternative* means by which men controlled women's work and wages within the capitalist labour market. Under this system women did not enter into a direct capital-labour relationship, rather their relationship with capital was mediated by the male sub-contractor, whose position in the capitalist labour process was derivative of his position in the patriarchal family/household. Thus, patriarchal relations *mediated* the relations between capital and labour. Women, and indeed children, were not fully 'proletarian'.

An adequate analysis of the family system of labour, we would argue, demands to be couched *within* categories of analysis derived from a theory of patriarchy. For this reason, we find Humphries' own analysis of the family system of labour incomplete and unconvincing. But when we turn to the reasons for the demise of the family system of labour in nineteenth-century coal mining, then we are also forced to question the pivotal role accorded by Hartmann (and others) to the pursuit of exclusionary strategies by male workers as the major source of patriarchal control over women's labour within patriarchal capitalist relations.

THE DEMISE OF THE FAMILY SYSTEM OF LABOUR IN COAL MINING

We now turn to an examination of the reasons for the demise of the family system of labour in coal mining, in an attempt to resolve Humphries' paradox. We focus on the male collier's stance on the proposed legislation to remove female and child labour from underground mining, as well as on the interaction between capitalist interests and patriarchal practices, which constituted the constellation of forces around the proposed legislation. Our argument questions the centrality of male workers' exclusionary strategies as the pivot of patriarchal control over women's labour within capitalist relations. In fact, we would find the support of male colliers for the proposed protective legislation as paradoxical as Humphries does, for male colliers *already* reaped benefits from the system of family labour.

Why, then, should male workers have supported state legislative measures which undermined male control over female labour in the capitalist labour process? Especially since it appears that the family system of labour both enhanced the earnings of male hewers and gave them an unprecedented degree of control over the work process. Using the evidence of the 1842 Commissioners we would suggest quite simply that in those coal mining areas where the system of family labour prevailed, male hewers did *not* support the attempts either by individual employers at the local level, or by the state at the national level, to remove female labour from the mines.

At the local level the evidence suggests that in those areas where the family system of labour prevailed, and where women did work underground, the opinion of male colliers was in favour of family labour:

> The existence of some opposing voices [to the use of female underground labour] in the Commissioners' reports does not therefore mean that the miners 'almost universally' opposed the work . . . other reactions such as the torrent of petitions against the legislation reveal some of the ambivalences and variations amongst the workforce (John, 1981, p. 107).

Given extreme local variation in the employment of women in coal mining, the locality is probably the most relevant level of analysis. In the east of Scotland, for instance, where females made up 35 per cent of the coal-mining workforce, one underlooker agreed with the subcommissioner for that area that female labour was not desirable. However, he explained:

> '. . . in the present feeling of the colliers *no individual would succeed in stopping it in a neighbourhood where it prevailed* because the men would immediately go to those pits where their daughters would be employed . . .' (P.P. XV, 1842, p. 32. Our emphasis)

That the locality was the relevant level of analysis was argued quite specifically in parliament, usually by opponents of the bill. For instance, the Earl of Fitzwilliam, replying in the Lords to a petition from Sittingbourne in favour of the Bill claimed: 'It was impossible for the people of Sittingbourne to have any but very vague ideas of the conditions of the people in the manufacturing districts' (Hansard, vol. LXXIII, c198.)

Opponents of the bill, well aware of the flood of moral indignation that followed the publication of the Commissioners' reports, argued that the practice of employing females was disappearing anyway and hence not worth legislating against. As the Earl of Radnor (from a non female-employing area) put it: 'In this particular instance they had an old practice, and a practice which was on the decline' (Hansard, vol. LXV, c584).

It was also argued that the clause preventing the employment of women was unrealistic, failing to take into account the realities of working-class life in some areas. The bill sacrificed realities for principles, and in doing so was likely to give rise to a good deal of hardship. A year after the Act was passed, C. Cumming Bruce raised a motion in the Commons for a relaxation of the clauses concerned with the employment of women, and some interesting debate took place around this. Bruce described the very real hardship that resulted from the exclusion of females in some areas and presented petitions from workpeople in collieries to this effect, signed by 'many hundreds of men' and 'upwards of 1,000 females' (Hansard, LXIX vol. 4, c431). Bruce claimed he was not arguing in favour of women's employment in mines, because he realised that public opinion was very strongly against it, and because the eventual cessation of all female labour in mines was inevitable. But in the course of his speech he, in fact, presented a very reasoned defence of women's work in colleries, claiming that the evidence of degradation of women's work in mines presented by the sub-commissioners in the east of Scotland was exaggerated, incorrect and clumsily used (Hansard, LXIX vol. 4, cc429–57).

For his part, Ashley, defending his measure, claimed that petitions in favour of women's labour in mines were got up by unscrupulous coal owners who wanted to retain the cheaper labour of females. But according to Bruce the petitions came from the workpeople themselves:

> This was no coal owner question. In the mines with which he was acquainted, the exclusion or retention of women employed . . . was as a matter of profit, one of very slight importance. He could truly assert that he had never received a single communication on the subject from a single coal owner in Scotland. He had taken it up solely at the earnest request of the colliers themselves (Hansard, LXIX vol. 4, c444).

The evidence suggests that precisely the reason it was necessary for *state* intervention in the labour affairs of the coal industry, to get women and children out of the mines, was because colliers themselves, and indeed other members of collier families, would not allow it. Given the choice, they preferred the existing system of family labour. As the Commissioners put it:

> The great obstacle to improvement is . . . the peculiar character of the working people themselves: obstinately attached to the old habits and customs, they persist in making their wives and children contribute to their support, as they themselves formerly contributed to the support of their parents . . . (P.P. 1842, vol. XVI, p. 406)

According to Hassam, some coal owners who had attempted to dismiss women were:

> thwarted by the opposition of employees. Moreover there was a disadvantage in becoming a pioneer, namely the loss of male labour to those enterprises where the dismissed women were still given work (Hassam, 1980, p. 78).

The same situation had arisen in Lancashire where:

> . . . when an attempt was made to employ boys instead of females, it was resisted by the men, who refused to work themselves unless the women were employed . . . it was impossible, without the assistance of the law, for masters to put a stop to this system (Hansard, LXIX, vol. 4, c477, Mr Brotherton).

Support for the bill came from Commissioners who believed that only when coal owners were forced to exclude the labour of women would they improve working conditions, and from owners of larger, more heavily capitalised pits who anticipated that the exclusion of women and children would force smaller rivals out of business (c.f. Hansard, LXIV, c616). Women (on the whole) were used in under-capitalised pits.

Some pit owners clearly believed that the exclusion of women and children, with its corollary of the collapse of the family system of labour, would put competing smaller pits out of business. The destruction of that system also served to take control of the work process out of the hands of the male colliers. The exclusion of women brought with it a more dependent and malleable breadwinning labour force. At the Rosewall and Barley Dean coal mines in Scotland, from which females had been excluded in 1838, the Commissioners were told:

> Men labour here regularly, and average eleven to twelve days in the fortnight, whereas when they depended on their wives and children, they rarely wrought nine days in the same period. (P.P. vol. XV, 1842, p. 34)

And it was also argued that the removal of the family system of labour would '. . . enable men who now only work three or four days a week to discover their own interests in regularly employing themselves' (P.P. vol. XV, 1842, p. 35).

Our argument undermines Hartmann's claim that one reason why male workers' organisations develop patriarchal strategies is the gender-blind nature of capital, which will tend to draw on cheaper labour, almost inevitably female. In the case of coal mining at least, this gender-blind tendency appears to be absent in practice; for it was coal masters and owners who argued for state intervention to get women out of the pits. Why this should be the case is initially puzzling, not least because in other circumstances, for instance in engineering (Walby, 1985) and in printing (Cockburn, 1983) women's cheaper labour was much preferred by employers. Why was this not the case in coal mining in 1842?

The late eighteenth and early nineteenth centuries saw a period of rapid restructuring in mining. Improved transport facilities, in the form of canals and railways, broke the old monopoly which the Tyne and Wear had held over the export of coal for the home market, allowing previously undreamed of expansion in inland coalfields. The eighteenth century had also seen the improvement of technological innovations which could be used to dig deeper shafts and extract more coal, especially the use of steam power for drainage. By the nineteenth century then, methods of mining in some areas were changing rapidly, requiring ever-larger amounts of capital investment.

As Campbell and Reid put it:

> The new highly capitalised, vertically integrated coal and iron companies geared their production to rhythms which differed completely from those of the small masters serving domestic consumption . . . their need was not for an independent, come-and-go-as-you-please contractor, but a wage-hand (Campbell and Reid, 1978, p. 69)

The values of the old 'independent collier', who saw himself not as a wage hand but as a tradesman contracting with a particular company to do a job, 'clashed at every point with the rationale of the new companies with their emphasis on work discipline and company paternalism' (*Ibid.*, p. 56).

We suggest that the independent miner expected to be his own master, choosing, to a certain extent, his hours of work and the amount of coal he put out, and that this independent miner was partly constituted through the family system of labour. As we have already demonstrated, the use of the labour of family members gave the miner unique control over the labour process, a control which must have become an increasing anachronism in the restructuring and increased capitalisation of mining. In the case of coal mining the exclusion of both women and children was in part a casualty of the attempt by a new style of coal owner to ensure a disciplined work force.

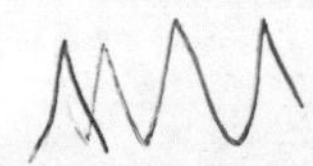

FORMS OF MALE CONTROL OVER FEMALE LABOUR IN NINETEENTH-CENTURY INDUSTRIAL CAPITALISM

We have shown that, in those areas where the family system of labour was in existence, there was an opposition on the part of the workforce to its proposed abolition. This is not surprising, because under this system of labour within coal-mining it was the principal male worker, the hewer, who exerted direct control over the family's labour. This control, as we have seen, may be described as patriarchal, inhering in the relations of the household outside the industrial work-place. We have demonstrated, for example, how the male hewer controlled both the distribution of economic rewards and the allocation of work tasks, as well as determining the effort-reward bargain that was struck between him and his family team. We have seen how, under the family system of labour, the male hewer determined his own work rhythm as well as that of other members of his family.

Employers, on the other hand, exerted only indirect control over the coal-mining labour process. With higher levels of capital investment and the necessity for increased and regular output, it was likely that this arrangement would no longer suit coal owners, who needed more intensive time-work discipline. While it would be naive to imply that the 1842 Mines Act was purely inspired by capital's needs for greater control over the mining workforce, it certainly did not frustrate that end. Humphries' paradox is therefore resolved in so far as male colliers, in those coalmining areas where women were working underground, did not support moves to abolish the system of family labour from which they benefited.

We now want to link our discussion of the case of family labour in nineteenth century coalmining to broader conceptual issues related to the theorisation of gender relations in patriarchal capitalism. The burden of our analysis of the family system of labour in coal mining has been to demonstrate that a historically grounded understanding of patriarchy is essential to understand the form in which female labour was utilised within coalmining, that is, through the family system of labour. In addition, we have shown the necessity of looking at the complex inter-relationships between patriarchal and capitalist relations, in order to untangle the constellation of forces behind both the existence and the eventual demise of the family system of labour in coal mining.

Our analysis differs in certain fundamental respects from that of Humphries, who rejects the notion of patriarchy on the grounds of its alleged trans-historicism, and wishes instead to see sexual divisions and antagonisms within the labour force as derivative of historically specific phases of capitalist development (Humphries, 1981, p. 5). Our argument has further interesting implications for Humphries' work (1977) on the persistence of the working class family, in which she analyses the relationship between male workers' exclusionary strategies, including their support for protective legislation, and the campaign for a family wage.

Here Humphries describes the unity of the working-class family and argues that the family was defended by all its members, men and women alike. Essentially, Humphries argues that the campaign waged by male trade unionists in the nineteenth century for a family wage, together with their support for escalating restrictions on the labour of women and children, had the effect of raising male wages and therefore improving the working-class standard of living as a whole. The working-class family, Humphries argues, 'traded off' the labour and wages of women for higher male wages that would support both the male labourer and his family. By contrast, we have shown that in the case of the 1842 legislation no such trade-off took place. Indeed, far from the exclusion of women being a source of working-class control over the supply of labour, as Humphries argues, it was the *inclusion* of family members within the family system of labour in sites of production which gave the working-class household, and especially the male head of household, enhanced autonomy, and which maximised household income. The exclusion of women, and indeed children (whose exclusion in the form of compulsory schooling was strenuously resisted by some sections of the working class in the 1870s and 1880s [Hurt, 1979]) made the working class household more rather than less vulnerable, while only the aristocracy of labour ever achieved a true family wage.

At the same time, our analysis of the constellation of forces around the 1842 Mines Regulation Act also signals caution with respect to Hartmann's overly general account of the behaviour of male workers as directed towards the *exclusion* of female workers from the workplace. Nor does it provide support for Walby's (1986) imputation of patriarchal interests at work in the framing of both the 1842 Mines Regulation Act and the 1847 Ten Hours Act. Nonetheless, it would be mistaken not to recognise that exclusionary strategies directed against female labour by working-class, and indeed middle-class men, *did* come to constitute a key means whereby male power was institutionalised within the labour market in the latter half of the nineteenth and early twentieth century. There is ample evidence for this in engineering trades (Drake, 1984; Walby, 1986), the printing trades (Cockburn, 1983) and in professional occupations such as medicine (Witz, 1986, 1988). We are suggesting, however, that this type of exclusionary strategy was pursued by working-class men only when women, as workers, came to be constituted as independent wage labourers rather than as subsidiary workers in the family system of labour.

The burden of our general argument raises the possibility of conceptualising and periodising shifts in the nature of male control over women's labour within both the capitalist labour market and the household. Indeed, just as shifting modes of capitalist control over the labour process have been identified (Edwards, 1979; Braverman, 1974; Littler, 1982), shifting modes of patriarchal control within capitalist workplace relations may also be identified. Within this conceptual framework, the family system of labour constitutes one mode of patriarchal control; one which does not depend upon the exclusion of women from the capitalist workplace. On the contrary, it is a mode of patriarchal control which operates by way of the *inclusion* of women and children within sites of capitalist production.

We suggest then that Britain has seen shifts through different modes of patriarchal control, within which the relationship between male workers, female workers and employers changes. Each shift has important and observable effects at the intersection between capitalist and patriarchal relations. As capital increases its direct control over the labour process, and as patriarchal control relations within the capitalist labour process, such as the family system of labour, are dismantled, male workers no longer directly control the labour of women within the labour process. It is only when women are more fully proletarianised, as they enter into a direct capital-labour relation, that they begin to pose a competitive threat to male workers, and patriarchal control comes to be exercised by means of exclusionary strategies both from particular jobs and from trade union organisation. In a recent article Seccombe (1986) suggests that the development of an ideology of the male-breadwinner norm around 1850 acted to 'stabilise' patriarchal relations, which were threatened by the challenge of wage-earning women. But rather than seeing exclusionary practices as bringing about a 'stabilisation' of patriarchal relations, as Seccombe does, we prefer to see the process as one of a *restructuring* rather than a *reassertion* of patriarchy.

These different modes of patriarchal control may be seen as linked to the transformation of the family-production relation during the development of modern capitalism. The existence of a family system of labour within the coal-mining labour process of the early nineteenth century adds an interesting new dimension or sub-phase to Medick's (1976) thesis of the proto-industrial family. The thesis of proto-industrialisation as a distinct 'protean' phase of industrial development in Europe, dating from the sixteenth to the early nineteenth century (Mendels, 1972; Medick *et al.*, 1976) focuses on the spread of rural domestic industry and the dynamics of transition to centralised production.

Medick (1976) argues that the macro-historical perspective of proto-industrialisation needs to be supplemented by a micro-historical viewpoint on the inner dynamics of the household/family, for proto-industry *was* family industry. Medick points out that, amidst the variations in proto-industrialisation according to region and craft, there remained one common structural foundation: 'This consisted in the close association between household production based on the family economy on the one hand, and the capitalist organisation of trade, putting-out and marketing of the products on the other.' (Medick, 1976, p. 296).

Medick suggests that during the proto-industrial phase the

family as a unit of production and consumption comes to be replaced by the family as a unit of labour. But, interestingly, the case of mining is held not to 'fit' the proto-industrialisation thesis at the macro-level (Medick, 1976, p. 296; Hudson, 1986, p. 11). Nonetheless, taking Medick's thesis concerning the constitution of the family as a unit of labour, then the existence of a family system of labour within the coal mining labour process of the early nineteenth century adds an interesting new dimension or sub-phase to the proto-industrialisation thesis. This is also suggested by Seccombe's (1986) work, in which he identifies five major strands of the proletariat-in-formation from 1750 to 1850: the proto-industrial households of cottage industry, the family hiring arrangements of agriculture, the family system of labour in coal mining, the family economy of early textile factories and, finally, the artisanal households of the skilled trades (Seccombe, 1976, 63–4).

But these five descriptive categories, we would argue, are not discrete. In all five categories, albeit in different ways, family labour was utilised as an enclave of patriarchal control within a primarily capitalist mode of production. What varies is the degree of spatial integration of the family unit of labour and capitalist relations of production. We suggest that the following three descriptive categories are useful: the proto-industrial family, the proto-proletarian family and the proletarian-industrial family.

The first, the proto-industrial family, is one where the family functions as a discrete unit of labour, but is functionally inter-related with capital in the manner suggested by Medick (1976), as capitalist organisation impacts upon household production. Patriarchal control relations will be dense and all pervasive. The second, the proto-proletarian family, emerges in regions where the family as a unit of labour becomes displaced into capitalist sites of production, although family members do not necessarily relate to capital in a 'proletarian' manner, i.e. as independent free wage labourers. The case of nineteenth-century coal mining provides an example of the male head of household operating as a sub-contractor and utilising the family as a unit of labour within a site of capitalist production. But other cases, for example tin mining in nineteenth-century Cornwall, will reveal further variations on the ways in which the family functions in a proto-proletarian manner.

Finally, the proletarian-industrial family is one where the individual family member functions as an independent wage labourer in sites of capitalist production. Family strategy becomes increasingly dependent on the wages of individual wage labourers, and this provides the material conditions for the historical construction of the norm of the male breadwinner, as discussed by Seccombe (1976).

Is there space for fruitful interchange between the macro-structural focus of patriarchy theory, which addresses the neglected question of a societal-wide system of male dominance, and the micro-historical viewpoint? We think there is, largely because of the unwholesome tendency to treat familial relations as 'naturalistic' and universal, contained within a historically variable 'shell'. Recent discussions of the importance of the system of internal contract as a mode of labour control which only declined in the last quarter of the nineteenth century, have also identified 'familial control' as one mode of control (Littler, 1982). But the slippery and unenlightening use of the term 'familial control' serves to obscure the fact that the family is a site of gender relations. In whom is this control vested? Who is controlling whom? Upon what basis is this control exercised? Such questions are evaded. Medick (1976) makes a nod in the direction of the issue of 'power relations' in the family, but claims then that the proto-industrial family as a unit of labour has 'slipped beyond the grasp of patriarchal domination' because marriage and family are no longer determined by property relationships (p. 303). But we have argued that the family system of labour in nineteenth-century coal mining was controlled by men, particularly in their capacities as husbands and fathers, and that this control derives from sets of patriarchal relations constituted outside of the workplace and reconstituted within the workplace in the form of internal contract.

Our argument has attempted to use sociological/theoretical perspectives and debates to examine historical evidence. But such an exercise is fruitless unless the evidence itself is allowed to inform or to reformulate those initial perspectives. At its worst, sociological history does little more than assemble historical evidence, sometimes from widely different historical periods and localities, to support sets of theoretical assumptions: an eclectic sift through the 'dustbin of history'. We hope we have avoided these pitfalls. We have started with the theoretical concerns of patriarchy, have reviewed these in the light of one particular historical instance, and have attempted to reformulate that concept to suggest that patriarchal processes are constituted in different and historically and socially specific ways in different periods and indeed in different places.

REFERENCES

ALEXANDER, S. and TAYLOR, B. (1981), 'In Defence of "Patriarchy"', in R. Samuel (ed.), *People's History and Socialist Theory* (London: Routledge & Kegan Paul).

BARRETT, M. and McINTOSH, M. (1980), 'The "family wage": some problems for socialists and feminists', *Capital and Class*, II, Summer.

BARRETT, M. (1980), *Women's Oppression Today* (London: Verso).

BEECHEY, V. (1979), 'On Patriarchy', *Feminist Review*, no. 3.

BRAVERMAN, H. (1974), *Labour and Monopoly Capital* (New York: Monthly Review Press).

BRENNER, J. and RAMAS, M. (1984), 'Rethinking women's oppression', *New Left Review*, no. 144.

CAMPBELL, A and REID, F. (1978), 'The Independent Collier in Scotland', in R. Harrison (ed.), *Independent Collier: The Coal Miner as Archetypal Proletarian Reconsidered* (Brighton: Harvester).

COCKBURN, C. (1983), *Brothers: Male Dominance and Technological Change* (London: Pluto).

DELPHY, C. (1984), 'The main enemy', in *Close to Home* (London: Hutchinson).

DRAKE, B. (1984), *Women in Trade Unions* (London: Virago).

EDWARDS, R. (1979), *Contested Terrain: The Transformation of the Workplace in the 20th Century* (New York: Basic Books).

EISENSTEIN, Z. R. (1981), *The Radical Future of Liberal Feminism* (London: Longman).

EISENSTEIN, Z. R. (1984), *Feminism and Sexual Equality: Crisis in Liberal America* (New York: Monthly Review Press).

FIRESTONE, S. (1970), *The Dialectic of Sex* (New York: Morrow).

HARTMANN, H. (1979), 'Capitalism, Patriarchy and Job Segregation by Sex', in Z. R. Eisenstein (ed.), *Capitalist Patriarchy and the*

Case for Socialist Feminism (New York and London: Monthly Review Press).

HARTMANN, H. (1980), 'The Unhappy Marriage of Marxism and Feminism: Towards a More Progressive Union', *Capitalism and Class*, no. 8.

HASSAN, J. A. (1980), 'The Landed Estate, Paternalism and the Coal Industry in Midlothian, 1800–1880', *Scottish Historical Review*, pp. 73–91.

HEESOM, A. J. (1980), 'The Northern Coal Owners and the Opposition to the Coal Mines Act of 1842', *International Review of Social History*, no. 25.

HEESOM, A. J. (1981), 'The Coal Mines Act of 1842, Social Reform and Social Control', *The Historical Journal*, 24, 1.

HOBSBAWM, E. J. (1964), *Labouring Men: Studies in the History of Labour* (London: Weidenfeld & Nicholson).

HUDSON, P. (1986), *The Genesis of Industrial Capital: a study of the West Riding Wool Textile Industry* (Cambridge University Press).

HUMPHRIES, J. (1977), 'Class Struggle and the Persistence of the Working-Class Family', *Cambridge Journal of Economics*, vol. 1, September.

HUMPHRIES, J. (1981), 'Protective Legislation, the Capitalist State, and Working Class Men: The Case of the 1842 Mines Regulation Act', *Feminist Review*, no. 7.

HURT, J. S. (1979), *Elementary Schooling and the Working Classes 1860–1918*, London.

JOHN, A. V. (1981), Letter in response to Jane Humphries, *Feminist Review*, no. 8, Autumn, pp. 100–9.

JOHN, A. V. (1984), *By the Sweat of their Brow: Women Workers at Victoria Coal Mines* (London: Routledge & Kegan Paul).

KUHN, A. and WOLPE, A. (eds) (1978), *Feminism and Materialism* (London: Routledge & Kegan Paul).

LAZONICK, W. H. (1976), *Historical Origins of the Sex Based Division of Labour Under Capitalism: a study of the British textile industry during the Industrial Revolution*, Harvard Institute of Economic Research Discussion Paper, no. 497.

LITTLER, C. R. (1982), *The Development of the Labour Process in Capitalist Societies* (London: Heinemann).

MEDICK, H. (1976), 'The proto-industrial family economy: the structural function of household and family during the transition from peasant society to industrial capitalism', *Social History*, vol. 1, no. 3.

MENDELS, F. (1972), 'Proto-industrialisation: the first phase of the industrialisation process', *Journal of Economic History*, vol. 32.

PINCHBECK, I. (1981), *Women Workers and the Industrial Revolution 1750–1850* (London: Virago).

RICH, A. (1980), 'Compulsory heterosexuality and Lesbian Existence', *Signs*, vol. 5, no. 4.

ROWBOTHAM, S. (1981), 'The Trouble with Patriarchy', in R. Samuel (ed.), *People's History and Socialist Theory* (London: Routledge & Kegan Paul).

SECCOMBE, W. (1986), 'Patriarchy Stabilized: the construction of the male breadwinner wage norm in nineteenth century Britain', *Social History*, vol. 11, no. 1.

SEN, G. (1980), 'The Sexual Division of Labor and the Working-Class Family: towards a conceptual synthesis of class relations and the subordinates of women', *The Review of Radical Political Economics*, vol. 12, no. 2.

SMELSER, N. J. (1959), *Social Change in the Industrial Revolution: an application of theory to the Lancashire cotton industry, 1770–1840* (London: Routledge & Kegan Paul).

TAYLOR, B. (1983), '"The Men Are as Bad as Their Masters . . .": Socialism, Feminism and Sexual Antagonism in the London Tailoring Trade in the 1830s', in J. L. Newton, M. P. Ryan and J. R. Walkowitz (eds), *Sex and Class in Women's History* (London: Routledge & Kegan Paul).

THOMPSON, E. P. (1974), 'Time, Work-Discipline and Industrial Capitalism', in M. W. Flinn and T. C. Smount (eds), *Essays in Social History* (Oxford: Clarendon Press).

VOGEL, L. (1983), *Marxism and the oppression of women: towards a unitary theory* (London: Pluto)

WALBY, S. (1986), *Patriarchy at Work* (Cambridge: Polity Press).

WIDDOWSON, F. (1983), *Going up into the Next Class: Women and Elementary Teacher Training 1840–1914* (London: Hutchinson).

WITZ, A. (1986), 'Patriarchy and the Labour Market: Occupational Control Strategies and the Medical Division of Labour', in D. Knight and J. Willmott (eds), *Gender and the Labour Process* (London: Gower Press).

7 Women's Employment and The Historical Periodisation of Patriarchy

Sylvia Walby

INTRODUCTION

Sociology has recently seen a renewed interest in macro-historical analysis; an exciting re-thinking of the major historical turning points and forms of social inequality (Lash and Urry, 1987; Giddens, 1981, 1985; Mann, 1986). However, most of this work has been lacking in any significant analysis of gender relations. For instance, in writing of the history of power from the beginning to 1760, Mann attempts to justify the omission of gender relations on the grounds that there has been no change in these in this period (p. 31).

In contrast, much of the recent historical writing on women has been very cautious about large-scale generalisations or theoretical development. There are exceptions to this, however, such as Kelly's (1984) reassessment of the changes for women during the renaissance, and Lerner's (1986) account of the development of patriarchy since the start of civilization. But these are few. Thus historical sociological accounts provide us with a picture of major changes in social structure, but little on gender changes, while gendered historical accounts tend to focus on detailed rather than macro changes.

This chapter will discuss historical change in gender relations from a sociological perspective. It will consider which are the main historical turning points for gender relations, asking whether they are different from those for class relations. The nature and causes of these changes are crucial for understanding that the deskilling of work and the take-over of household tasks by the capitalist economy creates a demand for cheap unskilled labour, and a supply in the form of women with less housework to do. A non-Marxist version can be found in the work of Bergmann (1986), who analyses the 'economic emergence of women' as a more general result of the expansion of the economy.

There is a further debate on the significance of the development of capitalism for gender relations, and employment in particular, in which there are two main positions. On the one hand writers have argued that capitalism led to the separation of home and work, with women being confined to the former (Tilly and Scott, 1978; Zaretsky, 1976; Oakley, 1976; Davidoff and Hall, 1987). On the other there are those who have argued that capitalism did not lead to such a separation because there was already a marked sexual division of labour (Middleton, 1981; Hartmann, 1979).

Most of the debate so far has been about the sexual division of labour. Some of the same major themes recur within a broader perspective on aspects of gender relations, albeit in slightly different form. Again they can be divided into two. Firstly, there are those who report on improvements in the position of women and the impact of the War (Marwick, 1968), and on the improvements brought about by modern medicine (Shorter, 1982). Secondly, there are those who suggest that every advance on one front is balanced by regression on another, for example, Millett (1977) and Faderman (1981), and their analyses of the sexual counter-revolution as a backlash to the advances of first-wave feminism; Brown (1981) in her suggestion that women only gain legal control over their children when they become a drain rather than a resource; and others in suggesting that women only gain entry to an occupation when its position is falling in the hierarchy of occupations. This twofold classification is, of course, over simple, and there are other themes such as the worsening of women's position with the development of capitalism; but I think these are the two major positions, and they represent a significant divergence in ways of understanding gender and history.

FORMS OF PATRIARCHY

I am defining patriarchy as a system of social relations through which men oppress and exploit women (see Walby, 1989a, 1989b for a defence of the concept). I want to distinguish conceptually between degrees and forms of patriarchy. The former refers to the intensity of the oppression of women and the latter the different shapes this takes.

I would suggest that the different forms are dependent upon the interaction of six key patriarchal structures. These are the patriarchal mode of production; patriarchal relations in paid work; patriarchal relations in the state; male violence; patriarchal relations in sexuality; patriarchal relations in cultural institutions including religions, media, education. (These are described more fully in Walby, 1989b).

In different times and places some of the structures are more important than others. The elimination of any one patriarchal structure does not lead to the demise of the system as a whole. Logically there could be many forms, since I have identified six structures of patriarchy, and two other major systems with which it has been in articulation. I am going to suggest that in recent Western history there have been two major forms. The purpose of doing this is to demonstrate that patriarchy is not an ahistoric, universalistic concept.

The two main types are those of public and private patriarchy. Private patriarchy is centred on the exclusion of women from arenas other than the household, with a patriarch appropriating a woman's services individually and directly, in the relatively private sphere of the home. In public patriarchy women are controlled in all sites and are not excluded from the public arenas. Here the appropriation of women by men is done collectively rather than individually.

Britain has seen a movement from a more public form of patriarchy to a more private one, during the eighteenth and nineteenth centuries, and from this private form to a public form since the turn of the last century.

THE MOVEMENT FROM PUBLIC TO PRIVATE PATRIARCHY?

Many writers have suggested that changes in gender relations during the last two centuries, such as the separation of home and work, can be attributed to the development of capitalism – as was noted earlier (Tilly and Scott, 1978; Zaretsky, 1976; Oakley, 1976; Davidoff and Hall, 1987). Against this there is a school of thought suggesting that the sexual division of labour pre-dated capitalism and cannot be considered to be caused by it (Middleton, 1981; Hartmann, 1979).

I shall argue that, while there have been significant changes in gender relations in the seventeenth and eighteenth centuries, the development of capitalism cannot be considered to be the main cause of them. Patriarchal relations pre-dated capitalism, and were not created by them. Nevertheless there were changes. The rise of capitalism was a factor in the development of a new form of patriarchy, but not in changing its basic structures.

The dominant account stresses the significance of the changes in gender relations with the rise of capitalism. It is argued that there was a separation of home and work, thereby creating the role of the housewife. This is considered to be a result of the development of capitalism which pulls men away from the household in search of work in the factories, and the growth of a domestic ideology which locates women as nurturers in the home. Some of the later writings (for example, Davidoff and Hall) pay particular attention to the class dynamics of this process, in which the most acute separation develops among the rising middle classes and bourgeoisie; this is then copied by and sometimes imposed on the working class.

I think this account is mistaken for the following reasons. Firstly, it underestimates the significance of the pre-capitalist sexual division of labour. Middleton has shown that in England there was a well developed sexual division of labour in both feudal and proto-industrial times (Middleton, 1981, 1985). Further, agricultural labour, in which the majority of the British population engaged prior to industrialisation, necessarily meant that men left the home in order to work, long before the advent of capitalist factories; the separation of home and work is not specific to capitalism. Domestic industries were not the only forms of occupation. Secondly, changes in the gender division of labour during the rise of capitalism are over-stated. Adult men constituted a minority of the workforce in the first industry of the industrial revolution. In cotton textiles adult men made up only 18 per cent of the factory workforce in 1819 (Hutchins, 1915: 72). Only in later industries were women excluded, and this was significantly a result of patriarchal pressures, not capitalist ones (see Walby, 1986). Poor women in pre-industrial England engaged in field labour; poor women in industrial England also engaged in work other than domestic work for their own families, ranging from cotton weaving, domestic service, and needlework to taking in laundry. Thirdly, changes in the household are over-stated. The English household had had a nuclear structure long prior to capitalism. Laslett (1971) finds this pattern in the sixteenth and seventeenth centuries, while McFarland (1978) finds this structure in the thirteenth century. Indeed Anderson (1971) shows that the household became less nuclear during industrialisation, with households in the cotton textile mills taking in additional members. Women married to men of the ruling class did not engage in 'work' in either period. As the size of the British empire grew so did the size of its ruling class, in proportion to the population of Britain. Fourthly, the practice of confining women to the domestic sphere, which is supposed to be the hallmark of gender relations after the rise of capitalism, is in fact found in its most developed forms in Islamic societies, both pre-capitalist and capitalist. Capitalism is not an exclusive hallmark of such patterns of gender relations; it cannot be treated as their cause.

Nevertheless, I am not wanting to argue that there were no changes in gender relations during the period of industrialisation. Rather, that they have been both massively over-stated and incorrectly explained.

These changes included the progressive loss by women of areas of work which had been deemed women's work, and the loss of certain legal rights that they had previously held over property (Pinchbeck, 1981; Schreiner, 1918). In looking at the shifting balance of power between women and men it is essential to examine the gains by men as well as the losses by women. The changes also included the one-sided gain by some men of privileged access to new spheres of power. For instance, the benefit of the development of credit, necessary for capitalist entrepreneurs, was restricted to men because of the limitations on the legal personhood of married women. Other examples include the development of formal, bureaucratised political arenas such as Parliament and state apparatus to which some men, but no women, had access.

Essentially in this period we see the development of many new bases of power, most of which might be considered to be in the 'public' sphere and from which women were debarred. The critical changes are not so much a new confinement of women to a private sphere, as the growth of the public sphere to which men had nearly exclusive access.

This is not to say that the proportion of English women who embraced a 'domestic ideology' did not increase. Neither is it to deny that the discourse became progressively more restrictive for the women living this 'domestic ideology'.

How do we understand these changes? I have argued elsewhere that there is no part of any logic of capitalism that would explain these changes (Walby, 1986). The benefits capital gains from the production of labour power from the patriarchal nuclear family are contingent, not necessary, and there are significant costs entailed. Is it then part of a logic of patriarchy? I think not, in the sense of inevitable laws of development of patriarchy. But I do think that it is a result of the shift of resources of male power consequent upon the development of capitalism, which led to changes in the critical sites of patriarchal power. The development of capitalism opened up new sites of power, and men colonised these because they were strategically placed to do so. This was not always achieved without a struggle, however, as the preferential employment of women by capitalists in early cotton textiles indicates. Simultaneously, the transformation of the domestic economy and domestic industries by capitalism contracted the bases of female power.

THE MOVEMENT FROM PRIVATE TO PUBLIC PATRIARCHY

While it is customary to argue that the rise of capitalism caused significant changes in gender relations, it is not often argued that there have been significant points of change since then. Indeed many writers suggest that we have seen few significant changes. Those who do argue that there have been changes, generally suggest that these have been gradual and cumulative developments in the direction of the emancipation of women. For instance, Stone (1977) argues that the growth of affective individualism has been to the benefit of women. There are a few exceptions, of course; for instance, Marwick (1968) considered that women made significant progress during the upheaval of the World Wars.

I want to argue that there has been a point of very significant change in gender relations. In particular, that there was a change in the direction of the development of patriarchy away from the trend towards the private form in the early nineteenth century, to that towards the public form. This is not merely a statement that there were important changes, but further, that the very direction of change was reversed. This turn has two moments, one located at the end of the turn of the nineteenth century into the twentieth, the other in the post-World War II period. There are two main reasons for this change: firstly, the capitalist demand for labour; secondly, feminist political activity. Both were pertinent at the two moments of this point of change. In the first moment women won political citizenship which gave them not only the vote, but education, and hence access to the professions, property ownership and the right to leave marriages. In the second moment women gained effective access to paid employment and the effective ability to leave marriages. The first moment was primarily a victory at the political level of the state; the second, at the economic level, provided the material possibility for the mass of women to take advantage of their legal independence. In the absence of the first, the political victory, the increase in women's wage labour of the second moment would have been merely additional exploitation.

CAPITALISM AND CHANGES IN THE FORM OF PATRIARCHY

The usual ways of analysing the impact of capitalism and industrialisation on gender inequality are either to argue that it worsened the position of women (as is described above), or improved it (see Perkin, 1969). I shall argue that neither is the correct view. Rather, there was a struggle between capitalist and patriarchal forces, the outcome of which was a change in the form of patriarchy from private to public. This change was not immediate and there was a prolonged period of dispute before the historical compromise was made.

The main basis of the tension between capitalism and patriarchy is the exploitation of women's labour. On the one hand capitalists have interests in the recruitment and exploitation of female labour, which is cheaper than that of men because of patriarchal structures. On the other hand there is resistance to this by patriarchal strategies which seek to maintain the exploitation of women in the household.

The first forms of capitalist industrialisation saw the successful recruitment of women (and children) into the cotton textile factories in greater numbers than men. Prolonged patriarchal resistance, through political pressure on the state to pass the Factory Acts, and by craft unions to bar women entry to specific jobs, was not able to do more than stabilise the situation in this industry. In other occupations that entered the capitalist factory later, such as skilled manual engineering work, the men's craft organisations were successful in excluding women during the nineteenth and early twentieth centuries. Indeed there was often a strong cross-class patriarchal alliance which supported the exclusion of women, even in the absence of strong male unions. However, this cross-class alliance had weaknesses when it cut across the interests of employers to recruit the cheaper labour of women. Conflict would break out, as it did over the recruitment of women into the munitions factories during World War I.

The exclusionary patriarchal strategy described above was not the only one. An alternative patriarchal strategy developed, generally later, of allowing women into paid employment, but segregating them from men and paying them less. Clerical work at the turn of the century is a good example of this process, where the male workers' organisations were insufficiently strong to defeat employers' insistent attempts to recruit women. This was resolved by a compromise, in which the employers ceased trying to substitute women directly for men and instead recruited women for new sub-occupations that were segregated from those of men, graded lower and paid less, while maintaining the men in the upper reaches of white collar work (see Walby, 1986).

Whether the exclusionary strategy or segregation strategy was followed depended upon the balance of capitalist and patriarchal forces in a particular industry in a particular locality. The exclusionary strategy was based upon a private form of patriarchy in which women were controlled by excluding them from the public sphere, especially from paid work. The segregation strategy was based upon a public form of patriarchy in which women were controlled within all spheres, not by excluding them from some. The power of capital precluded the successful maintenance of the exclusionary mode, except in certain small tight pockets of patriarchal power and resistance. For instance, the typesetters were able to sustain this until the last decade, as Cockburn (1983) has shown. The exclusionary form of patriarchy was also under attack by a large powerful feminist movement from the middle of the nineteenth century to the first quarter of the twentieth.

The development of the economic structures of capitalism was not sufficient by itself to cause the shift from private to public patriarchy. This could only occur in the context of a powerful feminist movement in Britain, and indeed most of the West. Where we find capitalism without a feminist movement, there is not such a change in the form of patriarchy. For instance, in some parts of the contemporary Third World young women have been pulled into wage labour for the capitalist factories of foreigners, yet are still subject to the patriarchal control of their fathers (Jayawardena, 1986; Mies, 1986). Wage labour by itself does not provide freedom from patriarchal control. In the case of Western industrialisation, first-wave feminism created a different balance of forces.

FIRST-WAVE FEMINISM

The political level of feminist organisation, and the capitalist system, with which patriarchy was in articulation, were vital in this change of direction from private to public patriarchy. First-wave feminism was a large, powerful movement which won citizenship rights for women and their formal entry into the public sphere. Its continuation in the form of welfare feminism, in alliance with the labour movement, was critical in the development of the Welfare State. The expansion of the capitalist economy was important through its dynamic restructuring of jobs and its increasing demand for labour, especially of the cheaper sort. This combination was key to the significant expansion of women's paid employment.

First-wave feminism is a significantly under-rated political movement; its extent, range and impact is rarely appreciated. It was a large, multi-faceted, long-lived and highly effective political phenomenon. It can be dated as extending from around 1850 to 1930 and it encompassed a wide range of political positions and campaigns (Banks, 1981; Hayden, 1981; Liddington and Norris, 1978; Schreiner, 1918; Spender, 1983; Strachey, 1978). Campaigns included not only the famous one for suffrage, but also for the containment of predatory male sexual behaviour (Christabel Pankhurst's slogan was 'Votes for women, chastity for men'), access to employment, to training and education, reform of the legal status of married women so that they could own property, for divorce and rights to legal separation at the woman's behest as well as that of the husband (Holcombe, 1983), and for the collective rather than private organisation of meal preparation (Gilman, 1966; Hayden, 1981).

This political movement made a major impact on the position of women and the forms of patriarchy. Women won political citizenship. In addition they won access to higher education, and hence to the professions. They won rights to legal personhood such as the right to sit on juries, to own property whatever their marital status, and hence to have access to credit. They won the right to leave a marriage, both by legal separation and by divorce.

These are considerable gains. They defeated the patriarchal strategy of restricting women to the private sphere of the home. Women had won access to the public sphere and claims to the rights and privileges of citizenship. They could no longer be legally subsumed to their husbands or fathers.

This is not to argue that women won equality with men, but it is to assert the significance of these victories in the public arenas relating to political citizenship and legal personhood. It is true that many things were still closed to women; the material and political conditions to guarantee full access in many areas were lacking. But nevertheless, the significance of these gains should not be under-estimated. They led women's entry into the public sphere and the change in forms of patriarchy from private to public. This political movement caused a change in the *form* of patriarchy as well as in degree.

While the movement constituted a turning point, the consequences of first-wave feminism took some time to be worked through. It is only with women's access both to waged labour and state welfare payments in the post-World War II period that the possibility of full economic as well as political citizenship is realised. The second moment of the turning point from private to public patriarchy is of critical importance. I shall discuss the changes for which the winning of political citizenship were vital, before moving on to a consideration of this second moment.

What is the connection between the first moment of the turning point that I have identified and future developments? A most important factor is the entry of women into decent paid employment; this could not have occurred without first-wave feminism. This struggle ended the closure of professions such as law and medicine, by the winning of women's access to the universities. While numerically this is not particularly significant, it is so in terms of women's collective access to the top jobs, which themselves are significant gatekeepers. Further, the state could no longer be used to back up a patriarchal exclusionary strategy by organised male workers to the same extent after women had won the vote. During the nineteenth century a series of Acts of Parliament had sought to restrict women's paid employment. These restricted the best, rather than worst, work available to women. They limited women's access to cotton mills and mines, which had shorter hours and better pay than domestic service and field labour (see Walby, 1986). During World War I male unions had been able to call on the state to back their demands that 'their' jobs be returned to them after the war, if they 'let' women take them for the duration of the hostilities (Braybon, 1981). Yet in the next World War, after women had won the vote, the same strategy was significantly less successful, and the state was much more reluctant to intervene to support the men's demands in the aftermath of the war (Braybon, 1981; Summerfield, 1984). Despite the enormous patriarchal pressure to exclude women (and especially married women) from paid work during the inter-war depression, the national state never passed legislation to enforce this. From the 1950s the state has been backing moves towards equality in paid work for men and women. The first groups of women workers to win equal pay were white collar government employees (teachers, civil servants etc).

I am not trying to argue that the state today is an anti-patriarchal state, rather that there was a significant change in its policy, from acting to enforce closure in employment against women, before women got the vote (in legislation such as the series of Factory Acts and the First World War Munitions Act), to a *laissez faire* policy in the inter-war period, and then to an active, albeit weak, endorsement of women's rights to employment from the 1950s onwards. Such closure that remains, and it is significant, is primarily enforced at a more decentralised level, in the structures constituting occupational segregation. I would argue that women's winning of political citizenship was crucial to these changes.

A further major change crucially affected by state policy is the ability of women both to leave marriages and to live with their children without a man. The legal right to leave an unwanted husband was won by first-wave feminism. In the nineteenth century a man could have a 'runaway' wife forcibly returned to him (see Holcombe, 1983; Strachey, 1978, for instances of this). First-wave feminism won the right of a woman to leave her husband if she so wanted. This was won, not only by means of the revisions to the divorce law, but also in those to legal separation, which brought this right within the financial reach of working-class women, who could only afford the procedures of the magistrates courts (Holcombe, 1983; Strachey, 1978). This right has been steadily extended ever since, in particular by the 1969 Divorce Reform Act which enabled divorce after two years separation if both parties agreed, and after five if one did not. While the legal right to divorce was won by first-wave feminism, it was not until the 1970s that divorce became widespread. This was partly due to the further reforms of the 1969 Act, but most especially because of the availability of economic support for women. It was only at this time that paid employment for married women became the majority pattern, and the option of supporting oneself and one's children by paid employment became a real possibility – though this employment is extremely restricted in the case of women with pre-school age children, who are less likely to be in paid work than women with husbands (Cohen and Clark, 1988). Material independence is also partly a result of state policy in the provision of support for a lone mother in the form of supplementary benefit payments. She is not obliged to seek the support of relatives or stay with an unwanted partner. In short, first-wave feminism won the right to escape an unwanted husband; this right has been steadily extended ever since, both in terms of ever more 'liberal' divorce legislation, and through the increasing possibility of material support as a lone woman and lone parent.

I am arguing that the entry of women to the state and political citizenship, via the vote, was a highly significant factor in changes in gender relations. However, there is a second moment to the change from private to public patriarchy; this is the increased access of women to paid employment, which took place after World War II and is still occurring.

In 1988 the majority of women are in paid employment, and make up 45 per cent of the paid workforce. Women having children in the 1980s take, on average, only five years out of the labour market (Martin and Roberts, 1984). Class differences are negligible. Ethnic differences are significant, with women of Afro-Caribbean origin being more likely to be in paid work, Moslem-Asian women least likely to be in public paid work, and white women in between these two groups.

This is significantly different from the peak of the private form of patriarchy in the middle of the nineteenth century when women of the middle and upper classes were less likely to be in paid work than either the working-class women of that time or the white and Afro-Caribbean women of today. Further, working-class women had restricted access to paid employment, with most of the best jobs barred to them on grounds of sex. For instance, all the skilled manual trades that demanded apprenticeships were closed to them. Among those that remained, the most important form of work, domestic service, entailed forms of control which were mid-way between paid work and housework, such as nearly continuous availability, supervision of 'private' life, living in, and not infrequent sexual demands. Further, most forms of formal paid employment, even those which gradually opened to women in the early decades of the twentieth century, had a marriage bar.

While some branches of paid employment were opened up to women in the decades following first-wave feminism, most retained the marriage bar. Most married women did not have access to formal paid employment until the removal of this bar during World War II, despite demands for this by working women's organisations. The expansion of women's paid employment could then only occur after World War II, when the marriage bar had been abolished.

Conventionally, the expansion of women's paid employment is seen, by both Marxists and neo-classical economists as a result of the expansion of the economy into which women get drawn. That is, the explanatory variable is the capitalist economy or market demand for labour. Some see this as a cyclical phenomenon, others a long-run one, as was indicated at the beginning. The problem with these ungendered accounts is that they are unable to deal with the fact that women are continuing to enter the paid workforce while men are leaving it in the current recession. Demand for labour is not a sufficient explanation.

The expansion of women's paid employment has often been considered to be a crucial step on the road to women's emancipation. Engels refers to the significance of the introduction of women to public industry. Young and Willmott

(1975) see it as an important factor in the development of the 'symmetrical family'. Bergmann (1986) sees the 'economic emergence' of women as key to their social emergence.

Yet this is controversial. Does the entry of women to paid work merely give them a 'double burden'? The experiences of women in Eastern Europe have sometimes been held up as a warning in this respect; there they are said to have paid work with only minimal reduction of their domestic work, and without political or social equality.

The question I want to ask is whether the entry to paid work is merely a different form of patriarchy, or whether it is a reduction in its degree. In summary form the changes in gender relations between the two centuries might be described as follows. Women's paid employment has grown significantly since the turn of the century. However, most of this increase did not occur till half a century later, after World War II. Marriage has been significantly affected, with one in two ending in divorce, and one quarter of children being born out of wedlock. Women have some minor level of representation at the level of the state. There is little evidence of change in the relations around male violence, except a very recent increase in the support given to women whose violent attackers are strangers. There have been significant changes in sexuality, with less stigmatisation of non-marital sexuality, combined with greater pressure to be engaged in some. Access to education has been very significantly improved.

There are two types of interpretations of these developments. On the one hand, they can be seen as a decline in the degree of patriarchy. On a set of indices relating to each of the six areas of gender inequality, this might be done. On the other, they can be seen as a change in form, not degree. I want to argue for both, although these two dimensions of change need to be identified separately.

In summary, women have found access to the public spheres of contemporary society from which they were previously barred. They have entered paid employment in large numbers. Women are able to leave marriages, and increasing numbers do. The forms of control are significantly fewer from a personal patriarch (the husband or father) and increasingly more from a collective or public patriarchy. For instance, sexuality is increasingly regulated outside the family.

These changes by themselves might appear to constitute a reduction in the degree of patriarchy. I think they do, but I also think that they simultaneously provoked a change in the form of patriarchy.

With the failure of the exclusionary strategy of private patriarchy, with its exclusion of women from the public sphere, we see the development of a new strategy of inclusion, but with new forms of control, with the development of public patriarchy. The argument is then that as some sites of patriarchy lose their salience as a result of feminist advances, others come to the fore.

Changes in household structure and composition form a further area of change, indicating a shift in the form of patriarchy as well as one of degree. Women's ability to leave unwanted marriages has so far been presented as a diminution in the degree of patriarchal control. However, it should also be considered as part of a change in the form of patriarchy. While in female-headed households women escape the duties of serving husbands, they also lose access to the income a husband might have brought to the household. Women without men usually live in poverty. Lone mothers with pre-school children are likely to live on social security payments. Even when in employment, many women will not earn much more than a poverty-level wage if they have children. Women typically have custody of children after divorce, and in practice look after them during separation. The absence of a husband does not mean that women are freed from the work, responsibilities and cost of child care. They still produce the next generation. While they lose their own individual patriarch, they do not lose their subordination to other patriarchal structures and practices. Indeed they become even more exposed to certain of the more diffused public sets of patriarchal practices. Their income level and standard of living are no longer determined primarily by that of their husband, but instead either by the patriarchal state, if they are dependent upon welfare benefits, or the patriarchally-structured labour market. It is the anonymous state and market rather than her private patriarch which determine the life of the lone mother. She substitutes public for private patriarchy.

CONCLUSION

Patriarchy comes in more than one form; each form can be found to different degrees. British history over the last couple of centuries or so has seen a shift to a more intense form of private patriarchy, and then a dramatic reversal of this, with a move towards public patriarchy. This latter shift was a result of the successes of first-wave feminism in the context of an expanding capitalist economy. The British form of public patriarchy involves the market as well as the state, while there is a different sub-type of public patriarchy in Eastern Europe, in which the state plays a more central part in comparison with the market.

The major historical changes are different for gender relations from those affecting capitalist class relations. Gender and class have independent historical dynamics, although of course they do have effects upon each other. The rise of capitalism transformed class relations, changing the very classes that constituted society. This historical shift did not have such dramatic effects upon gender relations: men remained the dominant gender; all six patriarchal structures continued across this period; only a minor shift occurred in the relative significance of public and private sites of patriarchy. The trajectory towards an intensified private form of patriarchy, which can be identified as far back as the seventeenth century (Charles and Duffin, 1985; Clark, 1982), accelerated.

The major change in the trajectory of the development of patriarchy, which took place through the turn of the century women's movement, has no real parallel in class relations. Its nearest equivalent is the granting of political citizenship to working-class men a few decades prior to that to women. This was of significance in shifting the balance of power between the bourgeoisie and the proletariat, but it did not have the dramatic effect upon the basic productive relations of capitalism that it did on the basic relations of patriarchy. Further, the struggles were separate, both in personnel and in time. Working-class men, like middle-class and bourgeois men, were not renowned for their support for feminist demands. The main turning points in gender relations cannot be read off from those of class relations. This independence of historical turning points is not unexpected given the analytic independence of patriarchy and capitalism.

REFERENCES

The original paper presented to the BSA conference was considerably longer than what is published here. The other part may be found in *Women's Studies International Forum*, Spring 1989. I should like to thank both *WSIF* and Helen Corr and Lynn Jamieson for allowing some repetition in the latter sections of the paper.

ANDERSON, M. (1971), *Family Structure in Nineteenth Century Lancashire* (Cambridge University Press).

ANDREWS, I. O. (1918), *Economic Effects of the War Upon Women and Children in Great Britain* (New York: Oxford University Press).

BANKS, O. (1981), *Faces of Feminism: A Study of Feminism as a Social Movement* (Oxford: Martin Robertson).

BEECHEY, V. (1977), 'Some notes on female wage labour in capitalist production', *Capital and Class*, no. 3, Autumn, 45–66.

BERGMANN, B. R. (1986), *The Economic Emergence of Women* (New York: Basic Books).

BRAVERMAN, H. (1974), *Labor and Monopoly Capital: The Degradation of Work in the Twentieth Century* (New York: Monthly Review Press).

BRAYBON, G. (1981), *Women Workers in the First World War: The British Experience* (London: Croom Helm).

BROWN, C. (1981), 'Mothers, fathers, and children: from private to public patriarchy' in L. Sargent (ed.), *Women and Revolution: The Unhappy Marriage of Marxism and Feminism* (London: Pluto).

BROWN, C. (1984), *Black and White Britain: The Third PSI Survey* (London: Heinemann).

BUTLER, J. (1896), *Personal Reminiscences of a Great Crusade* (London: Horace Marshall & Son).

CHARLES, L. and DUFFIN, L. (eds) (1985), *Women and Work in Pre-Industrial England* (London: Croom Helm).

CLARK, A. (1982), *Working Life of Women in the Seventeenth Century*

(London: Routledge & Kegan Paul); originally published in 1919.

COTT, N. (1978), 'Passionless: an interpretation of Victorian sexual ideology, 1790–1850', *Signs*, 4, 2, 219–36.

DAVIDOFF, L. and HALL, C. (1987), *Family Fortunes: Men and Women of the English Middle Class 1780–1850* (London: Hutchinson).

DRAKE, B. (1984), *Women in Trade Unions* (London: Virago); originally published by Labour Research Department and Allen & Unwin in 1920.

DWORKIN, A. (1983), *Right Wing Women: The Politics of Domesticated Females* (London: The Women's Press).

GIDDENS, A. (1981), *A Contemporary Critique of Historical Materialism*, vol. 1, *Power, Property and the State* (London: Macmillan).

GIDDENS, A. (1985), *A Contemporary Critique of historical Materialism* vol. 2, *The Nation State and Violence* (Cambridge: Polity).

GILMAN, C. P. (1966), *Women and Economics: A Study of the Economic Relation Between Men and Women as a Factor in Social Evolution* (New York: Harper Torchbooks).

HARTMANN, H. (1979), 'Capitalism, Patriarchy and Job Segregation by sex' in Z. R. Eisenstein (ed.), *Capitalist Patriarchy and the Case for Socialist Feminism* (New York: Monthly Review Press).

HAYDEN, D. (1981), *The Grand Domestic Revolution: A History of Feminist Designs for American Homes, Neighbourhoods, and Cities* (Cambridge, Mass.: MIT Press).

HOLCOMBE, L. (1983), *Wives and Property: Reform of the Married Women's Property Law in Nineteenth Century England* (Oxford: Martin Robertson).

HUTCHINS, B. L. (1915), *Women in Modern Industry* (London: G. Bell & Sons).

JAYAWARDENA, K. (1986), *Feminism and Nationalism in the Third World* (London: Zed Books).

KELLY, J. (1984), *Women, History and Theory: The Essays of Joan Kelly* (Chicago University Press).

LASLETT, P. (1977), *Family Life and Illicit Love in Earlier Generations: Essays in Historical Sociology* (Cambridge University Press).

LASH, S. and URRY, J. (1987), *The End of Organised Capitalism* (Cambridge: Polity Press).

LERNER, G. (1986), *The Creation of Patriarchy* (New York: Oxford University Press).

LIDDINGTON, J. and NORRIS, J. (1978), *One Hands Tied Behind Us: The Rise of the Women's Suffrage Movement* (London: Virago).

LEWENHAK, S. (1977), *Women and Trade Unions: An Outline History of Women in the British Trade Union Movement* (London: Ernest Benn).

MANN, M. (1986), *The Sources of Social Power* vol. 1, *A history of power from the beginning to A.D. 1760* (Cambridge University Press).

MARWICK, A. (1968), *Britain in the Century of Total War: War, Peace and Social Change, 1900–1967* (London: Bodley Head).

McFARLAND, A. (1978), *The Origins of English Individualism* (Oxford: Basil Blackwell).

MIDDLETON, C. (1981), 'Peasants, patriarchy and the feudal mode of production in England', *Sociological Review*, vol. 29, no. 1, 105–54.

MIDDLETON, C. (1985), 'Women's labour and the transition to pre-industrial capitalism', in L. Charles and L. Duffin (eds), *Women and Work in Pre-Industrial England* (London: Croom Helm).

MIES, M. (1986), *Patriarchy and Accumulation on a World Scale: Women in the International Division of Labour* (London: Zed Books).

MILLETT, K. (1977), *Sexual Politics* (London: Virago).

MINCER, J. (1962), 'Labour force participation of married women: A study of labour supply', in *Aspects of Labour Economics* (National Bureau of Economic Research: Princeton University Press).

MINCER, J. (1966), 'Labor-force participation and unemployment: a review of recent evidence' in R. Gordon and M. Gordon (eds), *Prosperity and Unemployment* (New York: John Wiley).

OAKLEY, A. (1976), *Housewife* (Harmondsworth: Penguin).

PANKHURST, S. (1977), *The Suffragette Movement: An Intimate Account of Persons and Ideals* (London: Virago); originally published in 1931 by Longman.

PERKIN, H. (1969), *The Origins of Modern English Society, 1780–1880* (London: Routledge).

PINCHBECK, I. (1981), *Women Workers and the Industrial Revolution, 1750–1850* (London: Virago); originally published in 1930.

SCHREINER, O. (1918), *Woman and Labour* (London: Fisher Unwin).

SHORTER, E. (1975), *The Making of the Modern Family* (New York: Basic Books).

SHORTER, E. (1982), *A History of Women's Bodies* (Harmondsworth: Penguin).

SOLDON, N. C. (1978), *Women in British Trade Unions 1874–1976* (Dublin: Gill and Macmillan).

SPENDER, D. (1983), *Women of Ideas (and what men have done to them)* (London: Ark).

SPENDER, D. (1984), *There's Always Been A Women's Movement This Century* (London: Routledge).

STONE, L. (1977), *The Family, Sex and Marriage in England 1500–1800* (London: Weidenfeld).

STRACHEY, R. (1978), *The Cause: A Short History of the Women's Movement in Great Britain* (London: Virago); originally published in 1928 by G. Bell.

SUMMERFIELD, P. (1984), *Women Workers in the Second World War* (London: Croom Helm).

TILLY, L. and SCOTT, J. (1978), *Women, Work and Family* (New York: Holt, Reinhart & Winston).

WALBY, S. (1986), *Patriarchy at Work: Patriarchal and Capitalist Relations in Employment* (Cambridge: Polity Press).

WALBY, S. (1989a), *Theorising Patriarchy* (Oxford: Basil Blackwell).

WALBY, S. (1989b), 'Theorising Patriarchy', *Sociology*, 23, 2, pp. 171–92.

WALKOWITZ, J. R. (1980), *Prostitution and Victorian Society: Women, Class and the State* (Cambridge University Press).

YOUNG, M. and WILLMOTT, P. (1975), *The Symmetrical Family: A Study of Work and Leisure in the London Region* (Harmondsworth: Penguin).

ZARETSKY, E. (1976), *Capitalism, the Family and Personal Life* (London: Pluto).

8 The Political and Workplace Culture of the Scottish Working Class, 1880–1914

William Knox

In the 1970s one of the perennial questions undergraduates faced on labour history question papers was 'Account for the rise of the Labour Party before 1914'. The question implied the inevitable and predictable rise and mass growth of Labour, and the subsequent decline of the Liberal Party as the chief casualty of the 'revolution' in British politics and society. The key factors in this process were the growth of class consciousness among workers, especially the unskilled, due to mass strikes in the last decades of the nineteenth century; unfavourable trade union legislation and adverse legal decisions which drove the unions into politics; changes in the franchise which brought more workers into the electoral system; and the activities of socialists and the ideology of marxism.

The way we thought about the origin and rise of the Labour Party was dominated by the writings of Pelling (1968) and Hobsbawm (1964), and their influence was evident even in the works of Tory historians such as Robert Rhodes James (1978). Since then social historians under the influence of Braverman's *Labour and Monopoly Capital* (1976) have sought also to include changes in the labour process that blurred the distinctive characteristics between skilled and unskilled workers by narrowing wage differentials and opening up skilled work to greater encroachment from the latter groups. The threat of technological displacement acted to radicalise the skilled workers in the direction of independent labour representation and class politics, thus breaking their allegiance to the liberal/capitalist framework of British society. As one of the foremost labour process historians, Richard Price, put it recently: 'in general terms socialism emerged as a response to the restructuring of the labour process' (Price, 1985, p. 147). Thus the explanatory balance is shifted from the sphere of politics to the sphere of production. The exploitation of the working class at the point of production becomes the fundamental basis of understanding political change and the growth of class consciousness. However, whatever explanatory position is taken, both scenarios would point to a working class becoming more conscious and militant, and it is this that leads to the formation of the Labour Party in 1906. The rest, as they say, is history.

By examining the political and workplace culture of the Scottish working class in the period 1880–1914, this chapter seeks to challenge these accounts of working-class history, particularly the latter. Specifically, it questions whether changes in the workplace are necessarily harbingers of change in political behaviour, arguing that it is important to see the process of political change as the product of a number of different and sometimes contradictory factors, of which the workplace is only one, albeit an important one. Thus the paper draws attention to the role of social agencies such as religion, temperance and gender in shaping the context of working-class political culture. It also examines the role of the more exclusively class institutions such as trade unions and political organisations in this process. However, although giving due recognition to changes in working-class political culture, particularly the rise of socialist politics in the late 1880s, emphasis will be placed on the continuance and strength of a political tradition traceable back to the radical struggles of the first half of the nineteenth century. The Pelling thesis on the inevitable rise of Labour will therefore be strongly contested. Although set firmly in the context of the Scottish experience, the argument does not adopt a parochial outlook. Society in Scotland was in many ways different from England, thus it is important to examine the Scottish experience as a counterpoint to national political trends, but it also has to be remembered that Scotland played a disproportionately large part in the formation and early growth of the British Labour Party. At the level of ideology and leadership the Scots were to the forefront of Labour's development in these crucial years (Fraser, 1985, pp. 38–63). Thus any conclusions reached in this paper will have important implications for those engaged in the broader national debate.

THE CHANGING CULTURE OF THE WORKPLACE

The culture of the workplace is structured through the interaction of five major influences; firstly, by the nature of the market for the product and the demands it makes on production; secondly, by the nature of work and its interplay with changing technology and methods of work; thirdly, by the social relationships between capital and labour, particularly in the vital area of the distribution of power and authority; fourthly, by the level of industrial conflict which manifests itself, institutionally, in trade unions and employers' associations, and, practically, in strikes and lockouts; and, fifthly, by relationships between and within different groups of workers and the wider society. It is contended by historians such as Price that the period 1880–1914 witnessed a fundamental restructuring of the social relationships of production, which resulted in the greater homogenisation of labour, through deskilling, and an upsurge in class conflict and solidarity among workers. As management sought to subordinate workers' aspirations and skills to the accumulation of capital in an increasingly intensive manner the level of class consciousness was correspondingly raised and this had important political ramifications, which we will deal with later.

Evidence would point to a general restructuring of skill and working methods in industry and an all-round tightening up of industrial discipline. Scottish industry, with its reliance on heavy industry, was exposed during the last quarter of the nineteenth century to shifts in world demand and increased foreign competition from the USA and Germany, at a time of rising labour costs, falling productivity, and high interest rates. Pressure was on employers to rationalise production and intensify the exploitation of labour if cost competitiveness was to be maintained (Campbell, 1980, pp. 68–73). Employers responded by introducing new semi-automatic machinery in engineering, shipbuilding and coalmining: by increasing the use of semi-skilled and unskilled labour in trades hitherto the preserve of skilled workers; by increasing the size of the unit of production to take advantage of economies of scale; by introducing new time measurement systems of payment such as the premium bonus system; and by creating new categories of specialist labour such as draughtsmen, production engineers, and so on. The question is how far did these changes lead to a general deskilling of time-served craftsmen and what effects did this have on skilled workers' notion of the 'trade' and the values and customs that underpinned it?

New Technology and Skill

In respect of the first question it has to be said that the impact of new technology on the level of skill across industry was less than even. In engineering, the introduction of the turret lathe and other specialised machines reduced the work of the skilled men to that of preparation, and led to an increase in the use of semi-skilled and apprentice labour (Levine, 1954, pp. 156–7, 462–3; Zeitlin, 1983, pp. 27–8). In shipbuilding, technological change was less uniformly applied, as trade fluctuations made employers reluctant to invest heavily in machines and tools, and this led to continued reliance on labour-intensive production methods. However, problems with the construction of large hulls by handwork led to the introduction of pneumatic rivet machines and electrically powered drills. The effect of these innovations was felt most strongly by the least skilled handworkers: riveters and caulkers (McLelland and Reid, 1985, pp. 173–4). Employers responded by making greater use of low-cost apprentice labour in these trades. As a Glasgow factory inspector observed in 1903: 'Jobs formerly done by journeymen can now be undertaken by apprentices' (Levine, 1954, p. 431). Encroachments into the realm of skilled work were occurring at a similar pace in other trades, including coal mining, construction, and printing (Slaven, 1975, p. 168; Dearle, 1908, pp. 46–51; Zeitlin, 1985, pp. 207–8).

Intensifying the division of labour was only part of a general process of greater exploitation of labour by capital. The introduction of the electric light made shiftwork more common, and excessive overtime working became a problem for trade unions. On the railways the average working week for drivers was 70 hours. One guard was led to complain that 'for twenty four to thirty shillings a week you give yourself up body and soul to the public service, and a good two-thirds of your life are spent in the guard's room' (ASRS, 1888, p. 6). The number of engineering workers subject to systematic overtime quadrupled between 1876 and 1892 (Price, 1986, p. 104). Tighter discipline also followed. The control system adopted by railway companies facilitated the establishment of a 'strictly enforced hierarchy of obedience and accountability' (Price, 1984, pp. 134–5). The engineering lock-out of 1897 won for management the right to control the labour process and 'introduce new systems of supervision' (Zeitlin, 1983, p. 38). Additionally, the extension of new incentive payments schemes was effective in intensifying the application of the worker to the task in hand. By 1914, 46 per cent of engineering fitters and 37 per cent of turners were on piece-rate payment, compared with only 5 per cent of all engineers and boilermakers in 1886 (Hobsbawm, 1964, p. 320).

The question which arises from this brief summary of change and innovation in the workplace is whether this resulted in deskilling the content of the time-served man's work. There is little doubt that these changes led to the greater specialisation of labour and to a shared feeling among craft workers of 'a loss of control over their methods of working' (Littler, 1982a, p. 137). As a symptom of this, apprenticeship became more exploitative and less paternalistic. The increasing lack of interest in work shown by apprentices is evidence of this. Dr Alexander Scott, certifying surgeon of Glasgow, estimated that in 1907 not more than 50 to 55 per cent of ship building apprentices completed their time (Scott, 1906–7, p. 167). Some years earlier James Jack, general secretary of the Associated Iron Moulders of Scotland, in evidence before the Royal Commission on Labour (1892), said that employers were not able to keep boys to a seven years' apprenticeship as they will 'shift about to where they can get more money' (Knox, 1986, p. 177). Among large firms on Clydeside Burgess found that the implementation of new technologies led to a 'majority of engineering tradesmen with average levels of skill . . . [being] exposed to some form of deskilling' (Burgess, 1985, p. 171–2). The case for deskilling seems to have a strong foundation and we will return to this issue when trade unionism is examined, but for the moment let us consider the effect it had on the inner life of the workplace.

Pressures and Customs

Traditionally, artisanal culture was bound up with ceremonials and rituals that acted as socialising agents in the creation of artisan solidarity, in defence of the customary expectations in respect of wages, hours and conditions. They also reaffirmed the traditional journeyman/apprentice hierarchy and determined the right to the use of the tools of the trade. Most of the ceremonials and rituals were linked to alcoholic excess. In the printing trade, for example, initiation was known as the 'General Indulgence' or the 'General Intoxication'. However, these forms of workplace behaviour were beginning to disappear from the larger works by the end of the nineteenth century. Engineering provides an excellent example of the process of decline. In the past, journeymen had been responsible for training apprentices, but this task was increasingly handed over to apprentice supervisors to instruct and teach, usually in separate parts of the establishment. What socialisation occurred evolved out of the interaction of the peer group with the imperatives of management. Journeymen tied to piece rate work and under greater supervision had less time to spend instructing apprentices or indulging in the elaborate initiation ceremonies and rituals, and the drinking sessions which accompanied them. (Knox, 1980, pp. 176–94). In his study of life in a railway factory, Alfred Williams noted that 'Under the new discipline the men are generally more sober and silent, though they are none the happier . . . The increased efforts they are bound to make at work and the higher speed of the machinery has caused them to become gloomy and very often peevish and irritable' (Williams, 1915, p. 267). Even in the smaller workshops the old system of socialisation was being stripped of intrinsic value. The washing of the mason's apron, an important event in the *rites de passage* of the apprentice, was abandoned and the 'more modern masons were satisfied by taking the youth to a public house and making him drink a pint of beer' (Gilchrist, 1940, p. 21). True the ritual smearing of the genitals with grease, oil or ink, depending on the trade involved, continued, but these actions were more the product of a closed male environment than surviving customs of a once powerful artisan culture of secret rituals, signs and initiations.

It would appear that work, through increased specialisation and tighter control, was becoming intrinsically less satisfying and that workers, particularly those employed on new incentive payments schemes, were adopting a more instrumental approach. Labour was being seen as a commodity to be sold to the highest bidder, rather than the skilled man's birthright or inheritance whose value was determined by non-market forces. This was the outcome of skill specialisation which enormously enlarged the numbers recruited to the trades, and, at the same time, destroyed the division of them into 'honourable' and 'dishonourable' sections. Labour mobility was enhanced as skills became more interchangeable. Workers were no longer tied to one firm or locality, and this resulted in a much greater sharing of experience – the foundation of solidarity. The shifting of the locus of authority from foreman to management specialists also helped to intensify bonds of solidarity among workers by making authority more impersonal and, at the same time, more visible.

The New Forms of Authority in the Workplace

The mid-century working class was confronted by a variety of figures representing the social authority of capital in the workplace. Prior to the changes outlined above, foremen exercised undue influence over the workforce. As one writer put it in the 1870s, 'In nine out of every ten establishments, one man – the foreman – has supreme control' (Anon, 1870,

p. 789). However, with the introduction of time measurement of tasks his all-round authority was being eroded as the new methods involved the separation of the planning and execution of work. Personal recruitment of labour was also gradually disappearing as firms set up personnel departments (Littler, 1982, pp. 87–8; Burgess, 1986, p. 266–7). These changes also had implications for internal subcontracting, whereby management contracted work to key employees who then proceeded to recruit and pay their own workers. This system was well entrenched in ship building and coal mining among the platers and colliers, as well as certain groups of iron workers. However, 'payment through the office' caused the system to decline with the result that the question of the work/effort ratio was lifted out of the realm of 'personalised disputes between a driving contractor and his men, into a more generalised struggle between employers and workers' (Littler, 1982, p. 83). Increasingly workers were confronted by capital or, at least, its managerial representatives, rather than by a host of authority figures. This was to sharpen class relations in the workplace.

Taken together these factors added up to a situation in which labour found itself increasingly subordinated to the imperatives of capital accumulation. Traditional skills were threatened by new technology; old customs and traditions were being obliterated by new working practices; shiftwork and excessive overtime working were intensifying the exploitation of labour; industrial discipline was being tightened by a greater drive towards managerial autonomy in the workplace; and, finally, class lines were being redrawn in a more overt way than ever before. This would seem to confirm the scenario put forward by social historians such as Richard Price as to a 'crisis in the social relations of production'. The question is whether these changes acted to raise the class consciousness of Scottish workers and if so what impact did this have on the institutional expressions of class awareness: trade unions and labour politics?

THE SCOTTISH TRADE UNION MOVEMENT

The first thing to note about Scottish trade unions in this period is that, in spite of the fact that they saw a growth in membership, they remained weak. The Webbs found that in Scotland in 1892 there were 147,000 trade unionists, which amounted to only 3.7 per cent of the total population. The corresponding figure for England and Wales was significantly higher at 4.9 per cent. More recent studies have shown that Scotland's level of trade union membership was half that of South Wales and Humberside, and only a quarter of the North East coast of England, all areas with broadly similar industrial structures (Campbell, 1985, p. 215; Southall, 1986, p. 189–93). The national figure, of course, disguises the higher density of union membership found in the Scottish capital goods sector, but even here it rarely accounted for more than 25 per cent of the workforce. Growth was experienced in the first decade of the twentieth century, particularly in the skilled trades, although this was subject to the ebb and flow of the trade cycle, the failure of a strike or the success of a lock-out; thus it was unstable. However, if we were to take a more elastic definition of labour organisation, as Price advocates, and include workplace resistance of an unofficial kind, then the response of workers to the new pressures is much stronger (Price, 1980, p. 62). Unofficial workplace organisation was demonstrated during strikes when unionists and non-unionists alike would down tools. For example, during the miners' strike of 1894 Page Arnot estimated that of the 70,000 Scottish miners taking action only 30,000 were union members (Arnot, 1955, p. 78). Although institutional assessments of workers' organisations have failed to give due attention to this form of unofficial collective defence, its existence does not dispose of the contention that labour organisation was weak, nor does it prove that the level of class awareness was high. It was the immediate workgroup, the locality, which was important in these struggles, rather than the class as a whole. There still remains the question why, in the face of more intensive exploitation, workers in Scotland were still weakly organised.

Firstly, the existence of downward pressures on skill needs to be viewed as more problematical than historians such as

Price would suggest. The ability of management to control the labour process and affect the level of skills is constrained by the nature of the product and the market, and, as far as British engineering and ship building were concerned, the product market was highly differentiated (Harley, 1973–74, pp. 391–414; Zeitlin, 1985, pp. 325–37; Pollard and Robertson, 1979, pp. 165–6; Reid, 1980, p. 199). This made it difficult for employers to implement techniques of mass production; ships, machines, railway engineers, boilers, had to be constructed according to the specific needs of the purchaser. The consumer orientation of construction and printing also imposed limitations on the use of labour saving technology in these industries. Consequently, employers still found it necessary to cede to labour a measure of control, and this suggests that the notion of deskilling has been carried too far. The impact was fragmentary and not all workers were threatened in the way Price suggests. The need for a united class response to downward pressures on skill and, therefore, wages was less than urgent.

Secondly, sectionalism was an acute problem among Scottish trade unionists. On Clydeside alone a hundred unions were active in the early years of the twentieth century, of which only twenty could claim five hundred or more members, and thirty-seven less than one hundred (Unger, 1979, pp. 257–8). The existence of a multitude of small unions led to numerous sectional disputes concerning the division of labour. Demarcation disputes were rife in shipbuilding and the metal trades (Robertson, 1975, pp. 220–35). The Webbs noted that 'blacklegging each other's disputes is a very frequent feature of all the minor trades, whilst the Amalgamated Society of Engineers is universally regarded, in this respect, the common enemy'. A similar situation existed in the building trade where demarcation disputes between masons and bricklayers were common (Webbs, vols. 10, 23). The smallness of Scottish unions not only made internecine strife inevitable, but it also encouraged an insular and localist approach to organisation. Local independence saw Scottish unions refuse to amalgamate or merge with national organisations. Anti-Englishness played a part in this and it was this feeling that led to the formation of the Scottish Trades Union Congress (STUC) in 1897, and to an attempt in the same year by the Clydebank section of the Boilermaker's society to form a breakaway Scottish union (Dickson, 1980, p. 267). Among Scottish miners, only the Stirlingshire association was affiliated to the Miners' Federation of Great Britain. The strength of national sentiment can be gauged from the fact that of the total number of trade unionists in 1892, two-thirds were organised in Scottish unions.

Thirdly, sectionalism was encouraged by sectarian rivalries among industrial workers. The depth of sectarian feeling in Scottish society should not be underestimated as it was a social phenomenon affecting all social classes. Helen Crawfurd, daughter of a small bakery owner and, later, suffragette and member of the Independent Labour Party (ILP), recalled in her unpublished autobiography, that she 'looked upon the Fenian and Catholic Irish as sub-human' (Crawfurd, no date, p. 13). David Kirkwood, of 'Red Clydeside' fame, said that 'It would be untrue to say we were one people. Religion and race . . . kept us apart' (Kirkwood, 1935, p. 60). Sectarianism was underpinned by the operation of the labour market which confined Catholics to low-skilled and less well paid work, and Protestants to enjoy a monopoly of the skilled jobs in engineering and shipbuilding (McShane and Smith, 1979, pp. 19, 76; Treble, 1978, pp. 121–2). A community divided on these lines found expression of solidarity difficult. It was said of the Lanarkshire coalfields that among Irish Catholics 'Protestantism was more obnoxious than low wages' (Stewart, 1921, pp. 11–12). The STUC further alienated the Catholic population when in 1913 they voted by a majority of 52–13 for the introduction of secular education in all state schools (Craigen, 1974, p. 93). Consequently, the Irish withdrew into their own community, which naturally centred on the Church and a reactionary priesthood suspicious of labour because of its links with atheistic socialism (Aspinwall, 1982, p. 53; Walker, 1979, p. 129).

Fourthly, there is the issue of gender. The occupational structure ensured that men occupied positions of dominance over women which reinforced societal notions of male authority and power over women. Even in the textile trades, where the overwhelming numbers of female industrial workers were concentrated, males occupied the post of overseer responsible for the supervision of the female spinners

(Freifeld, 1986, p. 431). Women's work was by definition unskilled; employers saw it as uneconomic to equip women with anything more than notional skills, since they assumed that marriage would lead to voluntary withdrawal from the labour market (Treble, 1986, p. 36). Scottish trade unions, by bargaining round the idea of the family wage, reinforced these divisions. Evidence also points to the active opposition of craft unions to female employment, particularly in the printing industry. The STUC endorsed the Scottish Typographical Association's attempts to exclude female compositors on the grounds that, as cheap labour, they posed a threat to the wages of the men (Gordon, 1988, p. 40). Some women did organise with the assistance of men, for example the Dundee jute industry (Walker, 1979, p. 152; Gordon, 1987, pp. 27–47), but it was only where they did not pose a direct threat to male autonomy. As Gordon shows in the second volume, even women's organisations attached to the labour movement, such as the Scottish Co-operative Women's Guild and the Women's Labour League, saw a woman's role principally as homemaker. Although the latter campaigned on behalf of unemployed women, its support for a woman's right to work was confined 'to spheres which were regarded as "Women's work"' (Gordon, 1989, pp. 15–20). On the whole, the biggest problem for the labour movement was how to keep women in the home. Thus women's issues were marginalised in the labour movement.

Finally, there is the question of the distribution of power and authority. In spite of being raised in the virtues of individualism and self-help, Scottish employers were strongly organised in associations and federations, in sharp contrast with the fragmented trade union movement. The Webbs described the engineering and shipbuilding employers of the west of Scotland as 'able and independent captains of industry, [whose] attitude with regard to all trade questions is one of "do what they like with their own"' (Webbs, vol. 23, ff. 209–14). A strong sense of managerial autonomy was also found among the interlocking coal and iron and steel companies, and this helped create a rock-like response to challenges to their authority from the workforce. It was not until the late 1880s that the Clydeside shipbuilding employers agreed to recognise the Boilermakers' society. But accompanying the abrasiveness was a kind of authoritarian paternalism which saw employers provide welfare in return for loyalty and obedience. Major companies had their own friendly societies and also provided housing (Hassan, 1980, p. 90; Melling, 1982, pp. 85–9). The latter was used as a direct form of social control, since striking workers and their families were liable for eviction, as happened in the 1891 Scottish railway strike and in numerous mining disputes. At the same time, employers used housing more subtly to reproduce the status hierarchies of the workplace in the wider society. John Brown's shipyard built new dwellings to end the practice of supervisory workers sharing the same tenement as journeymen. Railway companies divided their housing among their workers on the basis of occupational status, with the top drivers, engineers and supervisors receiving the better and more spacious flats (McKenna, 1980, pp. 52–3; Melling, 1981, pp. 280–1). For these reasons, in spite of new pressures, the trade union movement remained weak in Scotland. This, of course, may have been because the balance of power was heavily weighted against it, and the low density of union membership may not be an accurate indication of the level of class consciousness. As we have seen, industrial struggle was in many cases conducted outside the official movement. Consciousness may have translated itself more into political terms, since with the changes in the franchise, in 1867 and 1884, the worker confronted the boss in this arena on nominal terms of equality. Therefore, it is important to examine the political sphere in order to discover whether the anxieties created by changes in the labour process led to the growth of class politics in this period.

THE POLITICAL CULTURE OF THE SCOTTISH WORKERS

At the outset of the paper it was noted that labour process historians such as Price saw a causal link between the introduction of new technologies and work routines, the level of discontent this engendered in the work place, and the rise of socialism. What is clear in Scotland's case is that this scenario is inappropriate. Scottish workers remained committed to the Liberal Party. As the 1914 Labour Party conference commented 'unfortunately Scotland was so imbued with Liberal principles that it was a harder fight there than in any other part of the country' (Hutchinson, 1986, p. 264). What motivated the working class of Scotland politically, more than any other factor, was the struggle for democracy and the destruction of the vestigal remains of aristocratic power. The major political events in the period 1880–1914 were the demonstrations in favour of the Third Reform Bill of 1884 and the 1910 election campaigns to establish the People's Budget and reduce the powers of the House of Lords. In contrast, Labour's position was one of weakness. By 1914, there were only three MPs, trade unionists with declared Liberal sympathies, and a further two hundred councillors of various sorts. Why did the 'crisis in social relationships' which characterised the period, according to Price, not translate itself into a commitment to political change on a majority basis? What accounts for the continued hegemony of Liberalism? These important questions can only be answered by moving beyond the parameters of the workplace to examine the terrain of Scottish politics and society.

Religion is an obvious starting place. The Scots, as we have seen, were divided on sectarian lines. The major political problem for the emerging Labour Party was how to attract the sizeable Catholic Irish vote without alienating the indigenous Protestant population. Overtures in support of Irish Home Rule signalled the break-up of the British Empire, access to which was crucial in maintaining the jobs of the predominantly Protestant workers in the capital goods sector. Liberal Unionists were able to use this economic scenario to encourage the growth of anti-home rule sentiment in Scotland. Labour was, therefore, afraid of putting up Irish candidates for fear of a Protestant backlash. When it did so in the 1890s, the defeat of Hugh Murphy, a veteran member of the United Irish League (UIL), confirmed what Labour had only feared. But there was also the fear in the Irish community that to vote Labour would allow the Tories in, as happened in the 1892 general election (Wood, 1979, p. 78). As Liberal was the only party likely to deliver on the question of home rule, the Irish stayed loyal, and it was not until the partition of Ireland, after the end of the First World War, that they came over to Labour. Meanwhile it was Irish Home Rule and Liberalism towards which Catholic energies were directed.

The Scottish Liberal Party had been the dominant political force in Scotland since the 1832 Reform Act. It commanded widespread political support from skilled workers, particularly under Gladstone's leadership. Working-class support and involvement ensured that Scottish Liberalism was more radical than the English version. Glasgow Liberals made the city, according to *The Times*, 'the centre of the experiment in municipal socialism' (Middlemas, 1965, p. 17). Public ownership had been established in a wide range of utilities, including gas, water, tramways and telephones. As one contemporary noted, 'So long as textiles, shipbuilding, and the metallurgical and chemical industries were not interfered with, the standard Glasgow businessman . . . was willing to adopt collectivism (Leatham, 1924, p. 27–8). As the ILP was of the opinion that any 'municipalisation was socialism', the opportunity for providing an alternative to Liberalism was limited by the radicalism of the latter (Smith, 1980, p. 307). All that remained to Labour was the issue of housing.

The census of 1911 showed that over '62 per cent of Glasgow's population lived in one or two-roomed dwellings' (Butt, 1978, p. 152). As the unit of ownership was the tenement, working men rarely had the opportunity to buy their own home. In any case, cyclical fluctuations made this economically risky (Morris, 1983, pp. 13–4). Most of the housing was owned by small landlords who dominated local politics and gave their political support to the Liberal Party. By campaigning for housing reform, Labour was able to build support on the basis of anit-landlordism. They linked the struggle of the Irish peasants and Highland crofters against the rural landlords with the struggle against the urban landlord. This strategy appealed to both Catholic and Protestant alike since both communities endured these awful conditions. It also, as Gordon points out, allowed women, particularly housewives, a more active political role and they took the initiative on housing campaigns (Gordon, 1989, p. 4); Savage shows this to have been of crucial importance in explaining the political success of Labour in Preston and

Slough in the inter-war period (Savage, 1989). Inevitably this meant that housing agitation assumed greater political importance than the industrial struggle. From a theoretical standpoint this makes the relationship between economic and political change in the development of the Labour Party less straightforward and more problematical than the Pellings and Prices of this world would have us believe. The evidence would suggest that non-workplace relationships became the dominant concern of political activity. Indeed, members of the labour movement in Scotland failed adequately to theorise the relationship between the industrial and political struggle. The only capitalists attacked in the main Scottish ILP paper, *Forward*, were monopolistic mineowners (Smith, 1984, p. 35). It was only on the Marxist left that any attempt was made to link the struggles in the workplace with those in the wider society. Organisations such as the Socialist Labour Party had some impact among the young shop stewards, but it was not until during World War I that they exercised a direct influence on working-class action.

In the absence of a materialist political theory, the question of ethos and morality becomes of greater importance in understanding the political development of Labour. The leadership of ILP in Scotland was shaped at a fundamental level by the values of popular Liberalism. Socially, they were teetotal, rational, pacifist and evangelical in religion. Their heroes were Jesus, Shelly, Mazzini, Whitman, Carlyle and Burns (Lowe, 1919, p. 125). Attachment to temperance led them into campaigns to ban the sale of alcohol and to indict the Tory beer barons for the misery of the working class. *Forward* refused to accept adverts from the drinks trade, and while Hardie was leader of the Labour Party no Labour MP was allowed in the bar of the Commons. Indeed, Hardie often claimed that intemperance was the cause of working-class poverty; a view shared by many socialists who linked impoverishment and suffering to drunkeness (Knox, 1984, pp. 22–3; Wood, 1972, pp. 26–7). The stress on respectability led to assaults by the ILP on popular leisure pursuits, such as jazz, cinema, boxing and dog racing, which continued into the inter-war period. Cultural alternatives were offered by the Labour movement and included rambling clubs, choirs, art circles, handicraft classes and other forms of self-improvement (Knox, 1984, pp. 38–40). Evangelical religion was also an important influence. Ethical socialism was preached by the Labour leaders and was defined as an attempt to 'apply Christian principles to practical life' (Glasse, 1910, p. 19). As such the stress was placed on brotherly love and social justice rather than on class conflict. In Hardie's political philosophy the 'struggle for emancipation was a battle not between economic classes but between idlers and labour, managing employers being included under the term "labour" along with workmen' (Reid, 1978, p. 86).

The social ethos of Labour made it attractive to the middle class and allowed them to play a disproportionate part in shaping its development. Middle-class Glasgow Christian socialists provided the capital to launch Hardie's *Labour Leader* in 1893 (Reid, 1978, p. 139). Middle-class representation was strong in the area of leadership, and this applied also to the Marxist orientated organisations such as the Social Democratic Federation (SDF) and the British Socialist Party (Knox, 1984, p. 16). Reliance on middle-class financial and intellectual support strengthened the identification with popular Liberalism and the social ethos which underlay it. Thus the emerging Labour Party was a direct descendant of the class alliances which had formed the basis of the radical struggles for democracy dating back to the 1790s. In many ways it might be argued that Labour was the climax of the struggle for democracy as it wished to extend this from the realm of politics to the workplace itself. It was the failure of the Liberals to deliver in this area which led to the decline of its influence over the Labour movement.

The trade unions, in many cases only reluctantly, decided to support the struggle for independent labour representation in the Commons. Most were raised in the doctrines of free trade and self-help and were opposed to ideas of state intervention. Henry Tait, secretary of the Amalgamated Society of Railway Servants, summed up this view when he argued that state intervention was not necessary to solve the problem of overwork on the railways, believing that 'self-action is best suited for the case' (ASRS, 1888, p. 12). Belief in self-help meant that unions were reluctant to affiliate to the ILP or any other left-wing organisation. The Socialist

League and the SDF were shunned by the Glasgow Trades Council in 1885 when they tried to gain support in the general election. Three years later, exploiting the discontent over the Liberals' failure to support the miners in the 1884 strike, and the general lack of working class Liberal candidates, Hardie formed the Scottish Labour Party. But it also failed to win trade-union backing. Trades councils in Dundee, Edinburgh and Glasgow refused to affiliate to it (Fraser, 1979, p. 18). What changed the unions' mind were the legal setbacks suffered in the 1890s and early twentieth century, of which the Taff Vale judgement of 1901/2 was the most important in convincing them of the need for independent political representation, since the Liberals seemed unwilling or impotent to assist them. The more the state intervened in social relationships, especially in hostile ways, the more Labour needed political protection. Thus it would appear that it is the changes at the level of the state rather than the workplace which have a more radicalising effect on workers in this period. And if we were to address the weakness of Labour either in failing to respond with a more class-based set of politics, or, indeed, to capture the hearts and minds of the working class, then a study of non-workplace relationships and the ethos and value system of the leadership would pay dividends.

CONCLUSION

This chapter began by mentioning one of the perennial chestnuts of Labour history. The following discussion would suggest that the question ought to be re-phrased, at least in the case of Scotland, to read 'Account for the continuing strength of Liberal sympathies within the working class'. Liberalism and the values associated with it continued to attract widespread support because the political tradition of which it was a part resonated with the experience and aspirations of the working class. The Scottish working class was still committed to the values of the radical tradition, that is, democracy, republicanism, nationalism and the social ethos of popular Liberalism. These values were sufficiently vague as to be open to different interpretations, and elastic enough to be amenable to periodic negotiation and renegotiation. This was important, given the nature of political consciousness, which is shaped by a wide variety of social experiences including material conditions, religion, family life, language, geography, recreational and residential patterns, and past political experiences and memories. The Scottish working class in the period 1880–1914 was fragmented and culturally diverse and it was only a party that was ideologically eclectic and politically elastic that could weld the diversity of experience into a coherent political force. In spite of gradually increasing criticism and tensions, the Liberal Party performed that role and it was only the changes set in motion by World War I which led to the breakdown of its political hegemony.

The problem with workerist accounts of working-class political development is that exclusive concentration on the world of work omits consideration of these important political and cultural factors. It also fails to recognise the essentially dualistic impact change in the labour process has on the development of working-class consciousness. On the positive side, technological change, the intensification of industrial discipline and the work effort posed serious threats to the autonomy of skilled workers in the planning and execution of their work. The prospect of deskilling and reduction in status and earning power was real enough to lead to an amplification of industrial conflict. Such a situation allowed socialists the space to articulate a different version of class experience, but the effect, as Penn points out, was profoundly contradictory. Socialism stands for the unity and equality of all labour, something which poses a dilemma for craft workers in their desire to retain their status and pay differentials vis-a-vis other workers (Penn, 1982, pp. 100–1). Restructuring of the labour process also results in divisions being created within skilled trades. The move from wood to iron and, later, steel shipbuilding accelerated the frequency of demarcation disputes between shipwrights and boilermakers. Workers fought each other, rather than the boss, for the right to certain classes of work. Solidaristic outcomes of such changes in the world of work would therefore appear questionable. Experience of exploitation may define membership of the working class, but consciousness is the outcome of a much more complicated web of experiences and relationships. Social historians and sociologists have increasingly come to recognise this fact and are beginning to explore in greater detail the cultural and non-workplace relationships that are important to the understanding of political change and the creation of class consciousness. Savage's work on community politics (Savage, 1989), the various studies by feminist historians, such as Gordon (1989), and the work of Reid (1985) on the relationship between the state and working class organisations, have pioneered new ways of analysing the growth of class consciousness. Although all represent only partial accounts of this important development, they point the way to the evolution of a more coherent and sustainable account of working-class history.

REFERENCES

AMALGAMATED SOCIETY OF RAILWAY SERVANTS (1888), *Slavery on Scottish Railways* (Glasgow).

ARNOT, R. P. (1955), *A History of the Scottish Miners from the earliest times* (London: Lawrence & Wishart).

ASPINWALL, B. (1982), 'The Formation of the Catholic Community in the West of Scotland: some preliminary outlines', *Innes Review*, vol. XXXIII.

THE BUILDER (1870), vol. XXVIII.

BURGESS, K. (1985), 'New Unionism for Old? The Amalgamated Society of Engineers in Britain', in W. J. Mommsen and H. G. Husung (eds), *The Development of Trade Unionism in Great Britain and Germany, 1880–1914*.

BURGESS, K. (1986), 'Authority relations and the division of labour in British industry, with special reference to Clydeside, *c.*1860–1930', *Social History*, vol. 11, no. 2, May.

BUTT, J. (1978), 'Working Class Housing in Glasgow, 1900–1939', in I. MacDougall (ed.), *Essays in Scottish Labour History* (Edinburgh: John Donald).

CAMPBELL, R. H. (1980), *The Rise and Fall of Scottish Industry, 1707–1939* (Edinburgh: John Donald).

CAMPBELL, R. H. (1985) (ed.), *Scotland since 1707* (Edinburgh: John Donald).

CRAIGEN, J. M. (1974), 'The Scottish Trades Union Congress,

1897–1973: a study of a pressure group', M. Litt, (Heriot-Watt University).

CRAWFURD, H. (no date, *c*.1940), *Unpublished Autobiography*, (London: Marx Memorial Library). See also a biography of Helen Crawfurd by H. Corr, in W. W. Knox (1984), *Scottish Labour Leaders 1918–1939: A Biographical Dictionary* (Edinburgh: Mainstream Press).

DEARLE, N. B. (1908), *Problems of Unemployment in the London Building Trades* (London).

DICKSON, T. (1980), 'From Client to Supplicant: Capital and Labour in Scotland, 1870–1914', in T. Dickson (ed.), *Scottish Capitalism: class, state and nation from before the union to the present* (London: Lawrence & Wishart).

FRASER, W. H. (1978), 'Trades Councils in the Labour Movement in Nineteenth Century Scotland' in I. MacDougall (ed.), *Essays in Scottish Labour History* (Edinburgh: John Donald).

FRASER, W. H. (1985), 'The Labour Party in Scotland', in K. D. Brown (ed.), *The First Labour Party, 1906–1914* (London: Croom Helm).

FREIFELD, M. (1986), 'Technological change and the "self-acting" mule: a study of skill and the sexual division of labour', *Social History*, vol. 11, no. 3, October.

GILCHRIST, A. (1940), *Naethin' at A'* (Glasgow).

GLASSE, J. (1910), *The Relation of the Church to Socialism* (Edinburgh).

GORDON, E. (1987), 'Women, Work and Collective Action: Dundee Jute Workers, 1870–1906', *Journal of Social History*, vol. 21.

GORDON, E. (1988), 'The Scottish Trade Union Movement, Class and Gender, 1850–1914', *Journal of the Scottish Labour History Society*, no. 23.

GORDON, E. (1989), 'Working Class Politics, Feminism and Women Workers, 1900–1914', in L. Jamieson and H. Corr (eds), *State, Private Life and Political Change* (London: Macmillan).

HARLEY, C. K. (1973–4), 'Skilled Labour and the Choice of Technique in Edwardian Industry', *Explorations in Economic History*, vol. 11.

HASSAN, J. A. (1980), 'The landed estate, paternalism and the coal industry in Midlothian, 1880–1890', *Scottish Historical Review*, vol. LIX, no. 167, April.

HOBSBAWM, E. J. (1964), *Labouring Men* (London: Wiedenfeld & Nicholson).

HUTCHINSON, I. C. G. (1986), *A Political History of Scotland, 1832–1924: parties, elections and issues* (Edinburgh: John Donald).

JAMES, R. R. (1978), *The British Revolution: British Politics 1880–1939* (London: Methuen).

KIRKWOOD, D. (1935), *My Life of Revolt* (London: Harrap).

KNOX, W. (1980), 'British Apprenticeship, 1800–1914', Ph.D. University of Edinburgh.

KNOX, W. (1984), *Scottish Labour Leaders, 1918–1939: a biographical dictionary* (Edinburgh: Mainstream).

KNOX, W. (1986), 'Apprenticeship and De-skilling in Britain, 1850–1914', *International Review of Social History*, vol. XXXI.

LEATHAM, J. (1924), *Glasgow in the Limelight* (Turriff).

LEVINE, A. L. (1954), 'Industrial Change and its Affects upon Labour, 1900–1914', Ph.D. University of London.

LITTLER, C. R. (1982), *The Development of the Labour Process in Capitalist Societies: a comparative study of work organisation in Britain, Japan and the USA* (London: Gower).

LITTLER, C. R. (1982a), 'Deskilling and the changing structures of control', in S. Wood (ed.), *The Degradation of Work?* (London: Hutchinson).

McCLELLAND, K. and REID, A. (1985), 'Wood, Iron and Steel: technology, labour and trade union organisation in the shipbuilding industry, 1840–1914', in R. Harrison and J. Zeitlin (eds), *Divisions of Labour: skilled workers and technological change in nineteenth century Britain* (Brighton: Harvester).

McKENNA, F. (1980), *The Railway Workers, 1840–1970* (London: Faber).

McSHANE, H. and SMITH, J. (1978), *No Mean Fighter* (London: Pluto).

MELLING, J. (1981), 'Employers, Industrial Housing and the evolution of Company Welfare Policies in Britain's heavy industries, 1870–1920', *International Review of Social History*, vol. XXVI.

MELLING, J. (1982), 'Scottish Industrialists and the changing character of Class Relations in the Clyde Region, *c.*.1880–1918', in T. Dickson (ed.), *Capital and Class in Scotland* (Edinburgh: John Donald).

MIDDLEMAS, R. K. (1965), *The Clydesiders* (London: Hutchinson).

MORRIS, R. J. (1983), 'Skilled Workers and the Politics of the "Red Clyde"', *Journal of the Scottish Labour History Society*, no. 18.

PELLING, H. (1968 ed.), *A Short History of the Labour Party* (London: Macmillan).

PENN, R. (1982), 'The Contested Terrain: a critique of R. C. Edwards' theory of working class fractions and politics', in G. Day (ed.), *Diversity and Decomposition in the Labour Market* (Aldershot: Gower).

POLLARD, S. and ROBERTSON, P. L. (1979), *The British Shipbuilding Industry, 1870–1914* (Brighton: Harvester).

PRICE, R. (1980), *Masters, Unions and Men* (Cambridge University Press).

PRICE, R. (1984), 'Structures of subordination in nineteenth century British industry', in P. Thane, G. Crossick and R. Floud (eds), *The Power of the Past: essays for Eric Hobsbawm*, (Cambridge University Press).

PRICE, R. (1985), 'The New Unionism and the Labour Process', in W. J. Mommsen and H. G. Husung (eds), *The Development of Trade Unionism in Great Britain and Germany, 1880–1914* (London: Allen & Unwin).

PRICE, R. (1986), *Labour in British Society: and interpretive history* (London: Croom Helm).

REID, A. (1980), 'The Division of Labour in the British Shipbuilding Industry, 1880–1920: with special reference to Clydeside', Ph.D. Cambridge University.

REID, A. (1985), 'Politics and the Division of Labour, 1880–1920', in W. J. Mommsen and H. G. Husung (eds), *The Development of Trade Unionism in Great Britain and Germany*, (London: Allen & Unwin).

REID, F. (1978), *Keir Hardie* (London: Croom Helm).

ROBERTSON, P. L. (1975), 'Demarcation Disputes in British Shipbuilding before 1914', *International Review of Social History*, vol. XX.

SAVAGE, M. (1989), Urban Politics and the Rise of the Labour Party, 1919–1939', in L. Jamieson and H. Corr (eds), *State, Private Life and Political Change* (London: Macmillan).

SCOTT, A. (1906–7), 'The training of youth: supervision of lads from their fourteenth till their seventeenth year', *Proceedings of the Philosophical Society of Glasgow*, vol. XXXVII.

SLAVEN, A. (1975), *The Development of the West of Scotland: 1750–1960*, (London: Routledge & Kegan Paul).

SMITH, J. M. (1980), 'Commonsense Thought and Working Class Consciousness: some aspects of the Glasgow and Liverpool Labour Movements in the early years of the twentieth century', Ph.D. University of Edinburgh.

SMITH, J. M. (1984), 'Labour Tradition in Glasgow and Liverpool', *History Workshop*, no. 17.

SOUTHALL, H. (1986), 'Unionization', in J. Langton and R. J. Morris (eds), *Atlas of Industrializing Britain, 1780–1914* (London: Methuen).

STEWART, W. (1921), *Keir Hardie* (Glasgow).

TREBLE, J. H. (1978), 'The market for unskilled labour in Glasgow, 1891–1914', in I. MacDougall (ed.), *Essays in Scottish Labour History* (Edinburgh: John Donald).

TREBLE, J. H. (1986), 'The characteristics of the female unskilled labour market and the formation of the female causal labour market in Glasgow, 1891–1914', *Scottish Economic and Social History*, vol. 6.

UNGER, D. C. (1979), 'The Roots of Red Clydeside: economic and social relations and working class politics in the west of Scotland, 1900–1919', Ph.D. University of Texas.

WALKER, W. M. (1979), *Juteopolis: Dundee and its textile workers, 1885–1923* (Edinburgh: Scottish Academic Press).

WEBB, S. and WEBB, B., Collection on Trade Unions, London: British Library of Political and Economic Science.

WILLIAMS, A. (1915), *Life in a Railway Factory* (London).

WOOD, I. S. (1972), 'Drink, Temperance and the Labour Movement' *Journal of the Scottish Labour History Society*, no. 5.

WOOD, I. S. (1978), 'Irish Immigrants and Scottish Radicalism, 1880–1906', in I. MacDougall (ed.), *Essays in Scottish Labour History* (Edinburgh: John Donald).

ZEITLIN, J. (1983), 'The Labour Strategies of British Engineering Employers, 1890–1922', in H. F. Gospel and C. R. Littler (eds), *Managerial Strategies and Industrial Relations: an historical and comparative study* (Aldershot: Gower).

ZEITLIN, J. (1985), 'Industrial Structure, Employer Strategy and the Diffusion of Job Control in Britain, 1880–1920', in W. J. Mommsen and H. G. Husung (eds), *The Development of Trade Unionism in Great Britain and Germany, 1880–1914* (London: Allen & Unwin).

9 Politics of the Sexes in English and Scottish Teachers' Unions 1870–1914

Helen Corr

INTRODUCTION

There is a substantial body of historical and sociological literature which establishes that female employees have been less likely than males to join trade unions. A lower rate of trade union membership was a characteristic shared by women in a variety of manual and white collar occupations during the late nineteenth century. Most notably in the elementary school teaching profession, females formed the majority of the workforce in both England and Scotland, but were in a minority in the Educational Institute of Scotland (EIS) and the National Union of Teachers (NUT). The EIS and NUT constituted the largest professional organisations for elementary certificated teachers in Scotland and England in the late Victorian period. This paper will examine a series of ideological factors underpinning women teachers' reluctance to join professional organisations, and the controversial issue of equal pay will form the central theme.

The various attempts to explain the phenomenon of lower rates of union membership among women teachers are in themselves revealing. Until recently, eminent educational historians have explained the male monopoly of the NUT in terms of women teachers' apparent willingness to 'allow' men to be the dominant partners. Evocative words such as 'docility', 'passivity' and 'apathy' have been liberally applied by writers to describe women's role in the NUT. To a large extent, both historians and sociologists have inherited this set of pre-value judgements from their predecessors during the late nineteenth and early twentieth centuries. Thus, Asher

Tropp in his book, *The School Teachers* (1957), reproduced Beatrice Webb's criticisms of women teachers, published in *The New Statesman* in 1915. He wrote:

> Down to the end of the nineteenth century the women teachers seem to have been prepared to allow the men to monopolise the leadership of the NUT. They accepted without any recorded complaint, the lower scales of salaries and the lesser opportunities for promotion. They were less inclined to join the Union and played little part in the running of the Union. (p. 157)

This statement is riddled with inaccuracies. It will be seen later that women teachers repeatedly recorded their complaints about lower salary scales and that there was a highly active female lobby for equal pay in the NUT during the late nineteenth century; but myths die hard. More recently, Geoffrey Partington in his book, *Women Teachers in the Twentieth Century* (1976) declared:

> Most women teachers in Victorian society accepted their inferiority with docility. The NUT was dominated by men even though most of its members were women. (p. 9)

These historians' references to women teachers' alleged passivity tend to assume that it was essentially 'a woman's problem'. Other writers have pointed out that women regarded their employment as secondary to marital and child-rearing responsibilities and this in turn resulted in a lack of commitment towards membership and activism in white collar union organisations (Hyman and Price, 1983). At a theoretical level, however, insufficient emphasis has been placed on studying the male values which in turn inhibited the female involvement in a union structure. Male trade unionists have frequently displayed an ambivalent and hostile attitude towards female membership in trade unions. For example, Barbara Drake's pathbreaking study, *Women and Trade Unions* (1920) abounds in examples of the exclusion of women from many of the craft unions during the early phase of industrialisation. The rationale for the exclusion of women was male unionists' fears of dilution and the undercutting of their own wages.

To account for this, the concept of gender is seen here as

being of crucial theoretical importance in understanding the divisions between the sexes in the overlapping spheres of the workplace and union politics. Gender differences have had radical social implications in the structuring of diverging ideologies between the sexes on a range of issues such as equal pay, skill, promotion and marriage. The gendering process has been such that men have often sought to defend and advance their own material self-interest as a group in direct opposition to the perceived interests of female employees. Historically, this has meant that women have attached a quite different and distinct set of meanings from those of men to belonging to a union. My study of teachers' organisations in England and Scotland shows the complexity of gender relations in the workplace and in union politics.

WHY ARE WOMEN THE 'SILENT PARTNERS'?

The question of female membership first appeared to have been raised at a management level within the EIS during the 1870s. The EIS was formed in 1847 for 'teachers of all denominations' but in practice, its membership was hierarchical, male-specific, and restricted to burgh and parochial schoolmasters.

In 1874, the first applications for female membership were recorded and approved by the two largest associations, Glasgow and Edinburgh. This prompted further discussion as to whether the entry of women into the Institute should form part of its policy, and there was a consensus in favour of female membership. The entry of women teachers into the Institute was a historical landmark, in view of the fact that for the previous 27 years the EIS had been an all-male body. By contrast, one of the most striking features emerging from the NUT official reports was the lack of publicity devoted to the question of non-female membership prior to the 1890s. At its inception in 1870, the National Union of Elementary Teachers (NUET), as it was then known (it changed its name to the NUT in 1889), did open its doors to female certificated teachers. The fact that the NUT accepted female members from the outset may provide one explanation why female non-membership was not, initially at any rate, perceived as a contentious issue.

In Scotland, the leadership's principal motive for encouraging females to join the EIS was to swell membership figures. In 1876, the total teaching staff numbered over 13 000, and yet EIS membership barely reached 2000. A decade later, it was reported that women teachers constituted only 18 per cent of the total membership, despite their overall superiority in numbers in the teaching profession. Concern over the issue of 'lesser female membership' was increasingly expressed with many local branches of the EIS throughout urban and rural Scotland.

As a result of mounting pressure from individual chairmen of local EIS branches, a circular was sent out in 1897 requesting the compilation of statistics on non-membership and the reasons for . . . 'the comparatively small number of female teachers who are members of the Institute'. The statistics confirmed that women teachers generally displayed a greater reluctance than men to join the EIS; a total of 1791 females, compared with 769 men, had failed to join the Institute. A similar inquiry into non-membership had been conducted in the NUT in 1896. The issue of non-membership among female certificated teachers surfaced in much the same way as the EIS, namely as part of a more general concern about flagging membership rates.

At a grassroots level, a lively discussion was initiated between the sexes in *The Schoolmaster*, the official organ of the NUT, which stated:

> There are 17,000 certificated women teachers non-members of the Union. Why is it? (18 January 1896, p. 121).

Reactions to the question varied in accordance with gender, in England and Wales. Likewise in Scotland the reasons cited by disillusioned females for their non-involvement in the EIS were almost identical with those offered by their colleagues south of the border. A shared conviction was that women's separate grievances as a sex were either marginalised or ignored altogether by the male leadership. The theoretical parameters of the debate were succinctly highlighted by a female teacher when she pointed to the wide gulf in gender attitudes on political issues that affected women more adversely than men:

> When the interests of men and women are identical, the questions are taken up heartfully and successfully but that which affect women only are left alone entirely or else taken up in a lukewarm way (*The Schoolmaster* 8 February 1896, p. 232).

Seeds of Unrest

The major grievances expressed among women teachers concerned the imbalance of power in the sex-ratio of delegates elected to the Local and National Executive Committees and the failure of the male leadership to fight for better salaries for women. Optimists widely assumed that by securing a power base at a management level inside the EIS and NUT, women's demands for equal rights with men would win approval. In each of these endeavours, however, they faced a formidable struggle. During the first sixteen years of the NUT's history there were no female delegates whatsoever on the NUT Executive Committee. Women teachers did participate in the Union at a local level, but found it extremely difficult to overcome the psychological barrier of running for election to what had always been an all-male committee at a national level. For example, in 1883, one woman from Shrewsbury considered running for election to the Executive, but withdrew her application when she found out she was the only woman. Only two women, Mrs Burgwin (London) and Miss Isabel Cleghorn (Sheffield) managed to secure coveted positions on the NUT National Executive before the close of the late Victorian era.

An almost identical pattern of female under-representation on Management Committees prevailed in the EIS. Before the 1890s, not a single woman had ever been elected president of a Local Association. In 1896 Miss Flora Stevenson and Miss Stephens were elected Presidents of the Edinburgh and Morayshire EIS local branches respectively. Many women complained that their position was marginal in the mainstream organisational structure of the EIS. This feeling of impotence was intensified by men's image of women as the silent partners. In the context of encouraging women to join the Institute, senior male officials predicted that women teachers would refrain from voicing their opinions at EIS meetings, and that their 'silent presence' would have a pacifying effect on the discussions among male members (EIS Reports 1876, p. 12).

Men's image of women's 'presence' as 'passive', but at the same time constituting a moral restraining influence on the activities of its members, was an enduring one (EIS Reports 1888, p. 95). However, from the standpoint of many women teachers, it was precisely because their role was viewed in such passive terms that they 'did not see the use' of joining the EIS. An additional source of friction between the sexes concerned the leadership's failure in both teachers' organisations to support equal pay for women teachers.

Gender and Economic Inequality

During the late nineteenth century the salaries of women teachers were consistently lower than those received by men. In 1885, the mean salary of female certificated teachers in England was £74 per annum compared with the male equivalent of £121. In Scotland the respective figures were £65 for women and £135 for males. Statistical data indicates that women teachers in Scotland earned less than their female colleagues in England. Scottish female teachers who migrated to England in search of a teaching post found that they could earn higher average salaries than when working in Scotland. The opposite applied to men. The mean salaries of male certificated teachers in Scotland were considerably higher than that earned by their counterparts in English elementary schools. By the last decade of the nineteenth century, there was some token improvement in the national mean salaries of women certificated teachers in England, whereas in Scotland pay differentials continued to widen between certificated women and men teachers. However, in both countries, employers, the locally elected school boards, continued to advance a policy of sex discrimination in teachers' pay.

Before 1900 there was an active female lobby which campaigned for equal pay inside the NUT, whereas there appears to have been no equivalent pressure group activity in the EIS. This finding is itself surprising in view of the fact that Scottish women teachers were economically more disadvantaged than their English female counterparts. The equal pay movement was particularly strong in London and the Metropolitan Districts and weaker in most of the provincial cities and towns. Within the Scottish urban structure, the Glasgow branch of the EIS was the most progressive pacemaker for debating the equal pay issue after 1900, but elsewhere in the cities of Edinburgh, Dundee and Aberdeen, the issue failed to generate the same degree of publicity. Women's demands for equal pay were seldom recorded or publicised in the *Scottish Educational News*, the official organ of the EIS before 1900. By contrast, women teachers regularly publicised their views on equal pay in *The Schoolmaster*, albeit that many of the letters and correspondence remained anonymous.

However, it was not until the closing stages of World War I that equal pay became a national issue for debate in the schoolteaching profession and in white collar clerical occupations in Britain. Before 1900, much of the pressure for equal pay within the NUT stemmed from the male leadership's then current policy of reproducing sexual inequalities in teachers' pay. In challenging this policy, one female teacher in 1896 drew attention to the fact that . . . 'the claims of assistant masters to a higher maximum salary were being strenuously advocated by the Union and rightly so' . . . but she asked . . . 'why not those of women assistants when every argument for one holds good for the other?' (*The Schoolmaster* 8 February, p. 232).

Women teachers' consciousness of gender and economic inequality was visibly intensified by the leadership's fostering of sex discriminatory practices within the union structure itself. One glaring illustration of this was the unequal welfare benefits paid in the NUT. On the one hand, the unofficial policy of the Union was to oppose the principle of equal pay, but on the other, women were required to pay the same subscription fee as men for NUT membership. Another blatant form of sex discrimination was that men and women teachers paid an identical fee to the Benevolent and Orphan's fund, but the maximum benefit women received was £25 compared with £30 for men. Such policies did have repercussions by galvanising and organising women teachers' resistance against male unionists' staunchly-held views. It was no mere coincidence that the campaign for sex equality largely stemmed from women's demands for equal welfare benefits with male teachers from the Union's own charitable funds. This particular concession was finally achieved in 1903. The EIS leadership, by contrast, permitted women teachers to pay a lower annual subscription fee than men, and they self-consciously viewed this as a tactical measure to swell female entrants into the Institute (Corr, 1983). Overall, the leadership's failure to support women teachers' claims for higher salaries and equality of access to decision-making bodies in both England and Scotland was pinpointed by a female teacher in 1896; she was responding to the question of 'Why women don't join the Union':

> It is because the men do not stand by the women. Do not uphold them, do not vote them onto the Executive that the women are not Unionists (*The Schoolmaster* 1896, p. 164).

A positive outcome to these debates on female non-membership was the formation of Ladies Committees in the EIS and NUT respectively at the close of the nineteenth century. The dual task of these female pressure groups was to represent 'the special interests of women teachers', and each committee member was eligible for election to the National Executive of the EIS and the NUT. Female pioneers regarded their election to policy-making committees as a symbol of the advancement of women in spheres of public employment and teachers' organisations. An ideal shared by women activists across Scottish and English geographical boundaries was that of persuading men of the separate but equal treatment of 'women's issues' in the dual spheres of the home and the workplace.

However, different strategies were advanced by female activists in Scotland and England on how best to tackle the problem of discrimination and particularly so over the issue of equal pay. The female leadership of the NUT supported equal pay, whereas their Scottish counterparts in the EIS rejected this principle before World War I. The second half of the paper will explore some hypothetical explanations as to why female activists in the EIS and the NUT adopted conflicting strategies on the equal pay issue. Particular emphasis will be placed on the ideology of professionalisation of teaching in Scotland as a restrictive force in pressing for equal pay before 1914.

THE EQUAL PAY DEBATE 1900–1914: CONFLICT AND HARMONY BETWEEN THE SEXES

Based at its headquarters in Glasgow, the EIS Ladies Committee acted as the official mouthpiece for the mass female membership on women's issues. In theory, all EIS members were eligible for membership to the Central Ladies Committee, but in practice it was the preserve of a close-knit group of women, mainly from Dundee, Edinburgh, Glasgow and its hinterland. The elite nature of the group was such that almost all its members were also to be found on the central Ladies Committee of the Scottish Class Teachers Association (SCTA) formed in 1896. The social composition of the EIS Ladies Committee could be described in an almost identical way to their English counterparts. The membership of both groups was exceedingly cohesive, with a very small turnover in members of between four to six ladies over a 20-year period. A leading characteristic of each group was that nearly all of its members were spinsters, ambitious, well-qualified and extremely dedicated to the concept of a 'mixed' union of men and women. Unfortunately no information exists on the class background of these individuals.

In 1900 the Scottish and English Committees each drew up a list of topics defined as 'of special interest to women teachers'. Many of the topics were non-contentious and echoed a pastoral concern for women teachers within their respective communities. The schemes included making regular visits to teacher training colleges for recruitment purposes, and the promotion of domestic science for inclusion in the elementary school curriculum for older girls. A significant difference in pressure group activity was that the issues of salaries, equal pay, promotions, headships and the removal of an unofficial marriage bar in cities were rarely placed on the agenda of the Scottish women's meetings, whereas the opposite applied in the case of the NUT Committee.

The principle of equal pay was first raised for public debate by the local branch of the EIS and the Scottish Class Teachers' Association (SCTA) in Glasgow in 1914. The official policy of the Ladies Committee was to oppose this principle despite the fact that there was overwhelming grassroots support for equal pay among female teachers in Glasgow. The female leadership's reasons for rejecting equal pay were complex. One evident explanation for the Committee's failure to support equal pay was they were intent on avoiding conflict with men. The committee was aware that the official policy of the EIS was to support the retention of sex differentials in teachers' pay and it is conceivable that they avoided the topic because it aroused much acrimony and aggression from their male colleagues. Their first allegiance lay with the concept of a mixed union based on mutual co-operation with men.

The Ladies Committee's reluctance to embark on a campaign for equal pay was also bound up with the ideology of professionalisation of schoolteaching prevailing in Scotland.

The Search for Professional Status in elementary school teaching

The female leadership believed in elevating the status of the elementary schoolteaching profession in Scotland through winning the respect of the public, and this ideal became a major inhibiting force against organising a salaries campaign on behalf of women teachers. To illustrate this point, it is worthwhile examining the views of Miss Elizabeth Fish, who, in 1913, became the first female President of the EIS. In her presidential speech, Fish raised the question of equal pay, and she acknowledged that it was currently an issue of much controversy among members of the various Scottish and English Teachers' Associations. The female president supported higher salaries for women teachers but was vehemently opposed to the principle of equal pay. Her rationale for this stance was particularly related to the sex ratio of the labour force, with her claim that:

> It would be a disastrous thing for our country were the work of education to fall almost entirely into the hands of women . . . men teachers are scarce and their service can naturally command a higher price than that of women which is so abundantly offered (*Educational News* 9 January 1914, pp. 29–30).

The president's views on equal pay were in total harmony with the official policy of the male leadership. After dismissing counter-arguments in favour of equal pay, the so-called 'champion' for female teachers considered whether the EIS should adopt trade union methods and strike action, in line with their NUT colleagues. She rejected the adoption of trade union tactics and the concept of school teaching as a 'profession' was the main argument advanced:

> We must never be unmindful of our 'high calling' and the dignity of the profession . . . If teaching be indeed a profession and not be a mere trade, it must not resort to the methods of the trade unions in its demand for increased remuneration (*ibid.*).

Elizabeth Fish's preoccupation with professional status, class and public recognition was in keeping with the dominant values of EIS male leaders ever since its foundation in 1847. The Ladies' Committee inherited these goals of professional status and the improvement of teachers' social standing within the community as models for themselves. Moreover, the search for professional status among male EIS founder members was intricately bound up with their occupational position within the class structure of Scottish society. As Robert Anderson (1983) has pointed out, nineteenth-century Scotland was a society dominated by the values of the middle classes, emanating from Edinburgh as the centre of Medicine, Law and the clerics. In the earlier part of the century, it was the Edinburgh legal profession that had the power to make decisions about educational policy. They in turn were influenced by their own educational background, acquired through burgh or parochial schools or at one of the Scottish universities.

In contrast with England, where a system of national education was barely in existence, in Scotland there were close links between parish schools in the countryside, burgh schools and the universities, which helped to give some reality to the meritocratic ideal of education. In this respect, the Scots were much more in line with their continental allies, who shared a calvinistic appeal for intellectuality and individual merit. However, the position of the parochial schoolmaster within the Scottish educational structure was an ambivalent one. Many schoolmasters had not attended university long enough to qualify for the Ministry, or had failed to meet the necessary course requirements. Hence they entered teaching as a second choice and at a significantly lower salary than that paid to the clergy.

From its inception, claims for professional status constituted a major ideal of the EIS, and this was to remain a dominant concern in EIS politics throughout the nineteenth century, in spite of radical changes which were taking place in the structure of the teaching profession following the 1872 Education (Scotland) Act. Disillusionment at a grassroots level in the EIS grew more intense after 1872. This derived from a growing awareness that the rhetoric of professional status had a negative effect on teachers' demands for higher salaries and the abolition of local school board authorities. In England, school boards had been abolished in 1902 whereas this did not happen in Scotland until the 1918 Education (Scotland) Act.

Rank and File Unrest

Resentment was most pronounced among male assistant certificated teachers, since the salary and promotional prospects of this occupational group were the most severely restricted. With the creation of large public schools in Scotland during the late nineteenth century, many male certificated teachers in particular came to view themselves as 'permanent assistants' with little hope of achieving promotion to headships and more lucrative salary scales. The rift between the views of the leadership and the rank and file male and female membership on the issue of professionalisation was expressed in this statement in 1913:

> Neither in social standing nor in emoluments do we take our place among the professions' history . . . The intense feeling of unrest today is due to the conviction that the public have failed to realise the altered conditions of things (*Educational News*, p. 669).

Disenchantment with the absence of more decisive action on the salaries issue was aggravated by the teachers' strike in Herefordshire in 1913. The successful outcome of strike action convinced many Scottish teachers that the policies of the EIS were more conservative and antiquated than those of the NUT. This feeling was heightened by the leadership's persistent refusal to replace *Educational Institute* by the term *The Scottish Union of Teachers* in line with the *National Union of Teachers*. Strident demands for a Scottish Union of Teachers were being made against a background of industrial militancy and a wave of strikes in Britain in the years immediately before the outbreak of the War. It is significant that the EIS did not launch a teachers' strike until 1961, whereas the NUT had a legacy of supporting strike action stretching back to the Portsmouth strike in 1896.

A further complexity is that the rank and file female membership in Glasgow overwhelmingly supported equal pay and were opposed to the policies of the Ladies Committee on this issue before 1914.

A circular was sent out to all EIS and SCTA members in Glasgow to canvass opinion on the proposal of equality of pay for men and women teachers. The plebiscite revealed that 1608 members voted against the proposal for equal pay and 922 were in favour of it. However, the Glasgow Local Association failed to provide a statistical breakdown of the supporters and opponents according to sex, and it is therefore impossible to use voting returns to ascertain sexual polarity over this issue. Nonetheless, when a vote on equal pay was taken by the Glasgow branch of the SCTA, a breakdown was made according to gender, and hence the statistics are more revealing. The results showed that 1,478 women teachers were in favour of equal pay and 296 were against it, whereas the respective figures for male teachers was 160 in favour compared with 600 against it. The women teachers' overwhelming support serves as a decisive indication of the deep ideological schism which existed between the genders on equal pay in Glasgow. It also reflected the conflicting differences in opinion which existed between senior female representatives and the rank and file female membership of the SCTA. Official discussions on the subject of equal pay in the teaching profession were effectively squashed in Scotland before the outbreak of World War I. The EIS convening committee reported that a decrease in membership in 1914 had corresponded with debates on equal pay. However, if anything, male teachers' opposition to equal pay was even more pronounced and acrimonious inside the NUT. The conflict of interests beween the sexes was exacerbated by the Ladies Commitee's support of this principle at a senior level in the NUT.

Gender Conflict on Equal Pay and Suffrage in the NUT 1900–1914

Gender differences in outlook on equal pay surfaced at a meeting of the National Executive Committee as early as 1900. Miss Isabel Cleghorn proposed the following motion ... 'that women should be eligible for appointment on the staff of junior and senior clerks in this office [NUT] and at the same wages as men'. Supporting this measure, Cleghorn argued the NUT Executive would combat the prevalent argument that the 'Union did nothing to represent the interest of women teachers'. However, the response from male members of the committee was one of incredulous surprise that Isabel Cleghorn had raised equal pay as a serious issue. Mr Sandiford, who taught in a national school, Gosport, bluntly replied that the case was 'erroneous' and added that ... 'there were certain duties which could not possibly be performed by women. And really all things considered was there any need for this proposition at all' (NUT Minutes 1900).

In defending the stance of the Ladies Committee, Miss Hannah Williams (Cardiff) voiced her 'deep regret' that the motion for equal pay .. 'had not received the proper respect it deserved from their male colleagues'. She reminded them

... 'that precisely because the Union was mixed, it should provide a splendid opportunity for men and women to run with the other' (NUT Minutes 1900). It is conceivable that even the most experienced middle-class female public speaker would have felt intimidated by such a negative response, and not least because the lady members were in a minority of four compared with 38 men. Any further dialogue on the subject was squashed, on the grounds that no previous NUT conference had ever debated 'equal pay for equal work'. One direct outcome of this clash on equal pay was that the Ladies Committee received an explicit warning that the defence of this issue could lead to future bouts of unconcealed aggression among men at the most senior level of the NUT. After 1900, the discussion on equal pay temporarily receded. However, even if the NUT Ladies Committee had wished to avoid the equal pay topic, it could not do so, largely because of regular contacts with a network of Fabian and union organisations.

The female NUT leaders' involvement in a supportive network of industrial and white collar organisations in and around London was in marked contrast with the comparative isolation of the Scottish EIS women's group; this may in turn be a contributing factor in accounting for the relative weakness of the equal pay movement in Scotland during the early Edwardian period. Nearly all of the founder committee's members in England and Wales lived and taught in the provincial cities and towns but London formed the central arena for policy-making decisions. Among those organisations that cultivated close ties with the NUT committee was the National Union of Women Workers (NUWW). Miss Isabel Cleghorn and Miss Goodwin, another woman on the Executive, were appointed to the NUWW's national council. As Dina Copelman (1985) has pointed out, each of these activities indicated women teachers 'coming of political age'. When the United Kingdom Postal Clerk Associations sent a questionnaire to the NUT Ladies Committee on equal pay in 1909, it once again highlighted the sharp divergence in attitudes of this group with the male-dominated National NUT Executive. After reaffirming their support for equal pay 'where a woman is placed on the staff of a boys' department' the Ladies Committee conceded that the Union had not laid down any firm policy endorsing their own stance on this.

The position of women teachers at the centre of Union policies was characterised by self-conscious demands for separate but equal treatment with male teachers in public employment. Support for separate female headships of boys' and girls' departments was an overtly political expression of the viewpoint. Women teachers feared that 'mixed and combined' departments would adversely affect their own promotional prospects in favour of men (Oram 1984). Hence, the Ladies Committee campaigned for single sex departments for girls, under the headship of women teachers. The issue of 'mixed and combined' departments was a persistent theme in the writings of the NUT female leaders. Here, they were dependent on the support of their female colleagues in the London Teachers' Association (LTA) to drive for single sex departments for girls under the headships of women teachers. By contrast, the system of co-education existing in Scottish elementary schools did not arouse the same impassioned feelings of opposition among women teachers, perhaps because it was a long established and accepted feature of the Scots educational tradition. The quest for a separate identity through single sex departments in English schools was also due to the growing practice of substituting women teachers for men in boys' departments, at a lower salary. In London, there were ten assistant mistresses in boys' departments in county council schools in 1905, compared with 93 in 1907. This practice was strongly condemned on the grounds of the employers' procuration of a cheaper female labour force. Another example of the Ladies Committee's desire for a separate sphere of influence from men in schools was reflected in their ardent support for the teaching of domestic science to girls. Like so many of their peer group in the social-imperialist Edwardian era, the Ladies Committee believed that a girl's first duty was to prepare herself for her future role as wife and mother. Consequently Cleghorn in 1907 advocated that 'at least six months of a girl's school life should be taken up entirely with Housewifery, including cookery and laundry'. The fact that women teachers were to be entirely responsible for the instruction of girls in domestic subjects was in keeping with the women's active support for sex segregation (Corr 1983). A related motive of the Ladies Committee was to achieve an autonomous power base from men within elementary schools and in the Union.

The stress on women's special nature and needs during the Victorian and Edwardian period was integrally bound up with women's reactions to sex discrimination. Feminists' struggle for equal pay in the union co-existed with a broader campaign for the right to vote. In 1908 one suffragette in the NUT pointed out that while all 35,000 women members were expected to contribute two shillings a year towards the salary of the Union's MP, not a single woman was entitled to vote in parliamentary elections. The suffrage movement highlighted the capacity of women for self-organisation and protest in the political sphere dating from the mid-Victorian era. It was on the issue of suffrage that a major public argument exploded between the sexes at the annual NUT conference in Aberystwyth in 1911. Paradoxically, this row was preceded by jubilant celebrations among the women delegates following the election of Miss Isabel Cleghorn as the first Lady President in the Union's history.

What ought then to have been a week of personal triumph for Isabel Cleghorn and the women's movement in the event degenerated into a nightmarish experience. Ferocious antagonism was expressed by male unionists on the suffrage issue. The explosion was sparked off when Mr Croft, a member of the Executive, attempted to place a motion in support of women's suffrage. Uproar followed and for 30 minutes, hundreds of jeering men stamped, howled and hurled abuse at the women delegates in the conference hall. When peace was finally restored, the suffrage motion was decisively defeated by 40 653 votes to 12 276. The suffrage issue symbolised the obstacles which confronted women teachers in attempting to voice their grievances within their own Union organisation.

Cleghorn, however, refused to concede any feelings of disappointment, and her main message to women teachers was this:

> Defeat is sometimes a victory . . . and I am a more advanced suffragist to-day than when I came to Aberystwyth

> ... But ... Go Home to your Association and work for the Union. That is our line of policy ... Go back and tell them that you have been doing wrong in working for the suffrage movement and forgetting your Union, therefore losing influence in your Union ... I ask you to do all you can for the Union and then try to work through your Union to get redress for any grievance you consider you are suffering (NUT Minutes 1911).

Not every woman in the NUT however, shared Isabel Cleghorn's dedication to the principle of a 'mixed' union and this caused a deep ideological schism between women teachers. A lobby of women NUT activists thereafter pressed for the safeguard of a separate women's organisation to campaign for parity of treatment with men in the teaching profession and in the Labour movement. The breeding ground for the formation of an all female organisation was a pressure group known as the National Federation of Women Teachers (NFWT) (Pierotti 1963). It originated from the Equal Pay League inside the NUT in 1904. By 1910, the Federation was taking a more permanent form and it held its first independent conference in March of that year. As early as 1908, Isabel Cleghorn described the Federation as a 'menace' even though at that time she was sympathetic to its aims. During the latter part of her life Cleghorn changed her views on equal pay and, as a member of the Burnham Committee in 1919, she supported the nexus of women to men teachers' pay at a ratio of 4:5. In the Burnham inquiry the family wage was used as the chief ideological justification for gender inequality. This concept implied the notion of the male as the chief breadwinner and the woman as wife and dependent. The NUT leadership's lack of effective support for equal pay finally convinced a small but influential lobby of women teachers of the futility of remaining in a mixed union. In 1920, they officially severed links with the NUT and reformed themselves into an alternative organisation – the National Union of Women Teachers (NUWT). Individuals explained why they had left the Union. Miss Agnes Hewitt, a former president of the East Ham NUT branch, wrote:

> At last I become convinced that women teachers could not

> hope to find a legitimate expression through that organisation. It is a regrettable fact that the majority of men teachers do not yet recognise that the opinions and votes of their women colleagues are of the same value as their own [Pierotti, 1963].

An equally committed group was the National Association of Headmasters (NAS) (Littlewood, 1985). It was formed in 1919 with the express aim of opposing equal pay. The formation of two separate Unions symbolised the polarisation of gender conflict among teachers in the early twentieth century. In Scotland, there was no parallel formation of sex-specific Unions during the same era. Women teachers decided to remain in a mixed organisation, and the distinctive system of co-education, coupled with the professional ideals of different EIS leaders, may have militated against the radical formation of an independent Scottish Union of Women Teachers.

CONCLUSION

After a protracted history, equal pay was finally introduced for women in the teaching profession and in the civil service in 1961. This account of sexual politics has sought to highlight the dilemmas which women confronted in a male dominated power structure, and the various strategies open to them, leading for some to assimilation to the dominant values of the particular organisation and for others to outright rejection of those values and secession. The equal pay campaign raised the difficult ideological question of whether women should consider the ideals of the union as their first priority, and their own separate grievances as a sex secondary. In Scotland pressure group activity for equal pay was contained and restricted among the rank and file membership, whereas in England conflict on this issue was irrevocably to split women teachers among themselves. The purpose of this chapter has also been to refute the received view that women teachers have historically 'accepted their inferiority with docility' and to put on record their often painful struggles against discrimination.

NOTE

I would like to thank Penny Summerfield, Peter Gordon and Gian Poggi for their helpful comments. This chapter is based on an earlier version of an article in P. Summerfield (ed.) *Women, Education and the Professions* (History of Education Society, Occasional Publication No. 8, 1987).

REFERENCES

ANDERSON, R. (1983), *Education and Opportunity in Victorian Scotland* (Oxford: Clarendon Press).

COPELMAN, D. (1985), 'Women in the Classroom Struggle: Elementary Teachers in London', unpublished Ph.D. thesis,

CORR, H. (1983), The Gender Division of Labour in the Scottish Teaching Profession 1872–1914', unpublished Ph.D. thesis, Edinburgh University.

CORR, H. (1983), 'The schoolgirl's curriculum and the ideology of the home 1870–1914' in Glasgow Women's Studies Group (ed) *Uncharted lives* (Glasgow: Pressgang).

CORR, H. (1983), 'The Sexual Division of Labour in the Scottish Teaching Profession 1872–1914', in W. Humes and H. Paterson (eds), *Scottish Culture and Scottish Education, 1800–1980* (John Donald).

DRAKE, B. (1920), *Women in Trade Unions* (Labour Research Department).

HYMAN, R. and PRICE, R. (1983), *The New Working Class: White Collar Workers and their Organisations* (Basingstoke: Macmillan).

LITTLEWOOD, M. (1985), 'Makers of Men', *Trouble and Strife*, 5, Spring pp. 23–9.

ORAM, A. (1984), 'Sex Antagonism in the Teaching Profession: Employment issues and the woman teacher in Elementary Education 1910–1939', unpublished M.Sc. thesis, University of Bristol.

PARTINGTON, G. (1976), *Women teachers in the twentieth century* (National Foundation for Educational Research).

PIEROTTI, A. M. (1963), *The Story of the National Union of Women Teachers*, published by the NUWT.

TROPP, A. (1957), *The School Teachers* (London: William Heinemann).

WEBB, B. (1915), 'English Teachers and Their Professional Organisations', in *The New Statesman*, vol. 5 no. 129, special supplement.

10 Meanings of Class and Social Mobility: the Public and Private Lives of Female Civil Servants

Kay Sanderson

INTRODUCTION

> Every individual lives from one generation to the next in some society; he lives out a biography and he lives it out within some historical sequence (C. Wright Mills, 1959, p. 6).

This often cited, but rarely followed suggestion to consider history, biography and society together is the methodological key to this small scale study of women's social mobility. I shall suggest that social position and social mobility can usefully be seen as components of the biography of the individual; a biography constructed within the socio-economic constraints of the particular historical period within which the life-cycle is located. The study is a synthesis, therefore, of 'humanistic' sociology, social history and oral life-histories. It reflects the interactionist account of personality and the individual construction of reality, but places these 'constructions' within historical context.[1] Since this is not how social mobility is usually studied, some explanation for this theoretical and methodological deviance is required.

Women and social mobility

The publication, in 1980, of J. H. Goldthorpe's account of the research undertaken by the Social Mobility Group at Nuffield College during the 1970s, reactivated the debate about the position of women in stratification studies. This very extensive study of social mobility in Britain was a study of *male* mobility only. Goldthorpe's justification for excluding women, and the objections and discussions that followed, have already been extensively rehearsed (see, for example, the debate in *Sociology*, November 1983, May 1984, November 1984) and the issue remains unresolved. It has to be conceded, however, that there are real problems associated with integrating women into *traditional* studies. Briefly, women have an unstable attachment to the labour force, occupy different (and generally lower level) niches in the occupational structure, and, in any case, are generally assumed to share the class position of the male head of the household to which they belong. The latter objection is certainly open to debate, but the former problems seem intractable within the methodological and theoretical constraints of the traditional approach; an approach which identifies 'social mobility' with intra- and inter-generational movement within the occupational structure.

Nevertheless, excluding women from the field of study seems an unsatisfactory solution to the problems of including them. I have, therefore, made an *a priori* assumption that women *do* have social position (and in their own right)[2] and that, consequently, they can be socially mobile. However, this does imply some definitional changes: firstly 'position in the occupational structure' will be taken as only *one* of the indicators of social position, rather than as the sole determinant; the other socio-economic institutions within which individuals achieve social standing will also be considered. At the same time, the problematic will, as suggested in the introduction, be focused on the 'how' of social mobility: specifically – how do women establish, maintain and change their position in the social world they inhabit?

At this point it is already possible to suggest how a more interactionist account of women's social mobility might be developed. Firstly, the subject is redefined as 'becoming socially mobile – the process by which women negotiate the move between social classes'. Secondly, the study should take into account the social material from which women fashion their lives (including their social position) and the meaning this has for the individual. This social material includes the macro socio-economic world, which is historically specific, as well as the micro social world of their particular lives: family size, income and aspirations; geographical location; schooling and other influences. Finally, it should take into account the life-cycle related opportunities and constraints of early childhood, education, career, marriage, child-rearing and old age.

It is, perhaps, already clear why this approach to social mobility requires historical as well as sociological insight. Firstly, as suggested, individual lives are historically placed and only 'make sense' within this context. Secondly, a case study of individual social mobility that takes into account the constraints and opportunities of all the phases of the life cycle is, by definition, a study of now-elderly people whose lives were significantly affected by socio-economic developments which are rooted in the past. Thirdly, the institutions through which the individual passes during the life-cycle also change over time – they have their own histories. In short, the intersection of life cycle and the ever changing social institutions significantly affect life chances, outcomes and attitudes; it makes a difference when one is born.

SOCIAL MOBILITY: THE CASE OF CLERICAL WORKERS

The decision to study women ex-clerical workers, born around the time of World War I, was an obvious one. It was, as already mentioned, necessary to select women who had passed through most stages of the life-cycle; at the same time the expansion of educational opportunities and white collar work for women after World War I meant that this generation of women were quite likely to have had a better education and broader occupational choices than their parents. This paper concentrates on a particular sub-group within the broad heading 'clerical workers'.[3]

This sub-group consisted of women who had been clerical grade civil servants during some part of the years between 1925 and 1940. There were several reasons why this sub-group was selected for a more detailed case study. Firstly, I knew, and knew of, several women who had been civil servants between the wars and had formed the impressionistic view that they had been socially mobile into the service and that this part of their life-cycle had been very significant in terms of social identity. Secondly, the Civil Service was and is a record keeping institution, making it relatively easy to discover explicit accounts of employment policy and practice, an important consideration since, as discussed, part of the objective of the study was to explore the interaction between individuals and institutions.

The women were recruited through the good offices of the local Civil Service Fellowship[4] and a letter in 'Woman's Realm' magazine, which asked women who had been civil servants to contact the researcher. This prompted about 40 replies, including long descriptive letters about life in the service, which proved very valuable. The twelve women who were interviewed had all been selected for the Civil Service via competitive open examinations and were a relatively homogeneous group.

They were the daughters of small business or artisan fathers and mothers who had been in domestic service before marriage. The parents were all educated to elementary standard and had left school by 13 or 14. None of the families was well off and several were definitely hard up; nevertheless, the families were not at the extremes of poverty suffered by some families during the inter-war period. Importantly, all of the women had been born into small families; all, except one, were either only children or one of two female siblings, and this made possible a family investment of time and money – and personal support – that could not have been spread over a (more typical) family of four or more children.

This was not the only characteristic they had in common, there were other aspects of their childhood that facilitated their entry into secondary education – their first move into a middle-class institution. Firstly, all the families were self-consciously 'respectable' and some also had traces of the 'sunken middle class' also discerned by Jackson and Marsden (1962) among a later generation of grammar-school boys from working-class backgrounds. All of them feel, on reflection, that they were a cut above other families in the neighbourhood:

> Our family was a bit better off than the others really, mum was very houseproud, I think she got her standards from being in service.

> My mother was a skilled woman in a domestic sort of way and, well, I think, if anything, we were a bit, sort of, a bit higher class than the average sort of person to be quite honest. My father was a very intelligent man, though, as I say, I don't know what he did in the early days. (This father was nearly blind and did caretaking jobs).

> My mother didn't gossip or stand talking to people, partly because, I think, my mother's father was an engineer so, in a sense, she'd come from a more educated background, not necessarily financially so. I rather gather that her father was – that he squandered his money away.

Most of the mothers had been in service before marriage, and, indeed, this is what one would expect; in 1881, 80 per cent of all employed women were in occupations associated with the domestic sphere. These mothers were not entirely typical however. Those who had been in service had been employed in rather grand households and had achieved considerable success within the limitations of a career in domestic service:

> (mother) had been a cook in various large establishments, she worked for the First Lord of the Admiralty at one time, so she had a responsible sort of job; she had reached a pinnacle really . . . She thought she was superior, no doubt about that, she was in charge of the kitchen maids, they had to obey her, she was very young (25) to have a position like that.

> Over a period of years she went from job to job, until gradually she went up, so finally, when she was married, she was actually a cook in a very, you know, substantial household. That was the usual thing that happened to girls, and, really, you were lucky to be taken into service in a big house, because you were fed and, perhaps, had a higher standard of living than you did in your own home.

It has been argued that domestic service was not likely to lead to upward mobility (Higgs, 1986) since most domestics were employed as 'maids of all work' in modest middle-class homes. These mothers, however, had acquired high level domestic skills and had the drive to put them into practice in their own households. These rather formidable women set about creating a life style to match their aspirations, in spite of very modest incomes. This was, in part, manifested in the most rigorous cleaning and scrubbing of all surfaces, inanimate and animate. Clean net curtains, scrubbed doorsteps, blackleading and endless laundry figure in the memories of all the women. However, this is a well documented aspect of 'respectable' working class life of the inter-war period, and in many ways it demonstrated respectability to the outside world. But these particular households had other characteristics that differentiated them from others in a similar economic position.

The women were, as young girls, brought up to be accomplished as well as clever; musical instruments, elocution lessons or painting lessons, were part of rather genteel childhood experiences:

> I started to learn to play the piano when I was seven, I really pursued it, mind you I was made to do it in the early days . . .
>
> And, of course, when I started to play the violin, I was nine years old when I started, she was very anxious for me to play the violin; she was always very proud of the fact I played the fiddle and used to swank to other people about the fact that I could play.

Education

Mothers were also responsible for educational decisions. They chose the 'best' elementary schools and they encouraged the girls through their early years at school and into the 'scholarship' examinations at eleven. All of the women passed competitive examinations into old-foundation girls' grammar schools or (two cases) into new county secondary schools. This access to secondary education differentiated the women both from their parents' experience and that of their elementary school peers; secondary schooling represented the first step towards a more middle-class social position.

The educational system that the women experienced was not the same system that their parents had entered a quarter century earlier, and it had changed again by the time their children were of school age. When the women were at school (in the 1920s) the usual experience was an elementary school education until age fourteen, then entry into the labour market. Since this was the majority experience, as it had been the generation before, people of all levels of intellectual ability and talent 'were only elementary educated' (Mrs C. about her mother), and most jobs did not require a higher level of basic education. The careers that did require secondary education as a condition of entry were, therefore, a middle-class preserve and carried high social status. By the 1920s it was *possible* for poorer children to acquire the credential of a secondary education by passing a competitive 'scholarship' examination for a free or subsidised place. But the number of such free places remained small and fewer than 10 per cent of elementary children were able to move to the middle-class system.

For the women in this study, being 'scholarship girls' at grammar or independent schools had considerable consequences at the time, and at later stages in their lives. Their position at school was ambiguous. They had both academic superiority (they were 'the brains' of the school) and social disadvantage; they had a very deferential attitude towards the school and their teachers and, at the same time, had high standing in the family because of their achievement in passing the scholarship. Mrs H. describes her school, which was an 'old foundation' grammar school where the majority were fee-paying girls who were:

> . . . daughters of members of parliament, people like that; it was a beautiful school like an old house with a lovely garden. The private girls were all better off of course, you know, more middle class, I was definitely working class, my stockings were well darned, my knickers well patched. I had a uniform though, we made the blouses, I had a school hat and hat band so I was lucky. There was a silver badge, I had one eventually, but not to start with. When I was

almost leaving I had a bicycle, on the never-never of course.

Mrs H. was a talented artist (it is still her major activity) and this somewhat protected her from the class-based distinctions within her school:

> I got on well with all the girls, but I could draw. I could do that one thing well, and I enjoyed that.

Mrs B. was more aware of the class differences and did not associate very much with the fee-paying girls:

> There were three grades at the school 'A', 'B' and 'C'; all the 'A' grade were scholarship girls and the 'B' and 'C' paid so we were the minority, we had diplomat's daughters there you see, that sort of thing.
>
> K. S.: How did you get on with the fee-paying girls?
>
> They more or less left you alone. One girl said to me 'So you're a scholarship girl?' and I said, 'Yes' and she said, 'Oh dear' and I said, 'What do you mean?' and she said, 'I don't think this school likes scholarship girls' and I said, 'Yes they do, because we have to sign to say we'll stay until we're sixteen, they know they're going to get our fees'. I was so annoyed. Anyway, *we* were the brains of the school, of course we didn't have the same clothes as they did, no money or anything like that. But I was grateful, if you can understand, I was grateful for the opportunity, though I never felt I was on their level even though I went to their school.

This tension between academic superiority and social disadvantage, which Mrs B. articulates here, was a characteristic, to some degree, of the secondary school careers of all the women. None of them saw their education as a 'right', but rather as a privilege earned by academic ability; they all had – and have – a deferential attitude towards the institutions that selected them; a characteristic they retained when selected (also by competitive examination) for the Civil Service in their late teens. And, whatever their doubts about the fee-paying girls, none of the women had reservations about the schools. They were all very impressed by the education they were offered.

> Oh, it was a wonderful school, it really was! Well, in those days what we considered was the academic side of it, that's what we went for really. We had good teachers, all women of course, but if you wanted to learn, you could, they were there. If you wanted to consult them after school they would do that, if you were puzzled. As I say, I thought it a privilege to go there.

The teachers did not, however, offer much inspiration, or even information, about the working world and life after school. The only profession on offer was teaching, and the only alternative to that was to work in an office. None of the women looked to either alternative with any enthusiasm and some would have liked to continue studying. Mrs H., for example, was encouraged by her teacher to go to art school, Mrs B. wanted to be an analytical chemist and Mrs T. wanted to be a translator. However, none of the women came from the families that could afford a further investment in their daughter's education – they had already been at school for two years longer than their elementary school peers – and they knew that they would have to find a job and start contributing to the family income.

For each of the women the decision to enter for the Civil Service entrance examination was made by, or influenced by, their parents:

> He (father) made the choice for both of us (her sister too), he entered us for the Writing Assistants examination, and in those days, you did what you were told in practically every case. I had to take a one term's course at Clarks College to learn shorthand and book keeping, which I didn't like one little bit, but then the results came out (of the writing assistants examination – she passed) and I was shunted off to the Post Office Savings Bank.

> . . . he jibbed a bit at paying for shorthand and typing, he thought that if that was all I was going to do it was a waste of a long education, but he was quite happy when I got there (into the service), it was a good job for a girl in those days.

'Those days' were the late 1920s and early 1930s, a time when many skilled male workers and craftsmen were insecurely employed; the fathers of most of the women went through some periods of unemployment or under-employment, so it is not surprising that they encouraged their daughters to take up a position in the expanding clerical labour market. And the Civil Service, in particular, offered security, a respectable job and a moderately good salary – it was indeed a good job for a girl.

Working Life: The Civil Service

The women found themselves in an ambiguous situation when they became lower grade servants of the State. On the one hand they had been specifically selected through very competitive examinations, and were in more secure, higher status jobs than almost any of their female peers; on the other hand, within the Civil Service itself they were, as one of them described herself, 'the lowest form of human life'.

In fact their position in the Civil Service reflected the general position of women in the wider occupational structure; they filled the routine semi-skilled positions at the bottom of the hierarchy. The Writing Assistant class into which most of them were recruited was an all female 'dogsbody' grade, working mostly in large segregated offices doing routine clerical tasks generated by the larger departments, especially the Post Office and Post Office Savings Bank. All of the Writing Assistants (later called Clerical Assistants) were eventually promoted to 'Clerical Officer' a process that took about seven years of time-serving. Two of the women entered the Service as Clerical Officers, a grade also open to men.

Although, as suggested above, 'being a civil servant' was more significant for these women than 'doing clerical work', it is worthwhile to examine, briefly, what kind of tasks were considered suitable for grammar-school girls who were entering the white collar labour market in the 1920s and 1930s, the first generation of 'ordinary' girls to do so in large numbers.

Mrs L. was appointed as a Writing Assistant within the Post Office Savings Bank:

> It was a big place, well it had three thousand people there,

> it was the headquarters you see, it was four floors with big windows, bright offices; you could just see the end of the room from the other, a huge place. Of course in those days every error counted against you – you couldn't do it now – and also you were on a year's probation and could be turfed out after a year, so it was quite disciplined, but you see it was the depression and you hung on to your jobs . . .

Nor did the women recruited into other departments have more challenging jobs; two of the women recall doing simple accounts seated at a moving table – a conveyor belt bringing their work to them. They are, in old age, puzzled by the docility of their youthful selves, but at the same time they take pride in the fact that they 'put up with it'. They were over-qualified for the work they were doing; this was organised on the principles of Rational Management with work broken into simple routine tasks. Their work, in fact, had much in common with that of their peers in mass production industry; however, their prestige as white collar civil servants was not much affected by the actual nature of their work.

What the Civil Service offered these clever Grammar School girls was 'middle-class' status and respectability in exchange for docile, loyal and concientious time-serving. This bargain was sealed at the end of the women's service, when they retired into marriage, with a 'dowry' provided by the service in lieu of pension. This gratuity was paid to women when they resigned to get married, thus making them rather a good catch for an aspiring man. It was paid at the rate of one month's pay for each year of service, but not exceeding twelve month's pay. It was not finanically worthwhile for a woman to stay in the service beyond 12 years as the gratuity would cease to accumulate beyond this. After 12 years a woman would get only a proper return on her pension contributions if she stayed in the service to retirement, and stayed single. The 12 year limit was thus a subtle pressure on female civil servants to have short careers and to leave before they became too expensive to the State.

This regulation, and the Marriage Bar (which was not formally removed until after World War II), combined to reinforce the women's perception of their employment as a temporary phase. However, in spite of this, the years the women spent in the service were a critical part of their life cycle. They formed friendships with their fellow female clerks which, in many cases, still continue nearly 50 years later, and together they shared a common identity and social life. At the same time their relationships with parents and siblings declined in importance, and only one maintained close connections with the church of her youth.

This stage of their life was particularly important in the establishment of their new, more middle-class identity, an identity that certainly owed more to their fellow clerical civil servants than to the households in which they were brought up and still lived. They were forming themselves into a new, homogeneous 'class of their own', as young, well educated, career women, and this was not affected by the expectation that they would eventually leave the service for domestic life. Indeed it was their career experience that later influenced their ideas about suitable husband material and the nature of their subsequent married life. This identification with each other was strengthened by shared leisure activities after office hours, and the impression they had that they were '. . . all the same'. The actual differences in background were obscured by their common experience as ex-grammar school girls and civil servants. In some ways their experience in the service reproduced their rather ambiguous social position as clever scholarship girls; they were with, but not truly of, the middle-class establishment.

Finding, and Marrying, a Suitable Man

The business of meeting men, of finding a suitable husband, became something of a priority as the women approached 30. None of the women was anything like 'man-mad' or, apparently particularly interested in sex:

> In those days it wasn't sex, sex, all the time, we didn't really think about it.

> You'd be really loose if you . . . really distasteful, it really was . . . no more than kissing, but nothing like that (sex). I'm sure I'd have nothing to do with that. I'm sure that any of the girls I knew, I'm sure none of them would have had

> pre-marital sex, mind you I think as the War came along things got a bit looser. I'm sure that Stan and I were tempted, very tempted, for one thing you didn't know if you were going to see each other again.

This last speaker was a war-time bride, and her comments about changing sexual mores after the outbreak of war can be put in the context of other changes experienced by unmarried women at that time, when initiative came to be valued over docility, even for women. For the pre-war working girls, however, 'standards' were not being questioned. Certainly questions about the qualities they looked for in a man did not lead to comments about physical attraction, love or sex. To a question about 'desirable qualities' in a husband they replied:

> Somebody like oneself, the same educational background, say local government or the Civil Service, someone steady, with a similar attitude and outlook (Mrs M. married a Civil Servant).

> Well, we expected men to be tidy and well spoken, but not necessarily to share the interests of the girl's group – ballet and music and so on. (It was also necessary) . . . that he had a job that the two of you could exist on, because, in those days you left the office.

> I think you went out with men of your own class, more or less, yes, say office people; one I used to know worked for a solicitor, another was an optician, you see? Yes, and there were people from the Post Office, we met them, and my friend's brother, he was a jeweller in Regent Street, he had friends and we met them. They had good positions, we had all nice, what I call nice, people, they were decent people with decent manners and dressing, men with good steady jobs, with nice clean habits, clean hands (laugh) you see?

This, then, was not a youthful fancy for romance and a white wedding dress, but a desire to settle down in a nice house to a proper domestic career; and they were prepared to wait and save to achieve this objective.

> Well, that's what I wanted, more than anything, to be honest, to get married and have children. I loved children,

as you gather, that was my aim in life really.

> Given the choice we would rather have a short career and then get married, but short of that they (sic) would settle for a long career, settled in a secure job.

> Now there was a funny thing that happened then, we used to become engaged, then we'd save terribly hard for three or four years which you wouldn't dream of doing now . . . we saved hard to have nice homes to start off with – we all had a bottom drawer, it was called. It was such a thrill too, I can tell you (laugh). And the dowry was a great help too, mine was £169 if I remember.

> Once you were engaged, which gave you two years, you bought all your linen and bedding and curtaining, and my husband helped with those . . . Yes, we had made all our satin underwear, French knickers and petticoats and night-gowns, that is what you did in evenings in the winter and we made embroidered pictures for the wall, that sort of thing. . . . We had all our own furniture – we bought it with the dowry, it was about £100 – a three piece suite for £17, a dining suite for £17, a bedroom suite for £32, carpets for £3.10.0p and £4.

The dowry was, as we have seen, a gratuity in lieu of pension rights and was part of the regulations requiring a woman to resign on her marriage.[5] Nevertheless, none of the women called it a gratuity, indeed, they spoke of the dowry as if it was a gift, a bonus from their employer. None had it in mind that this 'dowry' was, in fact, based on their own contributions to the pension fund, nor that it was 'in lieu' of a pension. By accepting the 'dowry' the women forfeited any future entitlement to a pension. Two of the women had cause to regret this when, in later years, they once again took up employment in the public sector.

This is not to suggest that the women were ignorant about the actual nature of the gratuity, they had all worked out how much they were 'owed', based on a number of years service; nor is it clear where the term 'dowry' came from; but it is clear that the *idea* of the dowry not only reflected contemporary opinion about the proper role of women, but also perpetuated it.

These women seem to have happily abandoned their desks for the cosy homes which were made possible by the gratuity. In this way the gratuity was indeed a dowry, enabling the women civil servants, who for the most part had no expectations or income from their families, to start married life on a firm financial footing. Certainly none of the women felt any resentment at being retired so early. On the contrary:

> It didn't actually occur to me, or I'm sure to other people I worked with, that one should keep on a job, a woman I mean, after she got married. You felt running your house, properly, was required, and you didn't need a job after that, only if you were very poor, it was always running a house you see.

None of the women would have disagreed at all with this view of the Marriage Bar. Certainly the first response of these women to their new role of housewife was very positive. They felt pleasure in being independent from their parents, were relieved to get away from all the relentless travelling, and had a certain naive joy in 'showing-off' to their unmarried, less fortunate, workmates.

> Oh, yes, it was marvellous, I think that's what you wanted to do, to run your home, I always feel a little resentful of people who say you're a cabbage if you don't go to work.

> Usually you'd try, after you were married, to have some of your office friends down, to show off really, wasn't it? – your nice new home and all the nice things in it, you know (laugh) they'd think how lucky you are, hasn't she done well for herself (laugh). I did have a nice home as a matter of fact, all absolutely spot-new.

Mrs S. also tried to explain what 'the girls' thought about the obligations and duties of marriage, incidentally revealing the underlying attitudes that made the Marriage Bar a non-issue for these women.

> We all thought along the same lines, if you were getting married you were taking on another job, it was a job to you, and the job involved cooking, cleaning, baking and di da di da di da . . . in the house, the 1001 jobs to do in the house. It was all part and parcel of the job you've taken on and

> therefore it's up to you to do the job to the best of your ability, in return you had a home, a nice home, and you added to it, you discussed things with your husband, you got things . . . that's what I considered I ought to be doing and, really and truly, that ought to be absolutely foremost, as far as I was concerned at that time, and everything else should come second.

This mixture of description and polemic sums up the way all the women felt as they embarked upon their second, and 'proper', career as domestic unwaged labour.

Domestic Careers

The women, then, entered domestic life with enthusiasm. They saw themselves as having finally arrived at their proper and most fulfilling stage in life. Marriage had rescued them from the pressures of tedious clerical work and from a domestic life (in the natal home) over which they had little or no control. No wonder they, paradoxically, saw the move to financially dependent housekeeping as a significant move towards independence.

> We married ones never wanted to go back and do what they were doing in the office; we wouldn't have swapped with them (laugh). To own your own home was a kind of status you see . . . on marriage you changed your status and changed your life completely.

And, not surprisingly, these well educated civil servants did not intend to replicate the segregated 'old fashioned' marriages of their parents; these were to be marriages based on rational household management and 'different but equal' conjugal relationships. In short, the sort of marriage prescribed by, and for, the middle class.

For all of them, though, the war interrupted their plans, and those already married were unexpectedly returned to the public sphere for the duration. For those still unmarried, there were new opportunities within the Civil Service as women were recruited and promoted to cover for the absent men.

Three of the married, but childless, women were called up and returned to the Civil Service. Unlike the women who were still single at the outbreak of war, the married women were allocated routine low-skill tasks of a similar or lower level than they had achieved during their earlier career. For them the war did not have a radical effect on their lives, but was rather an experience to be endured until they were able to return to domestic life. However, for the women who were still single the war opened up opportunities for career advancement, and two reached the high level of Executive Grade:

> Normally to become an Executive officer you had to have been to university, there was an exam, but, really and truly, you needed the university education. But during the war, when all the men had gone you see, you could get it by promotion. And I got it by promotion.
>
> When my first promotion came it was a great joy – it all of a sudden became much more interesting, it was particularly challenging, you see, you were dealing with items in short supply and there was a lot of difficulties. But you just worked it out in your own way – this was rather fun actually.

The others found themselves in different and more interesting niches within the service.

These war time careers will not be discussed in detail, but it is worth considering the options facing the women whose careers developed during this period. They knew that their exciting working life would not survive a return to peace-time conditions and, in any case, none of them aspired to the life of a single career woman. Although the marriage bar was dropped after the war, married women were dis-established and offered work at a lower level, a 'dogsbody' job. In any case none of them considered that being married was compatible with having a career. As for remaining single, that was an increasingly unattractive proposition. Three of the women had become the most significant breadwinners in their natal families, they were beginning to feel the obligation to remain at home permanently and the status of 'spinster daughter' was not one that had any appeal. Not surprisingly, they, too, chose marriage and a home of their own.

Briefly, all the women had their lives disrupted in some way by the war, although four of them saw their jobs enhanced as a result. However, it would be wrong to see any of the changes as long-term or as offering new choices to the young women involved. At the end of the war they still lived in a world that offered women either a career, mostly in segregated, dead end, 'women's jobs', or a 'normal life' as full time wife and mother. All the pressures, both personal and social, led them, and most other women of their generation, to choose the latter alternative.

The husbands of the women in the study were, more or less, what they had been looking for. All the men had been to grammar school, seven were in public service, one was an optician and one worked at the Stock Exchange. Between them the women had 15 children, of these children (born between 1940–53) 13 passed the 11-plus examination to Grammar School and seven continued to University (which none of their parents had done).

The later stages of the life cycle – child-rearing, middle age and old age and retirement – will not be discussed in this paper; these stages can, in any case, be seen as a consolidation of the middle class position of early married life.

CONCLUSION

This case study of the lives of some women civil servants has tested the proposition that women 'belong' in the class structure, sociologically as well as socially. It has examined the ways in which these daughters of artisan fathers and domestic-servant mothers were able to cross from the respectable working class of their childhoods into the securely middle-class position of their adult lives. It has also suggested the importance of broader socio-historical change in the individual biography, and the need to consider the factors that facilitate (or hinder) social mobility.

As children in small, respectable working-class families, the women were well trained in the virtues of orderliness, thrift and the presentation of a respectable image in society.

By the time they transferred to secondary school at eleven they were, objectively as well as in their own estimation, moving onward from the social standing of early childhood. At secondary school they had a well defined role as the 'brains' of the school. They also learned that they were at least as clever (if not more clever) than the middle-class girls who were the traditional pupils of such schools. It was at this stage in their life-cycle that they started to develop a social position based on cleverness, ability to pass examinations and being 'selected' by middle class institutions.

Their entrance into the Civil Service (at that time still a prestigious employer) was also based on these characteristics. Once in the Service, middle-class standards of appearance, way of speaking and leisure activities prevailed, even though the actual work was routine and low-skilled. The women were creating and confirming a middle-class identity *in their own right* and prior to marriage to similarly placed men.

It was, in short, by their own efforts, by being suitable candidates for selection, by conforming to expectations and, at the same time, maintaining a strong sense of their own worth, that they successfully established themselves in the middle-class spheres of secondary education, the Civil Service and companionate marriage.

This focused case study has demonstrated how a particular, homogeneous cohort of women established their own social identity within the constraints of the social institutions through which they passed. At the same time it has tested a qualitative methodological approach to the issue of placing women in studies of class and social mobility. It has shown that women do, actively, contribute to their own class identity and must, therefore, be taken into account in such studies.

NOTES

The above chapter is based on an unpublished Ph.D. thesis: Social Mobility in the Life Cycle of Some Women Clerical Workers (1988), held at the University of Essex.

1. This is rather similar to the approach of Glen Elder (1981) who suggests that even 'personality' is likely to be historically

and cohort specific. He further suggests that the development of identity or notions of 'self' are closely related to the conjunction of life-cycle and historical events and developments: 'a historical perspective locates social structure, personality and actors in specific temporal contexts, and adds a processual dynamic to their interrelationship' (page 86).

2. The alternative – that they do not have a social position – is surely a solecism. In any case, Goldthorpe does not claim that women have no social position, rather that this is mediated through the male heads of households.
3. The early stages of the research were based on interviews with women who had been in clerical work between the wars; however, this group proved to be much more heterogeneous than had been predicted, and the detailed qualitative work concentrated on the smaller group of ex-civil servants.
4. It is particularly significant that these women *still* identified themselves as civil servants more than 40 years after they had retired to get married.
5. Samuel Cohn (1985) suggests that these formal marriage bars, or tenure bars, were of particular benefit to large scale employers, ensuring a high turnover of low level staff and the replacement of older expensive employees with lower-paid new recruits. As suggested, the division of labour within the service meant that 'experience' was not a particular valued characteristic in the lower grades.

REFERENCES

COHN, S. (1985), *The Process of Occupational Sex-Typing* (Philadelphia: Temple University Press).

ELDER, G. (1981), 'History and the life course', in D. Bertaux (ed.), *Biography and Society, the Life History Approach to the Social Sciences*, Sage studies in International Sociology, no. 23.

GOLDTHORPE, J. H. (1980), *Social Mobility and Class Structure in Modern Britain* (Oxford University Press).

JACKSON, B. and MARSDEN, D. (1962), *Education and the Working Class* (Harmondsworth: Penguin); revised edn 1966.

Part III
Sociology, History and the Question of Gender

11 'Adam spoke first and named the orders of the World': Masculine and Feminine Domains in History and Sociology[1]

Leonore Davidoff

Since the early 1970s there has been a move for social historians to free themselves from social science models and, making use of their own vast accumulation of social description, to generate their own theories (Zunz, 1985, p. 100). Embedded in this critique is a revulsion against unlinear, 'Big Bang' or 'before and after' models, whether modernisation or Marxist. Attention is drawn to a more holistic approach, the methodological metaphor is the 'single web of meaning' among innumerable variables.

This attitude has been accompanied by a slow but definite move from the liaison with sociology towards more humanistic, 'discursive' models culminating in the recent triumph of cultural history as part of a wider intellectual literary turn (Newton, 1989). However, it would be a sad mistake if in this climate sociologists allowed a rift to open between their subject and the practices of historical analysis, if not with historians themselves. For sociology can still look for enrichment by taking seriously the attention to wholes, to dealing with time, with relationships as process which are the stuff of responsible social history. And historians, however much they may be turning in on themselves, do recognise that the issues they choose to confront, if not the concepts they use, are ineluctably tied to concerns of present society.

There clearly remain important areas of common ground between the two disciplines. For example, the social construction of identity is an enduring theme of sociology as well as a vividly practiced concern of historians. This construction is itself a process of narrative, for there is really no other way for its expression except as the unfolding of a process which must, ultimately, be told as a story. But, contrary to much of our modern liberal inheritance, the story of identity is not neutral or disembodied, its construction is always gendered.

Gender categories generate social relations which, partially at least, constitute all other social relations and activities. As a basic axis of society, gender forms the social as well as linguistic air we breathe. A focus on gender illuminates the relationship between history and sociology and confirms Philip Abrams' dictum that in some fundamental respect, the two disciplines are trying to do the same thing and are employing the same logic of explanation to do so (Abrams, 1982, p. ix).

Our world has been constructed along gender lines at every level. Our everyday language, images and expressions carry a tint of oppositional masculinity and femininity but so, too, do concepts used in scholarly analysis. How can this fundamental pattern, now haltingly and laboriously uncovered by feminist thinkers, have been hidden for so long? A simplified answer to such a complicated question must include the fact that sexual categories are built in terms of super- and sub-ordination. It is the agency given to the powerful which has written the scores within which we produce our harmonies – and even our discordancies. Gendered ideas become themselves instruments of control over resources, over people and things and, especially, over the drawing of boundaries: between people, between things and between people and things. Those in positions of control have had no reason to look behind generalised 'given' categories, so often categories based on covert masculine identification. They have no motivation to seek out the supplementary, shadowy presences without which not only their working concepts but their whole cosmology would melt away (Scott, 1989).

Simmel long ago compared the power position between modern men and women to that of master and slave:

> One of the privileges of the master [is] that he does not always need to think about the fact that he is the master . . .

> there is no doubt that the woman loses a conscious sense of her being a female much more rarely than holds true for the man and his being as a male (Oaks, 1984, p. 103).

The derivation of the word 'gender', its relation to 'gens' or orders, indicates its centrality to classification systems depending on notions of difference. Gender, therefore, operates as a fundamental organising category, but also at the level of social relations and the structure of personal identity (Haraway, 1987). Given this range, it would be surprising if ideas about gender could be contained within a single disciplinary framework. On the other hand, feminist thinkers have recently turned from striving to build a monolithic grand theory and now emphasise the historically specific. In practice, historical research has been one of the most fruitful areas of feminist analysis (Gerson and Peiss, 1985; Stacey and Thorne, 1985).

There seem to be a number of reasons for this. As we have seen, recent social history has rejected static categorising; in particular it has abjured dichotomous models in favour of greater complexity. When historians have avoided functionalist explanations this leaves open a space to consider the role of the powerful and challenges to that power. It is perhaps easier to observe in the past how the living through of gender relationships is a process of negotiation, of contradiction between thought systems and between these systems and consequent behaviours. Like anthropologists, historians can reflect on their own categories when seen in an unfamiliar context. But more than anthropologists, they can then observe how these categories have been inherited and reworked in their own society.

No matter what the discipline, from the very nature of its subject matter, all feminist scholarship has tended to be more self conscious about the 'object of analysis', to break the subject/object dichotomy of the social, indeed all sciences (Signs, 1987). Feminist thinkers have had to live with a certain *inherent instability* in their categories (Harding, 1986). They have had to pay particular attention to boundaries, both the permeability and the limits of categories. In particular they have stressed the shifting definitions of identities, seeing the individual self as constantly reconstructed in various contexts and by various relationships. (de Lauretis,

1986). For example, family, marriage, kinship, sexuality and gender are seen as mutually constructed but also understood as drawn from a range of 'cultural domains', including the political/jural and economic (Landes, 1984). In turn these 'public spheres' cannot be understood without recognising their grounding in gender relations.

As if grasping these hidden interconnections were not arduous enough, the picture is further complicated by the fact that gender categories are so often 'embodied'. That is, they make use of putative characteristics of the body for signification, they use a language of the body. For example, building on the older notion of a 'body politic', literate English Victorians constantly spoke of their society as Head (man), Heart (women) and Hands (ungendered workers). Such conceptualisations carry powerful messages; gender and power are experienced through and by the body not only in appearance but also in stance, gait and even the physical space occupied (Connell, 1987).

Coming to terms with the flux and variation in gender relationships has not come easily. It has to be understood that boundaries and locations can shift, yet a system of masculine superordination remains intact. For example, it has begun to be recognised that the shift of women into or out of wage work has made only marginal differences to their life chances since the structure and meaning of wage work itself is already gendered.

Unfortunately, feminists ourselves have not always followed the logic of these insights. Understandably, most started where women were found – in the family, kinship, questions about sexuality – in other words, what was already defined as the private sphere. But in continuing to concentrate on these locations, masculine privilege as unproblematic, as somehow exempt from determination by gender, has been perpetuated (Flax, 1987). To put it at its starkest formulation, in our concentration on making clear that women's connection with the private, the identification of women with the 'natural', has been socially constructed, we have risked the nonsense of allowing men to be regarded as 'naturally cultural', as 'naturally rational' beings (Mathieu, 1978).[2]

On the contrary, masculinity, in particular full adult

masculine status, has always been defined in relation to women (as well as in relations between different categories of men). Far from being the ungendered norm, a whole range of structures, ideas and individual attributes in the economic, political, religious, moral as well as domestic domains have been gendered territories staked out and fiercely contested, a process in which the creation and maintenance of masculine identity has often played a central role (Morgan, 1987; Hearn, 1987). Masculinity, like femininity, comes in a variety of contradictory forms. For example, the manliness of the early nineteenth-century middle class embraced the man so easily moved to tears while simultaneously acting as household head and as 'fit and proper person' to hold public office. In the words of a contemporary, a 'real manliness as consisting of all that is pure and true and strong and tender' (Davidoff and Hall, 1987, p. 110).

It is in historical examples such as these that the links between categories of 'men' and 'women', 'masculinity' and 'feminity' and their intermeshing with other categories of class, ethnicity and race will be discerned. The effort to conceive gender as an abstract logical grid, without a notion of historical process, is doomed for the categories are only worked out during that process. The links, even at the conceptual level, have to be considered as emergent in social practices, gender groups 'as they are constituted and as they constitute themselves' (Connell, 1983, p. 37).

One of the most important of such constitutions, was the seventeenth-century formulation which cast sexual difference as the basis of political definition, crediting a masculine capacity to active agency with political rights including rights over the persons of others (Pateman, 1989). Here it was not so much that women were omitted entirely as that they were placed at the farthest end of a continuum of sociality. (Riley, 1988, p. 15). This idea of masculine potency and enactment was central to the transformations of the seventeenth and eighteenth centuries and forms the heritage of both history and sociology today. Building on that heritage, even the assumed division between abstract concepts and accounts of the everyday has its roots in a gendered epistemology (Caplan, 1988; Smith, 1988; Stinchcombe, 1984).

In this chapter, in brief and schematic form, I will look first at a series of concepts related by a core of unacknowledged, gendered assumptions which came to dominate the thought and institutions of powerful literate élites in Western thought from the seventeenth to the nineteenth century. But I also call attention to alternative voices which have been almost completely silenced in our twentieth century inheritance.

The final section situates these thought patterns in the early and mid-nineteenth century, the period when sociology was being formed as a discipline. In bringing out the centrality of gender to this story, I shall deliberately concentrate on the moulding of masculine identities since, paradoxically, this has been the unnamed premise on which the whole saga has rested.

A number of related ideas and practices had emerged from pre-nineteenth century developments and centred in the concepts of *rationality, the individual, the market* and *property*. To each of these I will briefly turn, keeping in mind that such ideas and their practical implementation were embedded in a prior culture, a culture already deeply imbued with gender differentiations.

The sixteenth and seventeenth centuries had witnessed a gradual shift from the idea that good or bad fortune, white witches and wizards or evil agencies, resided in people to a realisation that what befell individuals and groups might be due to environmental effects. Here is found the 'nascent statistical sense' which saw patterns in seemingly random behaviours (Thomas, 1971, p. 656).

This emerging objectivity in scientific, commercial and other bodies of knowledge, claimed a universality, but as Simmel has said, in actual historical configurations the idea of rationality was masculine throughout (Oaks, 1984). The dichotomous categories of science and nature, of rational thought and morality/spirituality flooded the world view of literate European élites, oppositions which were used and transformed in many contexts over the next two centuries but whose dualistic form remained.

Rational expertise as in science, medicine and the legal system gradually became the major source of intellectual authority using a statement of universal laws to draw ever further from what was seen as the ignorance of 'Old Wives Tales' (sic), while in the economic sphere, the rational calculation of income was torn away from the moral community.

The effort to maintain such dualities raised many contradictions. One of the most important was the jostling together of an idea of the feminine as both natural *and* moral in its role as 'other' to the masculine educated knower (Jordanova, 1989).[3] The feminine became identified with all that enlightened knowledge had left behind as well as the object of scientific enquiry as in a feminised concept of 'Nature' (Brown and Jordanova, 1981). But men, too, were both a-moral operators in the economy *and* represented the highest form of morality as free citizens of the polity.

In these oppositions, adult rational masculinity withdrew from the body. And with its disembodiment went a casting off of sexuality so that by the early nineteenth century, only women were constituted as sexual beings. Indeed in Victorian parlance, women were THE SEX. As we shall see, men's sexuality was then reincarnated in a naturalised biology (Bock, 1989).

Max Weber, the greatest student of rationality, who was more insightful, if more troubled, about such matters, stated the opposition with its implied gender connotations:

> Rational ascetic alertness, self-control and methodical planning of life are threatened most by the peculiar irrationality of the sexual act which is ultimately and uniquely unsusceptible to rational organization (Weber, 1968, vol. II, p. 603).

The importance of meanings assigned to the body can be followed into the political arena. The eighteenth-century tradition of civic humanism was concerned with obligations of citizens to a political community and implied the ultimate defence of that community through the ability to bear arms (Hont and Ignatieff, 1983). Such a contribution was, by deep seated custom, denied to women who were only recognised in a narrow inferior form as mothers, through the bearing of new citizens. As Carole Pateman argues, it was not the fact of physical birth which created this difference but rather that no recognition, no 'political significance', was given to this particular ability of women which men lacked (Pateman, 1988, p. 96).

The core idea associated with the drive to rationality was *the individual*, the self conceived as the source of knowledge and meaning. It was only individuals who could enter into civil and commercial contracts; it was the individual, rational and free, who represented both political and moral authority. The individual, however, had by definition to focus on *difference*; individuality was predicated on the idea of a 'dichotomous other' which carried a covert dimension of power (Luhman, 1986). Down through the nineteenth century, the 'otherness' of designated non-individuals can be traced in the construction of class and racial categories as well as gender.

Rational individuals through their free status and power of knowledge were independent of other men's will or influence. And the public domain was defined by the presence of such individuals. That domain was now firmly also where 'the economy' was placed (Appleby, 1978). It must follow that the private domain would be where the category 'women' would be found. Nevertheless, the exact equation of the public with the masculine and the private with the feminine is too simplistic. Aside from other considerations, in both ideal and practice, men were able to move between both spheres, while in fact, many women glided into the public from time to time although their legitimacy was always questioned – note the term 'public women' or 'women of the streets' for prostitutes (Stacey, 1986).

The masculinity of the individual rested on the double meaning contained in the concept of *subject*. The subject could be an initiator, the subject who acts, but that actor needed a subject upon which to act, who was subjected to his authority. It is as if a man's self-fabricated subjecthood could only be attained at the cost of another – so often a feminine other's – subjection, 'of the realization of her nature in the private realm' (Landes, 1984, p. 29). Individuality implied mastery over others conceived as objects and dependants. Thus, the two meanings of subject were fractured along gender lines from the start.

It was above all within marriage that women's subjecthood was evident, both symbolically and in action. Married women, under the doctrine of *coveture* died a kind of civil death, losing any capacity for active agency in either civil or commercial life (Pateman, 1987; Davidoff and Hall, 1987).

By the 1820s when the term 'individualism' had come into

more general use, the idealised individual subject, the maker of the world, the genius and extramundane of the Romantic hero, was conceived as transcendant to particular milieu or even physical space. Framed in these terms, it was evident that he could only be masculine whether he appeared in 'ethical responsibility, civic identity, artistic representation or economic behaviour' (Heller and Wellberry, 1986, p. 1).

The core notion of independent integrity from subjection to the will of others is evident in concomitant discussions about the meaning of childhood and adult status. These discussions, too, reveal a deep unease about dealing with embodied, live human beings who are yet often treated as commodities (Jordanova, 1986). But whatever defined the individuality of the child, if a boy, time would bring full adulthood. Coleridge, significantly, claimed that the obverse of manliness was childishness (Conder, 1857). It may be of some significance that boys who spent their first five or six years wearing little skirts with leading strings tied to their shoulders were ceremonially 'breeched' into adult masculine garb when they passed out of the hands of mothers and nurses to masculine instructors while girls remained in petticoats all their years. Another group where dependence and gender were increasingly at odds was the nineteenth-century male domestic servant who displayed his master's authority in the ribbons on his shoulders and the colours of his livery. He had an image of being both sexually disruptive and effeminate; the bird in a cage (an image also applied to wives), he was derogated as 'the flunkey', opposite to the manly independent worker.[4]

From such examples it may be seen how ideas about dependence and gender ran deep into the consciousness, the mental maps, of the articulate and powerful. It was the collection of masculine personnas, the individuals inhabiting a range of domains, which made up the potential public of the community and the nation. Women, children, servants, the poor, were seen as having no community; they were mobile as they followed their natural masters.

But the relationship of gender to the concept of self was more complicated than in formulations of political theory or classical economics. Alongside the rational masculine individual, there followed a shadowy figure based on a different order of morality, an a-political, less bounded, self associated with personal emotion, parenthood and increasingly with notions of good taste. Its highest expression came to be the bodily incarnation of delicate Victorian womanhood. Exponents of classical liberalism and utilitarian thinkers alike were happy to leave the sphere of 'moral or domestic economy' to the natural order of the family or the still powerful order of religious institutions (Jaggar, 1984). Indeed it is within the radical proselytising language of the late eighteenth-century Evangelical movement that some of the most intense and revealing contradictions about the notion of self appear. An apotheosis of selflessness in the service of God demanded constant examinations *of* the self. Men, in particular, were under great tension between the demands of masculine self-assertion and agency on the one hand and the obliteration of self in the service of Jesus Christ. Religion embraced both public and private spheres (Davidoff and Hall, 1987, Part I).

By the early nineteenth century, however, the religious domain was firmly excluded from the ideas and institutions which above all validated the rational individual, that of *the market*. Before the seventeenth century, the periodic chaos and uncontrollability, the 'fickleness', of commercial transactions had at times been associated with femininity. But as more commercial links were made the key relationship between production and consumption was removed from everyday, literal market place transactions to more abstract forces and symbolic representations. Price rates and credit began to stand in for the *personal* contact of bargain and exchange of material goods (Appleby, 1978).

There was still much suspicion about the growing 'paper screen' of credit mechanisms and a fierce antagonism to the new breed of agents, 'factors' and money men who operated the system. Nevertheless, a conception of inexorable laws, cast more like the mechanical laws of gravity – rational, immutable and masculine, only open to interpretation and manipulation by the knowing subject – developed alongside institutions such as banks, stock exchanges, corn and other commodity markets. Such laws were predicated on quantitative properties in people as well as land and moveable goods; all included a common denominator of price. The assignment of a calculable value to more and more areas of lived experience grew with the increase in the circulation of money throughout the eighteenth century. Money was becoming a currency to measure all value but what could not (or what was ruled as should not) be so measured, what did not have a price, now seemed to have no value (Appleby, 1978). The private sphere was outside the possibility of such value; that was its attraction, even its justification (Davidoff, 1990). As for the woman embedded in the domesticity coming to epitomise the private domain, her 'price was above rubies'.[5]

The discussion of the market and its relationship to morality became – as it has remained to this day – a 'matter of continuing contention' (Gray, 1987, p. 178). As Robert Gray has shown, a-moral liberal economics remained tied to a moral social organicism, echoed in the struggle to divide production and consumption, commerce and philanthropy. These sets of gendered dualisms were evident in early nineteenth-century iconography of the pitiless employer exploiting the defenceless female factory child. Here, too, were echoes of earlier representations of exploitation in the sexual seduction of the poor rural maiden by the aristocratic rake, a convention often used in political struggles (Clark, 1987).

But adult married women, too, were seen as marginal to production (although of course they actually continued to act as 'producers'). They could not make binding contracts, could not sue or be sued. They could only enter the economic circuit as consumers or in the specialised 'business' of philanthropy (Prochaska, 1980; Ryan, 1981).

A world divided between production and consumption could not have been assembled without changes in the fundamental institutions of *property*. In the seventeenth century the conception of property began to shift from a set of rights to a thing. Rights to property were now seen as 'unlimited in amount, unconditional in the performance of social functions and freely transferable' (Sugarman and Rubin, 1924, p. 27). By the eighteenth century, absolute property, originally conceived as land, extended to the growing forms of liquid capital in real estate, stock and plant, bonds and shares.

Property relations, too, were firmly based on the idea of a rational, free individual acting through contract and thus by definition, excluding women. But women, via the family and as producers of male children, played a vital role as *conduits* of property. Despite their grave legal disabilities, they did have certain, highly circumscribed, rights as property owners.

Paradoxically, hiding behind the paper screen of credit and market mechanisms, female capital could circulate widely. However, by the nineteenth century, new forms of middle class property organisation, in particular the revamping of the aristocratic trust, made certain that women's property ownership remained primarily in the form of consumption, making 'women's active generation of lasting wealth virtually impossible' (Davidoff and Hall, 1987, p. 451). Since in Britain citizenship, the inclusion in the body politic, rested on an independence given by the ownership of property, these initial limitations created a built-in stumbling block to women's claims for full civil participation.

In popular mythology as well as legal conception, the single, individualistic and self-generated entrepreneur came to embody the man of property. These features became the essence of that quintessentially Victorian concept, 'Character'. His supporting network of female kin, their labour and the contribution of their property were obliterated (Davidoff and Hall, 1987, Part II).

The original formulation of a free, rational individual gave men one further vital capacity – property in their own labour and in their own skill. Indeed, this capacity highly coloured definitions of skill. Women, subordinated by personal bonds to father, brother or husband, could never alienate their labour in this way. To a certain extent they resembled paupers, those outside the labour contract. Within the growing sphere of waged labour, wages not only gave means of subsistence but were the 'true sign of exchange' between employer and workman (sic) rather than a relationship of master and servant (husband and wife) (Pateman, 1987; Davidoff, 1986).

The father, as value creator and as supporter/protector of his dependants, became the legitimate worker entitled to a 'family wage'. These capacities were used by working class men to override the powerful derogation of manual work.

The ambivalences as well as gendered overtones gathered around the concept of *work* in the Victorian period are evident in elaborate meanings ascribed to hands – their whiteness, smoothness or roughness and dirt – as visible signs of non-labour but also of femininity.[6] (Davidoff, 1983).

If we accept the premise that the individual self was based on difference, in particular sexual difference, then it follows that views of sexuality must also have changed during this period. From the limited attention paid to this question so far, it would seem that in the seventeenth century, it was recognised that both women and men had carnal appetites, but sexuality was not yet an entity divorced from other parts of life. Within this view, however, women were held to be especially sexually voracious, their appetites especially threatening (Porter, 1982). At the end of the eighteenth century an idea of 'sexuality' as a separate entity began to appear, yet 'sex expanded differently into the old fields of body and soul' for women than for men (Riley, 1988, p. 104).

By the beginning of the nineteenth century, lines of sexual identity were hardening. Femininity – at least for the literate classes – had evolved into a passionless maternity or weak sensuality, only roused by men's action. Such a view may seem to sit strangely with the positing of women as 'the sex'. The key to such an involuted construction lies in the disembodied masculinity we have been examining. Rational, individual man had become a 'Cartesian mind that happened to be located in biological matter in motion' (Harding, 1986, p. 661). Male sexuality was banished to a naturalised 'biological' realm and was often visualised as an hydraulic model or, in keeping with the dominant market metaphor, a spermatic economy of saving and spending (Barker-Benfield, 1973).

During the nineteenth century, for men, the location and timing of work processes and sexuality became more compartmentalised. Play and leisure were now the opposite of *occupation*, ergo, sexuality was equated with the frivolous, the childish, the feminine. Beauty and desire were confined to women's bodies and if promoted by men's bodies, such desire transmuted to a fascination with muscularity or romanticised physical strength.

The interplay of views about individuality, rationality and sexuality can be followed in the complicated tapestry of gendered meanings mapped out on the grid of the human body (Connell, 1987). Like the prototypical 'other', woman might not only be the tender heart to man's cool directing head, but sometimes was cast along with social outcasts such as paupers and gypsies in unsavoury nether regions below the waist (Himmelfarb, 1971).

The placing of these groups was also fixed in geographical space which took on bodily overtones. For example, there were the men-only public arenas of office and club as well as wealthy homes divided between lady's boudoir, gentleman's smoking room or study and the back passages or basements inhabited by servants (Davidoff, 1983; Davidoff, 1986b). Such subliminal imagery of hierarchy could arouse strong emotions of power and desire, repugnance and fascination, which can be sensed in the intricate social metaphors of dirt and pollution which exude from so many Victorian texts (Stallybrass and White, 1986). Beyond even this shadowy realm of symbol and image which reflected, but also sometimes fractured, the conception of rational individuality, there were echoes of other voices telling other stories or reworking elements of the dominant narrative.

The alternatives posed by Owenite socialists, including a questioning of gender patterns, have been given some attention (Taylor, 1983). But there were other, still less audible opinions from non-literate peoples among the urban poor as well as in rural areas, cultures with their own, sometimes very different, gender cosmologies (Phythian-Adams, 1980). It has been argued, for example, that working class women held a notion of self which created mutuality as a form of individuality based on interdependence, the recognition of other agents as part of one's own agency (Smith and Valence, 1988, p. 296). But these expressions had no significance from the perspective of the authoritative centre; they have been given little historical credence or moral status.

The faintness of contesting views from the periphery alerts us to the power abrogated by the numerous 'Adams' over the years in the naming of the social world. The fictions of disembodied actors, the fable of capacity to sell labour away from the person – and the body – of the labourer, gained a currency by the third quarter of the nineteenth century which has provided the architecture of our thoughts about the social world. These ideas were inevitably carried forward by the discipline which was formulated in that period – sociology.

Nevertheless, the constructors of high theory did not succeed completely in framing the social world. A detailed examination of the varieties of masculinities in the early and mid-nineteenth century brings out some unacknowledged contradictions which historians as well as sociologists must confront.

From the 1830s, in Britain, the themes of work and sexuality were endlessly sought out, defined and debated. Some of these discussions can be read through developments in state engrossment, in the Factory Acts, and above all, in that extraordinary scheme of legislation, the New Poor Law of 1834. It was particularly here that the ideal of a male breadwinner working a fully defined day/week and the dependence of wives and children was made manifest. Respectable sexual mores, too, permeated ordinances of Workhouse administration, out-relief and in the notorious Bastardy Clause.

The step towards Civil Registration of births, death and marriages in 1837, the closing off of opportunities for more loosely defined plebian marriages chronicled by John Gillis, as well as moves to control if not eradicate non-familial households through the lodging house legislation of the 1840s and 1850s reflect the way definitions of individuality filtered through the framing of family, kinship and work (Gillis, 1985; Davidoff, 1979).

By and large, these were the products of middle class men's beliefs and actions. By the late 1830s, both symbolised and reinforced by the 1832 Reform Act, a middle-class conception of masculinity began to permeate large parts of British society. From the late eighteenth century middle class claims had been directed against both aristocratic status flowing from land ownership and the culture of an emergent working class. Middle class efforts instead focused on religious redemption – 'the aristocracy of the saved' – and the independence gained through ownership and manipulation of liquid capital or professional expertise.

The particular task confronting middle class men was to

redefine the notion of work, with its demeaning connotations of subordination. This they vigorously accomplished within the evangelical religious dimension but also within the newly minted individuality of political economy. Gradually what middle class men did to gain a livelihood shifted from a *situation* under clientage, to an *occupation*. Occupation was, and has remained, quintessentially masculine. It called forth qualities regarded as opposite to the feminine in a conception of *Manhood* which was at the furthest remove from the dependency of women through marriage.

But, as we have seen, Manhood, in fact, vitally depended on female support. The struggle to differentiate the masculine arena from the feminised was, thus, intense and appears in many guises. It is evident in the dramatic shift in middle class men's clothing. In the eighteenth century, the ideal for male attire included ruffled shirts, lace, silks and bright colours. Close fitting stockings and knee breeches showed off shapely limbs and gave a hint of sexual display, hair was long and curled, cheeks smooth shaven. Within a generation, a radical transformation took place leading to the dark, shapeless and utilitarian trousered suit, tall hat and heavy whiskers of the 1850s in deliberate strong contrast to the bell-shaped crinolined, ringleted, colourful female image (Davidoff and Hall, 1987). Yet these changes were accompanied by a wave of pseudo-chivalric masculine fantasies of combat and honour far removed from the daily world of counting house or office (Girouard, 1981).

By mid-century, the belief in an individual as captain of his fate bit deeper into the social fabric. Some working class men had begun to repudiate notions of manhood based on physical prowess or honour and focused on control of passion, sobriety and a form of domesticity which even among radicals, cast women as sisters and wives to the artisan community rather than actors in their own right (Clark, 1987).

As Barbara Taylor has shown, the short-lived Owenite feminist effort was superseded by men eager to defend their honourable status from cheap female and juvenile labour as well as to create a standard of domestic comfort based on wives' home-making commensurate with their status in the working class community (Taylor, 1983). Gradually the notion of *competence* changed its meaning from a man's ability to earn a comfortable subsistence for self and family through the practice of an entire craft, to simply the ability lodged in an *individual's* labour (Baron, 1990). For the notion of the male breadwinner was not only imposed from above. Rather a negotiated version of middle-class domesticity was adopted within large sections of the working class despite the fact that only a narrow strata could afford to put it into practice (McClelland, 1989; Danon, 1985).

Numerous nineteenth-century struggles over control of the labour process, the ability of working men to set the price and conditions of their labour, were also regarded as fighting off attempts to degrade and insult Manhood. The all-male experience of apprenticeship had taught the boy to be a man in class terms and to be a worker in gender terms (Baron, 1990). Men engaged with tools and materials in the workplace. Long experience of work processes shaped their 'property in skill' which underlay claims to masculine exclusivity (Rule, 1987). The very products of manufacture were coloured by gender connotations, most explicitly in entirely masculine arenas such as metal working, engineering and the railway which had evolved from the closed crafts of smiths, wheelwrights and millwrights. But even in workshops or factories where both men and women were employed, men usually made large or elaborated goods, women the plain and small. Men made outer garments, women underclothing and children's wear.

By the 1880s more men were claiming a property in work, and on this basis entry into the political community, pushed forward in the awarding of the franchise to successive waves of working class men in 1867 and 1884. Their claim to citizenship was on the basis of a manhood which refused to be judged less of a man because of differences in wealth (Tholfsen, 1976). In their case, collective organisation rather than thrusting entrepreneurship underpinned masculine independence, so vital to this property in labour (McClelland, 1989, p. 150; Rose, 1988). The male domestic servant, that 'creature' of his master, was the last to gain full citizenship; only he had not been transformed by the labour contract which had culminated in the 1870s Employers and Workmen's Acts which had replaced that of Master and Servant.

It should come as no surprise, then, that by the later

nineteenth century, the designation *working woman* has an uneasy, contradictory sound (Papanek, 1979). To many, women, by definition, were incapable of creating the same kind of value as men and thus could never be 'workers' (Scott, 1987a). Historians have begun to recognise how these formulations have effected their basic data such as the construction of census categories (Higgs, 1987). Working class women may have known that they must be at least self supporting during much of the life cycle, but they too, gained from pinning at least part of that support on the breadwinning family members (Osterud, 1986). And in a labour market framed by these assumptions, the threat of the unattached working woman, the 'independent factory girl', so often seen by middle class observers as one step from the prostitute, was also a potential hazard to working men (Cockburn, 1989).

If this were the only form in which masculinity appeared in nineteenth-century society, our understanding would be relatively straightforward. But older traditions, other groups, offered a range of competing masculinities. There was, for example, also a romanticised anti-work, anti-domestic ethos centred on the public house, the race course and the prize fight. (The whole area of sport and its relationship to masculinity has hardly been recognised.) Admiration for physical prowess and sexual adventuring did not simply disappear in the face of middle class proselytizing. A myth of coalition between the aristocrat and the working class man – 'nature's gentleman' – which ridiculed the sedentary, hen-pecked middle-class homebody dies hard. It was reincarnated in more democratic myths of mateship in the homosocial ambience of the Australian outback and the American West (Lake, 1986).

Even middle class men, however, with their devotion to Hearth and Home, joined in the many extra familial all-male locations where their identities were also forged, from the West End Club to the voluntary society, from the nascent public schools to the Oxford Movement within the Anglican Church. Spaces for male bonding removed from feminine influence abounded in what by the late nineteenth century was a highly sexually segregated society. Such organisations as the Freemasons and other fraternal orders specifically claimed a brotherhood overarched by masculine hierarchy.

In some cases these became a pseudo-family of brothers joined together in 'bonds of sentiment, loyalty and obligation' (Clawson, 1986, p. 689). It is significant that, once again, male domestic servants were pointedly excluded from the Freemasons.

We have followed the creation of a masculine identity, or rather identities, through a variety of settings. We have seen how these culminated in the claims – not necessarily the actual exercise – of manhood suffrage and a citizenship based on men's property in their labour, their self-defined role in the production of wealth. These rights, accruing to men, implied negative qualities in women. Just as women's dependency was sometimes portrayed as a brake on progress in the middle class, so among radical working men, women's putative ignorance and involvement in the minutiae of the domestic, were seen as a drag on the politically conscious working class.

The late nineteenth-century feminist movement, for all the progress made in the quality of women's lives, was never able to come to terms with the deeply masculine concept of citizenship which set the terms for the 60-year-long struggle for women's suffrage. In the same period and with a mutual influence not often recognised, a rising militarism brought to the surface implicit, taken for granted, ideas about the relationship of gender, citizenship and its ultimate expression – war.

As a feminist theorist has pointed out, belief in the masculinity of war was created precisely by leaving that which was seen as feminine behind, by the putative capacity to rise above what femaleness symbolically represented. In this conception, men in war moved into the universal and truly ethical because they transcended 'womanhood'. Women were seen as the embodiment (sic) of the individual body, of natural feelings and private interests. They were only able to serve their nation by negation, by giving up what was most precious in the private sphere (Lloyd, 1986). Thus, in the famous recruiting poster which became an enduring image of the Great War of 1914–18, the women of England were urged to say 'GO' to their menfolk. It was only by giving the fruits of their bodies, their sons, that women could achieve a kind of patriotism, although one utterly different from that of men. It was on the basis of this exclusion from full membership in the community and its centres of wealth and power that some women opposed war, not only on some mystical attachment to the giving and preserving of life (Pierson, 1987).

This cursory survey has examined some core ideas of our Western heritage and the consequent view of masculinity deriving from them. It has briefly touched on some of the institutions in which they were embedded and by which they were modified. It has indicated alternative visions extant in our recent past and now silenced.

The concept of the rational individual and his domain, the category of public sociality, became not only an idealisation of nineteenth-century society in general but the primary orientation of social scientific enquiry (Yeatman, 1984b). The fledgling discipline of sociology was moulded during the volatile decades of the early nineteenth century, coterminus with and contributing to the struggles for dominance of these concepts. The keystone of the sociological edifice, the concept of *class*, was based on the premise of a totally separate productive order.[7] Family and kinship were taken as necessary but natural corollaries of this order and were constructed around a similar concept of the individual self (Collier and Yaragisako, 1987). Within the construct of family the category 'woman' was explicitly located just as 'man' was assumed within the economy, polity and the realms of knowledge. Sociologists (and historians influenced by them) have assumed the family as secondary and peripheral, always responsive to changes in the public sphere although some latter-day social historians have begun to argue that in special cases, lines of influence might have run the other way.

Both assumptions rest on the original gendered dualisms going back to the seventeenth century. The proliferation of 'hyphen solutions' to bind together the separate spheres such as Marxist-feminism have not proved very satisfactory. It is increasingly evident that the most valiant attempts to extend concepts of rationality or universalism to women, to embrace them in the class system, are bound to founder on the fact that, as Joan Scott reminds us, these 'languages' are already dualistic and already gendered (Scott, 1987b, p. 44).

Acknowledging the need to find a different language, to

seek a variety of approaches, to admit permeable and pervasive relationships, should not be seen as failure but as the possibility of new beginnings (Flax, 1987). Here the sociologist's drive towards parsimony may have to be balanced by a nodding towards the more descriptive seamless web of the historian.

The effort to rise above the notion of the unitary individual self and give genuine recognition to the 'other', to the periphery, may break the rational mode. In the long run, however, it could provide a 'more inclusive, more democratic, less monovocal analysis which will capture the irregularities, particularities and contradictions which make up the whole of social life' (Yeatman, 1987, pp. 7–9).

Philip Abrams, echoing C. Wright-Mills, called for a sociology which would 'enable all men (sic) to become aware of historical structures and of their own place within them' (Abrams, 1982, p. 17). But such a call must be based on a genuine recognition of those whose place up to now has been in the shadows of the non-social, a designation which may lead all too easily into the darkness of the non-human.

NOTES

1. The title is taken from a lecture given by the Rev. Richard Cobbold on 'The Character of Women' for the benefit of the Governesses Benevolent Institution of London, in 1848. This paper was first presented as the Philip Abrams Memorial Lecture at the British Sociological Association in Edinburgh, March 1988. I would like to thank the following for ideas, suggestions and criticisms: Ava Baron, Paola DiCori, Catherine Hall, Donna Haraway, Ludmilla Jordanova, Jane Lewis, Carole Pateman, Sonya Rose, Joan Scott, Carroll Smith-Rosenberg and Judith Walkowitz. I am especially grateful to Helen Corr and Lynn Jamieson for editorial perception and patience.
2. It has been pointed out that there is a contradiction in recognising a politico-jural dimension to kinship while leaving the private domain, such as the family and sexuality, in a 'natural' limbo (Yeatman, 1984b).
3. This formulation appears repeatedly in the Madonna and Whore motifs assigned to women in the iconography inherited from religious tradition.

4. The stereotypical name for a male domestic servant, often used by employers instead of his given name, was *John Thomas*. It may be significant that to this day, 'John Thomas' is a British euphemism for penis. Here the servant is identified as the ultimate 'tool' of his master. There is no such connotation for the female analogue, 'Mary Ann'.
5. Early nineteenth-century clergymen such as the Anglican, Richard Cobbold, and his City of London Independent colleague, Thomas Binney, reinterpreted these Biblical views to emphasise that modern British wives were not expected to 'labour in the vineyards'. The timing of these conceptual shifts, starting in the early seventeenth century, has often been confused with the *actual* separation of home and workplace, a development which became widespread only in the early nineteenth century.
6. The well known, large mural entitled 'Work' painted by Ford Maddox Brown in the early 1960s gives some of the complicated readings surrounding that concept. The painting includes portraits of Charles Kingsley and Thomas Carlyle who framed some of the most potent doctrines about work at the time.
7. It is revealing that those groups whose incomes and access to resources are so limited that they cannot even be measured by using the usual indices, have been regarded as outside class analysis, placed back in a more common sense holistic realm. For example, the very poor in nineteenth-century Britain or blacks in early twentieth-century America were assigned a social status by sociologists, following popular custom, by concentrating on manners, cleanliness and other tokens of domesticity. These criteria have been conspicuously absent for those (men) taken to be *within* the working class (Higgenbotham, 1989).

BIBLIOGRAPHY

ABRAMS, P. (1982), *Historical Sociology* (Shepton Mallet, Somerset, England: Open Books Publishing).

APPLEBY, J. O. (1978), *Economic Thought and Ideology in 17th Century England* (Princeton N.J.: Princeton University Press).

BARKER-BENFIELD, B. (1973), 'The Spermatic Economy: A Nineteenth-Century View of Sexuality' in M. Gordon (ed.), *The*

American Family in Social-Historical Perspective (New York: St Martins Press).

BARON, A. (1990), 'An "Other" Side of Gender Antagonism at Work: Men, Boys and the Remasculinization of Work in the Printing Trade 1880 – 1920' in A. Baron (ed.), *Work Engendered: Towards a New Understanding of Men, Women and Work* (Ithaca, New York: Cornell University Press).

BOCK, G. (1989), 'Women's History and Gender History: Aspects of an International Debate', *Gender and History*, vol. 1, no. 1, Spring.

BROWN, P. and JORDANOVA, L. (1980), 'Oppressive Dichotomies: the Nature/Culture Debate', Cambridge Women's Studies Group, *Women in Society: Interdisciplinary Essays* (London: Virago).

CAPLAN, P. (1988), 'Engendering Knowledge: The Politics of Ethnography' *Anthropology Today*, vol. 14, nos. 5 & 6.

CLARK, A. (1987), *Women's Silence, Men's Violence: Sexual Assault in England 1770–1840* (London: Pandora).

CLAWSON, M. A. (1986), 'Nineteenth-Century Women's Auxiliaries and Fraternal Orders', *Signs: Journal of Women in Culture and Society*, vol. 12, no. 1, Autumn.

COCKBURN, C. (1989), 'Formations of Masculinity – Introduction', *Gender and History*, vol. 1, no. 2, Autumn.

COLLIER, J. F. and YANAGISAKO, S. (eds) (1987), 'Introduction', *Gender and Kinship: Essays Toward a Unified Analysis* (Stanford: Stanford University Press).

CONDER, E. (1857), *Josiah Conder: A Memoir* (London: John Snow).

CONNELL, R. W. (1983), 'How should we theorise patriarchy?' in R. W. Connell (ed.), *Which Way is Up? Essays on Class, Sex and Culture* (Sydney: Allen & Unwin).

CONNELL, R. W. (1987), *Gender and Power* (Cambridge: Polity Press).

DANON, R. (1985). *Work in the English Novel: the Myth of Vocation* (London: Croom-Helm).

DAVIDOFF, L. (1979), 'The Separation of Home and Work? Landladies and Lodgers in Nineteenth and Twentieth Century England' in S. Burman, *Fit Work For Women* (London: Croom Helm).

DAVIDOFF, L. (1983), 'Class and Gender in Victorian England', in J. Newton *et al.* (eds), *Sex and Class in Victorian Britain* (London: Routledge).

DAVIDOFF, L. (1986a), 'Mastered for Life: Servant and Wife in Victorian and Edwardian England', in P. Thane and A. Sutcliffe (eds) *Essays in Social History*, vol. II (Oxford: Oxford University Press).

DAVIDOFF, L. (1986b), *The Best Circles: 'Society', Etiquette and the Season* (London: Hutchinson).

DAVIDOFF, L. and HALL, C. (1987), *Family Fortunes: Men and Women of the English Middle Class, 1780–1850* (London: Hutchinson).

DAVIDOFF, L. (1990), 'The Rationalization of Housework', D. Leonard and S. Allen (eds), *Sexual Divisions Revisited* (London: Macmillan).

DE LAURETIS, T. (1986). *Feminist Studies/Critical Studies* (Bloomington, Indiana: Indiana University Press).

FLAX, J. (1987), 'Postmodernism and Gender Relations in Feminist Theory', *Signs: Journal of Women in Culture and Society*, vol. 12, no. 4, Summer.

GERSON, S. and PEISS, K. (1985), 'Boundaries, Negotiation, Consciousness: Reconceptualising Gender Relations', *Social Problems*, vol. 32, no. 4, April.

GILLIS, J. (1985), *For Better For Worse: British Marriages 1600 to the Present* (Oxford: Oxford University Press).

GIROUARD, M. (1981), *The Return to Camelot: Chivalry and the English Gentleman* (New Haven: Yale University Press).

GRAY, R. (1987). 'The languages of factory reform in Britain, c. 1830–1860', in P. Joyce (ed.), *The Historical Meaning of Work* (Cambridge: Cambridge University Press).

HARAWAY, D. (1987), 'Geschlecht' in W. F. Haug (ed.), *Kritisches Wörterbuch des Marxismus*, vol. I (Berlin).

HARDING, S. (1986), 'The Instability of the Analytical Categories of Feminist Theory', *Signs: Journal of Women in Culture and Society*, vol. 11, no. 4, Summer.

HEARN, J. (1987), *The Gender of Oppression: Men, Masculinity and the Critique of Marxism* (Brighton: Wheatsheaf).

HELLER, T. and WELLBERRY, D. E. (eds), (1986), *Restructuring Individualism: Autonomy and the Self in Western Thought* (Stanford: Stanford University Press).

HIGGINBOTHAM, E. B. (1989), 'Beyond the Sound of Silence: Afro-American Women's History', *Gender and History*, vol. 1, no. 1, Spring.

HIGGS, E. (1987), 'Women, Occupations and Work in the 19th Century Census', *History Workshop Journal*, no. 23, Spring.

HIMMELFARB, G. (1971), 'Mayhew's Poor: A Problem of Identity', *Victorian Studies*, vol. 14, March.

HONT, I. and IGNATIEFF, M. (1983), *Wealth and Virtue* (Cambridge: Cambridge University Press).

JAGGAR, A. M. (1984), *Feminist Politics and Human Nature* (Brighton: Wheatsheaf).

JORDANOVA, L. (1987), 'Conceptualizing Childhood in the 18th

Century: The Problem of Child Labour, *British Journal for Eighteenth Century Studies*, vol. 10.

JORDANOVA, L. (1989), *Sexual Visions: Images of Gender in Science and Medicine Between the Eighteenth and Twentieth Centuries* (Hemel Hempstead, England: Harvester Wheatsheaf).

LAKE, M. (1986), 'The Politics of Respectability: Identifying the Masculinist Context', *Historical Studies*, vol. 22, no. 86, April.

LANDES, J. (1984), 'Women and the Public Sphere: A Modern Perspective', *Social Analysis: Journal of Cultural and Social Practice*, no. 15, August.

LLOYD, G. (1986), 'Selfhood, War and Masculinity', in C. Pateman and E. Gross (eds), *Feminist Challenges* (Sydney: Allen & Unwin).

LUHMAN, N. (1986), 'The Individuality of the Individual: Historical Meanings and Contemporary Problems', in T. Heller and D. Wellberry (eds), *Reconstructing Individualism: Autonomy, Individuality and Self in Western Thought* (Stanford: Stanford University Press).

MATHIEU, N. C. (1978), 'Man-Culture and Woman-Natureo?', *Women's Studies International Quarterly*, vol. 1, no. 1.

McCLELLAND, D. (1989), 'Some Thoughts on Masculinity and the "Representative Artisan" in Britain 1850–1880', *Gender and History*, vol. 1, no. 2, Summer.

MORGAN, D. (1987), *It Will Make A Man of You: Notes on National Service Masculinity and Autobiography* (Manchester: Studies in Sexual Politics, University of Manchester), no. 17.

NEWTON, J. (1988), '"History as Usual?": Feminism and the "New Historicism",' *Cultural Critique*, no. 9, Spring.

OAKS, G. (1984), *Georg Simmel: On Women, Sexuality and Love* (New Haven: Yale University Press).

OSTERUD, N. G. (1986), 'Gender Divisions and the Organization of Work in the Leicester Hosiery Industry' in A. V. John, *Unequal Opportunities: Women's Employment in England 1800–1918* (Oxford: Blackwell).

PAPANEK, H. (1979), 'Family Status Production: the work and non-work of Women', *Signs: Journal of Women in Culture and Society*, vol. 4, no. 4.

PATEMAN, C. (1988), *The Sexual Contract* (Cambridge: Polity Press).

PATEMAN, C. (1989), 'The Paradox of Women's Citizenship', paper delivered at the Swedish Collegium for Advanced Study in the Social Sciences, Uppsala, Sweden, April.

PIERSON, R. (1987), '"Did Your Mother Wear Army Boots?": Feminist Theory and Women's Relation to War, Peace and Revolution' in S. Macdonald *et al.*, *Images of Women in Peace and War: Cross-Cultural and Historical Perspectives* (London: Macmillan).

PORTER, R. (1982), 'Mixed Feelings: the Enlightenment and Sexuality in Eighteenth Century Britain', in P.-G. Bouce (ed.), *Sexuality in Eighteenth Century Britain* (Manchester: Manchester University Press).

PROCHASKA, F. K. (1980), *Women and Philanthropy in 19th Century England* (Oxford: Oxford University Press).

PYTHIAN-ADAMS, C. (1980), 'Rural Culture' in G. Mingay (ed.), *The Victorian Countryside*, vol. II.

RILEY, D. (1988), *'Am I that Name?': Feminism and the Category of 'Women' in History* (London: Macmillan).

ROSE, S. (1988), 'Gender Antagonism and Class Conflict: Exclusionary Tactics of Male Trade Unionists in 19th Century Britain', *Social History*, vol. 13, no. 2, May.

RULE, J. (1987), 'The property of skill' in P. Joyce (ed.), *The Historical Meaning of Work* (Cambridge: Cambridge University Press).

RYAN, M. (1981), *Cradle of the Middle Class: The Family in Oneida County, New York 1790–1865* (Cambridge: Cambridge University Press).

SCOTT, J. (1987a), '"L'ouvriere! Mot impie, sordide . . ." Women workers in the discourse of French political economy 1840–1860', in P. Joyce (ed.), *The Historical Meaning of Work* (Cambridge: Cambridge University Press).

SCOTT, J. (1987b), 'A Reply to Criticism', *International Labour and Working Class History*, no. 32, Fall.

SCOTT, J. (1989), 'Women's History' in P. Burke (ed.), *New Perspectives on Historical Writing* (Cambridge: Polity Press).

Signs: Journal of Women in Culture and Society (1987), 'Editorial Introduction', vol. 12, no. 4, Summer.

SMITH, D. (1988), *The Everyday World As Problematic: A Feminist Sociology* (Milton Keynes: Open University Press).

SMITH, R. L. and VALENZE, D. M. (1988), 'Mutuality and Marginality: Liberal Moral Theory and Working Class Women in 19th Century England', *Signs: Journal of Women in Culture and Society*, vol. 13, no. 2, Winter.

STACEY, J. and THORNE, B. (1985), 'The Missing Feminist Revolution in Sociology', *Social Problems*, vol. 32, no. 4, April.

STACEY, M. (1986), 'Gender and Stratification: One Central Issue or Two', in R. Crompton and M. Mann (eds), *Gender and Stratification* (Cambridge: Polity Press).

STALLYBRASS, P. and WHITE, A. (1986), *The Politics and Poetics of Transgression* (Cambridge: Cambridge University Press).

STINCHCOMBE, A. L. (1984), 'The Origins of Sociology as a Discipline', *ACTA Sociologica*, vol. 27, no. 1.

SUGARMAN, D. and RUBIN, G. R. (eds) (1984), 'Introduction', *Law, Economy and Society: Essays in the History of English Law* (London: Professional Books).

THOLFSEN, T. R. (1976), *Working Class Radicalism in Mid-Victorian England* (London: Croom Helm).

TAYLOR, B. (1983), *Eve and the New Jerusalem. Socialism and Feminism in the 19th Century* (London: Virago).

WEBER, M. (1968), 'Religious Ethics and the World: Sexuality and Art', G. Roth and C. Wittich (eds), *Economy and Society*, vol. II.

YEATMAN, A. (1984a), 'Introduction', 'Gender and Social Life', Special Issue, *Social Analysis: Journal of Cultural and Social Practice*, Number 15, August.

YEATMAN, A. (1984b), 'Gender Differentiation of Social Life in Public and Domestic Domains', *Social Analysis: Journal of Cultural and Social Practice*, Number 15, August.

YEATMAN, A. (1987), 'A Feminist Theory of Social Differentiation', paper presented at the American Sociological Association Conference, August.

ZUNZ, O. (1985), *Reliving the Past: The Worlds of Social History* (Chappell Hill, North Carolina University Press).

Index